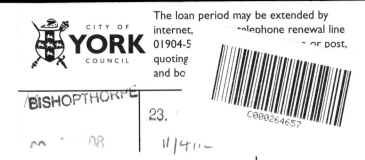
The Woven Basket

Cover photograph taken by David McCracken

The Woven Basket

By

Joyce Thackeray

Stamford House Publishing
Second Edition 2007

A CIP catalogue record for this title is
available from the British Library

ISBN 978-1-904985-46-4

Printed and Bound in Great Britain
by
Stamford House Publishing
Remus house,
Coltsfoot Drive,
Woodston,
Peterborough
PE2 9JX

Dedication

This book is dedicated, with love,
to my late husband, John.

Joyce Thackeray was born in Alexandria. The daughter of a senior Colonial Prison Officer, she was raised in the foothills of Kilimanjaro until her late teens. When independence came to East Africa, she moved to Cheshire with her family.

She married an RAF Regiment Officer, John Thackeray, whom she had met whilst he was Assistant Superintendent of Police in Tanganyika.

Over the next thirty-five years, they enjoyed life on a variety of Royal Air Force Stations, both at home and abroad. On retirement from the regiment, her husband took up a post at the Civil Defence Staff College, North Yorkshire.

The mother of three sons and grandmother to Nathan and Alice Hannah, Joyce decided to write of her memories after the death of her husband in 1997.

Acknowledgements

I should like to thank my family, who I love very much. Without them, there would be no story to tell. Also my friends, Brigadier Bill Hiles, who so painstakingly looked through my work and offered advice, which I was happy to take on board. I love him dearly for his kindness, and his wife, Betty, for her encouragement. Dear friends, Air Commodore Anderson, Group Captain Kingsley Oliver and Air Commodore Witherow for some of the material. Beverley Walker and her son, Mark, and friend, Simon, for being such 'whiz-kids' with the computer and scanner and turning out the photos for me. My love and a big thank you have to go to dear Judy and Rod Donnelly, not least for the love and support that they gave me when John died, but especially as Judy was to bury her mother that same week. I also owe a lot of thanks to my friends, Clare Cafferkey and Jocelyn Pearson for their help and kindness at that time.

I would also have to thank Michael Palin for making his wonderful travel videos, and Tim Sebastian for his HARDtalk programme, both of which kept me entertained as I sat up in the unsociable early hours of the morning, drinking cups of tea, when I couldn't sleep.

I thank Dorethea Rimmer for steering me towards Blackie & Co Publishers Ltd and their Consultant Commissioning Editor, Bettina Croft, and Dr Susan Forsyth, who both looked at my work and decided that perhaps I did have a story to tell.

History of Changi by Sqn Ldr Probert has been a valuable resource for this work.

Preface

My use of the analogy of the woven basket indicates that in life we often remember the best and the worst of events. The happy memories stay with us and are carried around, and the not so happy slowly dribble and fade through the mesh of life to become less painful.

In my life I have been extremely privileged to meet people from all walks of life through just being my father's daughter; from Island Governors to Tribal Chiefs, and when I married an RAF Officer, once again another strand intertwined with my life. There were royal garden parties and tennis with nobility. In reality, it shows that it doesn't matter who we are, for in life we rub shoulders with many people, though seldom do we take the time to get to know many of them well; yet our lives are inextricably linked. We experience many coincidences. In fact, our lives are woven and intertwined like the weave in a basket, for at no time are any of us more than a handshake away from friends we have passed by along the way.

Almost four years on now since John died and I still feel the loss. Nathan, my grandson, finished primary education and, as we had planned earlier, he left the quiet of Easingwold to live in Nottingham with his Daddy, my son Richard. Of course, at the beginning I missed him terribly, for while he was with me I had another body to love and take care of. I enjoyed our holidays to Tavira and our games of tennis. Nathan was always good fun to be with.

I have become used to the word WIDOW – it doesn't

sound so frightening anymore. Time heals, everyone says – whoever thought of those words I wonder? I'm not so sure. Does time heal, or do we rely on friends to chivvy us out of ourselves, or do we just throw ourselves into frenzies of hours of doing things to try to cover the hours of remembering? I cannot forget, but to try to ease the pain, I decided to buy myself a computer and put my thoughts on to paper. To a certain extent it has been very therapeutic. What next, I wonder, when the work is done. Maybe take myself to where my life began – back to Africa, perhaps put my nursing to good use?

Funnily enough, I picture myself eventually looking out from some hotel balcony overlooking the great Rift Valley in Africa and watching the golden sunrise over the hill, uttering the words that Alice spoke in White Mischief, 'Oh God… Not another bloody beautiful day!' Meanwhile my time is interspersed with visits to see the family and helping my sister, Joan, with her work at her restaurant in Liskeard in Cornwall.

*

The words, "Never put off until tomorrow what you can do today," were never more poignant, than when I found myself on my own. I had always said that I never regretted the things I had done, but there were many things that I regretted not having done.

I have had an interesting life which I wanted to share with my children and my family. I began to make a few notes in a pad a couple of years ago, of the more unusual events that had occurred, in the hope that, one day, I would have enough material to write a journal or perhaps a book. My husband, John, who was such a major part of my life and a great inspiration, had said that he would contribute some of the material. This would include stories my father had told to him about his life in the Coldstream Guards, and also experiences that they had shared in the Colonial Police and Prison Service in Tanganyika. Both men had a lot in common, having been in the military, and colonial service.

Many a time, I would hear peals of laughter coming from the drawing room or kitchen, where they could be heard talking of their different experiences over a jar – or two; stories I would love to include, but now, I could not possibly do them justice. Alas, sadly I left it all too late to begin writing, for I lost my dearest friend, my husband, in July of 1997: a man with a generous nature and enough wisdom and kindness in his soul to be a fair critic of my work!

I never kept a diary. Incidents in my childhood keep moving around in circles, so times and dates are somewhat irrelevant, but some events and dates can never be forgotten and remain always. My story has no real beginning for what is a beginning? Only what can be remembered. I am sure that my family would recall or interpret happenings in a slightly different way, but this is MY story!

My father died in 1991, so to help me piece together his earlier war-time service, I wrote to London, to see if I could obtain his service records. All I had to hand was my birth certificate, issued in Alexandria where I was born, which included my father's service number. I had a few old war-time photographs of him and his comrades which had been taken in the Middle East. I had these photocopied and enlarged, and sent them with a covering letter, to the Brigade of Guards in London. I was delighted to receive a reply and photocopies of my father's service records from the Regimental Headquarters of the Coldstream Guards.

Chapter One

When I first set foot on English soil in the autumn of 1945, with my elder sister Joan and my parents, it was to meet my paternal grandparents, George Joseph and Blanche, and in spite of a few photographs, which were reminders that I had been with them at the time, I remember nothing at all of my stay with them as a child.

My grandparents lived in a large, middle-terraced house in Small-Heath on the outskirts of the city of Birmingham, where they had begun their married life. They had three sons: my father, Basil, was the eldest, then came David, and another brother, who, sadly, died in infancy.

My father went to the local school, and was encouraged to attend the local church of St. Oswald's. As he grew up, he began to excel at sport, eventually representing his school and the city in swimming. On leaving school, he became a typewriter mechanic, following in the footsteps of a good pedigree of engineers – my grandfather was a master craftsman tool maker: his father was also an engineer, who worked on some of the contemporary armaments innovations, including the Lewis gun.

The family were hard workers, and my father and his brother were encouraged to work hard too. My grandfather, George, was a strict disciplinarian with strong Victorian values, tempered with down-to-earth warmth and kindness. Both sons were encouraged to take up other interests when they were not at work – idle hands and all that! So stamp collecting became a favourite hobby of my father, and the house was never without the current copy of the Stanley Gibbons catalogue! But perhaps my father's most favourite pastime when he was growing up, was going fishing with his brother, David, along the city canals.

At the time my father was eighteen, many of his friends had enlisted in the armed forces but he had been content and happy with the comforts of home life until he developed feelings of emotion towards the ladies (of which he had previously been ignorant and naive – certainly matters of the fair sex were never discussed at home). In a society where simply holding hands with a girlfriend in the open was regarded as terribly forward and taboo, and where strict moral codes prevailed, he plucked up the courage and asked a young lady for a date and, on the way home, he kissed her passionately and thought he had made her pregnant – those were my father's words! He was left with such feelings of guilt and impending retribution, that he rushed off immediately to enlist in the army.

So began his career with the 2nd Battalion of the Coldstream Guards at Pirbright. When war came, he saw service in Egypt, Syria, Palestine, North Africa and Italy. He served his country proudly and was awarded the General Service Medal with clasp, the Palestine Medal (of which he was particularly proud), the Africa Star and the Defence Medal. The comment from his Commanding Officer of his assessment at the time of his demobilisation was 'exemplary'! During his time in the army, his records showed that he was run over by a tank whilst in a shallow dugout in the desert and sustained a crushed thorax. He never spoke about it, but I should like to think that it was the enemy that was responsible for the dastardly deed, because this injury was a contributory factor to his death in July of 1991. He loved his service life and the comradeship of his friends, many of whom did not make it through the war.

While serving with his Brigade, he met and married a pretty, petite, dark-haired Maltese lady, five years his senior, called Mathilda. She lived and worked in Alexandria as an interpreter and secretary. At four feet eleven inches tall, she was tiny compared to his six feet five inches in height. She was fashionable and chic, and when she wore her elegant high heels, she could make five feet two. She spoke seven languages fluently, and my father said that he was attracted to her beauty as well as her great sense of fun. When they decided to get married at the church of St. George, Mustapha Barrracks in Alexandria, neither of them realised that the Catholic Church would pour scorn on their actions, regarding the ceremony as improper because they had not gone through the full nuptial mass. They eventually went through a further ceremony at the Catholic Church, and at the altar, they both had to endure a talk on morals. Turning to Mathilda, the priest continued, "and YOU my child, have been living in SIN!" to which she convulsed into a fit of uncontrollable giggling, as my father stood beside her, trying to look composed and desperately trying not to laugh.

By the time of their marriage in 1940, the war in Europe had already begun, and England prepared itself for the awesome ordeal that lay ahead. With air-raid shelters being built and trenches dug, while hundreds of cigar shaped barrage balloons loomed in the sky above London, people prepared for the worst and food rationing began.

By the time my sister, Joan, was born in 1942 at the Anglo-Swiss hospital in Alexandria, the war was well under way in the Middle East as well. Mussolini's troops had joined forces with Germany and attacked Egypt.

My father was away fighting with his unit at the time of my birth in February 1943 in Alexandria. As the British troops fought in the desert, the Eighth army marched to capture Tripoli and reached the borders of Tunisia, the German army finally surrendering in April. Meanwhile, across the other side of the world, the Americans, who came into the war after the bombing of Pearl Harbour, were heavily involved in the war in the Pacific.

My parents had earlier moved into a high-rise apartment block in the suburbs of Alexandria. Living in a high-rise flat was fine with tiny babies, until they began to crawl and explore! I understand that, one day, Joan, who was only about eighteen months old, had gradually manoeuvred a chair to the balcony, and, to the astonishment and horror of onlookers, she was seen crawling along the ledge some four stories up. The neighbours began searching frantically for anything that they could hold outstretched in case she fell, and my mother Mathilda stood a distance away, not daring to say a word to distract her. Finally, after a few very anxious moments, Joan calmly climbed down from the balcony ledge and on to the chair again, perhaps wondering what all the fuss had been about!

The family stayed in Egypt, until my father's demobilisation, when he left the battalion to take up a post with the Colonial Service in East Africa. They bade a tearful farewell to my grandfather, Darmanin, my mother's father, not realising at that time that it would be his final farewell to his daughter.

So, after our flying visit to England, in 1946, my parents embarked on a new life overseas in Africa with my sister, Joan, four, and me, three years old.

It was to be quite an adventure for all of us, not least because it was a whole new start for my father, who was due to take up a position as a Prison Officer with the Colonial Prison Service at Kingolwira, near Morogoro, tucked into the foothills of the Uluguru Mountains, in southern Tanganyika.

Our new home was a short distance from the prison. Mr. Price, who was the Deputy Commissioner of Prisons, and his wife lived near to us. Mr. Price was a short, portly, jovial gentleman with a moustache, and his wife a tall, trim lady with a pleasant gentle face and a cheerful, caring nature. Having no children of their own, they quickly took Joan and me under their wing and I was fond of both of them. Don Price and my father had a great deal of respect for each other and the two men became firm friends.

Kingolwira prison was not a new prison, but at the time it was a new concept in prison reform. As reported in a local newspaper of the time, it was a "prison without walls" a place "where men and women who had committed offences against the laws of the country, or against tribal usage, are serving out sentences meted out to them, ranging from a matter of months to imprisonment for life, under conditions which make the old-fashioned walled structures look medieval."

The house that was to become our home for at least three years was a large whitewashed building with steps leading up to an arched entrance into the main drawing room, and had a bedroom at each end of the house. The windows had no glass, only netting to keep out the insects, and there were cane shutters to keep the rooms cool against the hot afternoon sun. All around were neat lawns and flowering hedges. From the house, men working hard with their picks and hoes, could be seen daily, digging away vegetation, watched by the ever alert warders. Discipline was always a high priority, with consideration being given to the complex relationship between those on the wrong side of the law, and those whose duty it was to make sure that the inmates carried out a full day's work at all times. The overall authority came from the Commissioner of Prisons, Mr. Dawson, who had his headquarters in Dar-es-Salaam, and I remember that it was always a cause for celebration at home when an inspection from the Commissioner had gone well!

Mathilda, or 'Matty' as she became known to everyone, became very involved in the local Catholic Church, and she formed a strong bond with the White Fathers, an Irish order at the mission. Twice on Sunday, clutching her small, white, ivory-bound prayer book, she would leave the house to walk to the top of the hill to the church to worship. When I became seriously ill with amoebic dysentery shortly after arriving in Kingolwira, and it looked as if I would not survive the fever; it was the church she turned to for comfort and help, and a priest was called to administer the last rites to me. Being quite a tubby child with an obviously strong constitution, the long term recovery in the local hospital left me feeling comfortable, albeit a little thinner!

It was always the normal form that house servants were employed on the recommendation of homeward-bound European families, and Luke, a nice-looking, ebony-coloured native with a broad smile, was recommended to join the staff at the house as the cook. Other more menial tasks were usually carried out by specially selected and trusted prisoners, and one such was Joseph, who mainly tended the garden and kept the lawns watered. Occasionally Luke used him as general help in the kitchen. Luke was a kindly man who spoke reasonable English, which he had learned from his time at Mission school. He was a good cook, and, armed with the trusty copy of the 'Kenya Cook Book', he could turn his hand to anything from hot, wholesome suppers to the most delicate crêpes and cakes, and the visitors to the house always praised his efforts – some even tried to steal him away.

By the end of about three years, thousands of acres of land in and around the prison had been sufficiently cleared to force the tsetse fly to seek refuge elsewhere, and even more land was being stumped and transformed in order to plant maize, millet and sunflower seed. There were no bulldozers or tractors to help with the massive amount of clearing and felling of trees; only labour from the inmates and yoked oxen, who moved tons of earth and rock over wide areas, supervised throughout by the African warders.

Clearing of the dense undergrowth inevitably brought its animal casualties, this time in the form of two tiny, fluffy serval kittens, which were brought to the house in a kikapu (basket) covered with dry leaves, after their mother had been shot when she tried to attack one of the warders. The kittens had been found some time later, huddled under heavy undergrowth, close to where the inmates had been clearing bush. They were not yet weaned, and had to be coaxed by Matty to feed from a doll's pipette containing milk, and it was touch and go as to whether these tiny, fluffy kittens would survive; but survive they did, being hand-reared for weeks, until they could finally tolerate digesting bits of chopped meat.

In the reclaimed cleared areas of ground, hundreds of tons of maize, potatoes and pawpaw trees, cotton and ground nut continued to be planted and harvested. The land was so fertile that practically anything could be grown in it. Bore holes were sunk and dams built to conserve water supplies for drinking and watering, and, with the tsetse fly driven from the main areas, the local native, hump-backed zebu cattle were introduced, providing meat and milk for the whole prison camp. Later, chickens and ducks and rabbits were introduced, so there was a plentiful supply of mixed protein for the inmates. All the tasks were supervised by unarmed native warders within the main prison areas, but arms were carried when clearing the bush to cope with snakes and other wildlife.

Vegetables and millet fed the prisoners, and any surplus was disposed of to the prison authorities. Gallons of milk, far in excess of requirements, were sold to bring in even more government revenue, and each day a small token of fresh meat and milk, were delivered to our house for our use as well as for the servants.

At the prison, there was always a strict segregation of the sexes. Men carried out all the hard work, and the women cultivated the shambas (gardens). Every day, strict discipline was tempered by the human element, in the hope of influencing the inmates to a better way of life. After harvesting the cotton, the raw material was sent to the women's prison nearby, where it was woven into cloths and mats. Nothing on the land went to waste, even the maize stalks and leaves were used for cattle bedding. Mrs. Price regularly visited the women's prison to check on their welfare, and she also helped to supervise the teaching of cooking and sewing.

In February 1948, the twins, Martin and Mary, were born in the hospital in Morogoro. Mary was a pretty, plump baby with fair hair, but Martin was a sickly child, which caused my parents terrible anguish, until a doctor finally diagnosed that his failure to thrive was due to a gluten allergy. Now with four of us to look after, a native Ayah (nanny) was taken on to help with our care. She was a short, slim, woman with heavily lined tissue-thin skin which gave her a severe, mean-looking appearance. Strict and lacking any sense of fun, Joan and I were secretly rather scared of her. Her possessiveness over the twins was irksome and she wouldn't allow either Joan or myself to pick them up or cradle them on our knees, which we both longed to do. I cannot remember what her real name was, we simply knew her as 'Ayah'.

We had an Alsatian dog at the time called 'Poppet'. She had been chosen by my father from a litter of four puppies, because she was the smallest and prettiest-looking of the litter, with a dark coat and light muzzle. As she grew, her sleek coat and tan markings gave her a handsome appearance, and she too loved the twins, and would sit for hours beside the pram as if guarding them. Joan and I always had a strong bond with the dog, but Ayah was a little nervous and unsure of her, so if Ayah had given us a particularly hard time, we teased her unmercifully with the dog, making Poppet growl at her when she got near to the pram – well at least it gave us some small satisfaction to have someone on our side.

Matty spent many hours working amongst the flowers in the garden; she loved the outdoors, and the plants, and would sometimes sit outside the house, with her canvas or pad and paint them. Poppet would keep her company, lying alongside her chair, happily gnawing on a large ox-bone, which Luke would throw out on to the lawn for her. A variety of prettily coloured birds flew in daily to feed from the bird table nearby, wary of the sleeping servals. The whole place gave an air of complete tranquillity, disrupted only by the boisterous troop of visiting green monkeys, who would sit looking down from the overhanging tree branches. Each afternoon at about the same time, the same ritual was played out by the monkeys with barks and shouts. The only obstacle on their way to the trees at the far end of the garden was Poppet; so they would thrash about in the trees, rushing around, throwing down twigs or any missile they could reach, to try to get her to move. She wised-up to them early on, most of the time ignoring their antics, but when they pushed her too far she would move and wait until they came down from the trees to dart across the garden, whereupon she would give chase, scattering them in all directions. She was an excellent guard dog, and was very tolerant of the two cats, who by now were fully-grown and could fend for themselves. Their large ears and tiny, perky faces, gave them a comical appearance. They seemed happy enough in their human surroundings and became quite tame, having ample freedom to roam around or make their escape into the wild during the day, although at night they were penned. They scrambled around in the undergrowth, sparring with and teasing each other, while Poppet looked on, unamused, from a discreet distance, rarely having much to do with them: they seemed to respect each other's space.

Everywhere we went Poppet accompanied us, either in the car or when going for walks; and she especially loved the beach at the coast, chasing the surf and crabs amongst the rock pools. She was the right height for us to handle, and we always felt safe and comfortable in her company. Although fiercely loyal, and a good guard dog, she was also gentle and very friendly.

One day, Luke came to tell us that Poppet appeared listless and unwell and refused to eat anything despite all his efforts to try to coax her; we thought it was perhaps the heat that had got to her. Through the day, she lay under the shade of her favourite bush, and, despite the heat of the afternoon sun, she declined to drink the water which was placed in her bowl in front of her. Veterinary surgeons were few and far between in those days, and when an animal became very ill, the kindest thing to do was always to shoot them. My father hesitated to take such a drastic step with Poppet as she was a faithful animal so my parents stayed up through the night with her, trying to get her to at least drink. Finally, he was spared any such decision to shoot her, because by the early hours of the following morning, Poppet had given up her fight for life. She had, in fact, died of tick fever.

The house and gardens became a lonelier place without her around; she was no longer there to run to greet my father as he drove up the drive, or to accompany him when he went shooting, or to wag her tail outside the kitchen whenever she saw Luke appear with a bone. Our trips to the beach would never be so much fun again. Joan and I sobbed for days afterwards at losing her, and I often wondered later if, had she still been alive, the events that took place later in October of that year, would have turned out differently.

In many ways, Joan and I were like the country we lived in; we were both a little wild, often going about bare foot, wearing only a pair of pants for modesty. When my parents had visitors to the house, we had to 'dress up' – as we put it, which we hated, for it seemed quite unnatural for us to have to resort to being on display, playing with our old dolls and being posh and dressed when the visitors came. We both preferred the freedom of the outdoors and running about with the animals, especially Poppet. But with her now gone, we became quite resourceful, even commandeering the odd rabbit from the pen and taking it for walks in the doll's pram. We were delighted when Luke appeared one day with a beaming smile on his face, carrying a small vervet monkey in his arms. I was about to enquire where he got it from, when Joan eagerly scooped it out of his arms, immediately staking her claim on him, and the tiny creature was hastily brought indoors. The dolls and everything else were soon put aside and forgotten to make way for the new 'toy', and the dolls' clothes were unceremoniously tipped from their box on to the floor, only to be put on to this tiny uncomplaining monkey. I have to say, that he looked cute in his new wardrobe! We thoroughly enjoyed our trips to the coast with him as he ran around with a long lead attached to his waist, and we felt reasonably confident that there were no other monkeys around to entice him away. One day however, I let the lead accidentally slip from my hands – incurring the wrath of my older sister – as the little monkey made his bid for freedom, still wearing his clothes of the day!

Across, from the house, the maize plantation was due to be harvested, the tufts on the heads gently waving in the breeze. It took eighty days from planting to picking, I remember my father saying. We often enjoyed having 'corn-on-the-cob' for tea, and I offered to go into the field of maize (the stalks were a great deal taller than me) to pick some. After pulling out as many as I could carry, I emerged into the open once again, and as I did so one of the serval cats attacked me. I felt helpless as the animal, half my size, clung on to my arms, its claws digging deeper into my flesh from its sheer weight. My distant screams brought my father running from the house with his rifle in his hand. Shooting once into the air caused the cat to jump down off me, leaving me bleeding and bemused, and a second shot felled the animal as it tried to escape behind the house. Still clutching the armful of maize, I ran to where the serval lay dead. I couldn't for the life of me, understand why it had attacked me. I could only think that I had perhaps startled it, with the rustling noise of the leaves and stalks as I brushed against them and emerged into the open. Whatever it was, I felt dreadfully responsible for the poor cat's death – we had played so freely with these animals, forgetting one important factor – they were wild! The second serval was left outside at night and made its own way to freedom a couple of days later. My wounds took some time to heal but, thankfully, I was left unscarred.

Where we lived, the climate was tropical with little variation, save for the rainy seasons, of which there were two; one in November, and the other from February to May, although these varied slightly from place to place and year to year. In the hot dry season temperatures could reach the nineties, and nearer the coast it could be higher, with the atmosphere more heavy and humid. So it was not unusual to find most European families (who were not away working) taking a short siesta somewhere between the hours of midday to four. It certainly wasn't unusual for Matty to take to the cool of her bedroom to read or paint; sometimes we even joined her on her bed for a story, but mostly we preferred to be left to play outside in the shade, on our makeshift seesaw and swing. Ayah would either sit resting against the tree nearby, rocking the twins in their pram, or she would while away her time weaving. Our world was peaceful, laid-back and unhurried.

The afternoon of the 14th of October 1948, I remember, was warm and comfortable, but unusually breezy; the eerie wind whistled noisily around the side of the house, as it so often did before an impending rainstorm – in fact it was a relief to feel a cool breeze. So Ayah decided to take Joan and myself for a walk, and she allowed us on this day to take it in turns to push the twins in their pram. They were able to sit up now, strapped into the pram facing each other. As we walked away from the house, we could hear Luke, working away in the kitchen preparing the evening meal. There was the usual sound of escaping water down the drain and the clatter of pans being moved around.

Some moments later there were raised angry voices. We all stopped to listen for a moment, then walked on. Ayah wasn't duly alarmed; Luke often fell out with the staff if he felt they were either usurping his authority, or simply not pulling their weight and getting on with their allocated tasks for the day. He could be a hard taskmaster, often berating the native helpers for their idleness. Within a short time, the shouting became fierce, followed by what sounded like men scuffling; then there were faint moans, then silence. Ayah, not wishing to get involved, made some light-hearted comment in Swahili, like, "Luke, is really having a go at someone!". As we walked away, there came the most horrific screams from inside the house, so terrifying that at once we knew there was something horribly wrong.

Suddenly we were stunned into silence and terror.

Ayah, thinking quickly, pushed the sleeping twins in their pram into the safety of the bushes, and she and Joan went into the house. I ran into the kitchen to get help, but I was shocked at what I saw. Luke was clutching his chest, with blood pouring from between his fingers. He stumbled towards me, crumpling his shirt as he tried to stem the flow. I tried desperately to hold him up, to listen to what he was trying to say to me, but his limp body was too heavy for me and, as I held him, we both sank down on to the cold, grey, concrete floor. Pointing with his outstretched arm, he was able to tell me that Joseph had asked for a knife and when Luke questioned him as to why he needed it, the knife was wrestled from him. As he lay dying, his last words were for the safety of my mother. I ran towards the house, and before I could reach the steps, I came face to face with Joseph, half-naked from the waist down and heavily blood stained. He paused, then looked straight at me, his eyes wide open and wild. Brushing past me, he made off across the garden and into the field, as I looked on in horror and disbelief.

I was unprepared for what I saw next. On the bedroom floor lay pools of blood, and in my eagerness to get to my mother's side, I slipped and fell. Joan was at the top of the bed stroking Matty's hair. I remember that we exchanged a few words, and I picked up a small white enamel bowl, went to fill it from the cold water tap outside, and with the water we gently wiped her face, but that only revealed her badly lacerated cheeks and throat. "Don't worry," she said in a quiet voice: they were the last words she spoke. It had not occurred to me at this point, that she may die – mothers don't die – I was sure that my father would make her better when he came home.

Ayah grabbed the pram, and she and Joan hurried down the road towards the prison, shouting for help.

Down at the prison, I learned later, my father and Mr. Price were taking a stroll around the cattle boma and had paused for some time to watch a dung beetle rolling its ball of dung down a hole. They were quite absorbed in its antics, when they saw Ayah, who was now in shock, calling to them. She could hardly get the words out of her mouth, and they both realised that something dreadful had happened. Jumping into the car, they drove home as fast as they could and called the doctor. My father stood at the bedside, and with tears running down his cheeks he looked down upon the once beautiful face of his young wife, and bent over and kissed her. Everything had happened so quickly, and I cannot remember crying until I saw my daddy cry. Suddenly I was gripped with overwhelming fear, of what exactly I didn't know.

Doctor Smart, a family friend, arrived in his black Ford car. Wrapped up in her bedding, my mother was carried to the car and laid on the back seat with her head resting on Joan's knee for the journey to the European hospital. The doctor had deduced that despite her small frame she had put up an incredibly brave fight against her much larger attacker, but she died before reaching hospital, from severe haemorrhaging.

During the frenzied attack, the killer had lost part of his index finger, evidence that would trap him some time later.

We left the house and went to stay with Mr. and Mrs. Price. Joan began to tell of her terrifying encounter with the killer in the bedroom; how she had been chased around the room, but had been too quick for him; and how he had given up on her and run off.

As darkness fell, the Prices house seemed full of people coming and going; Joan and I were put to bed, but neither of us could sleep. The fears of the awful events of the day returned; fears that we were maybe being watched from the darkness outside. I remember being so petrified, even to go to the bathroom, that I lay and wet the bed, for which I felt horribly ashamed – what would Mrs. Price think of me? I lay there, still with the haunting whistle of the wind in my memory.

My father's well-ordered and happy life was now turned upside-down, and he was faced with the task of bringing up a very young family of four on his own. Mrs. Price had tried to explain the death of our mummy to us, in the kindest way possible, which must have been difficult for her; and I well remember imagining the vision of Matty meeting these angels with floating white wings in heaven and becoming one of them – which somehow brought some comfort and made it easier to understand. The Prices had been good friends to my parents, and now my father needed their help and support more than ever. About a day later we were flown by private plane to stay with Mr. and Mrs. Dawson, the Prison Commissioner and his wife, who lived in Dar-es-Salaam on the east coast; the twins and Ayah stayed at the British Consul's residence close by.

My father flew back to Kingolwira a few days later

where he had a number of things to do including sorting out the funeral arrangements. The nuns from the Catholic Church offered to take care of the twins and bring them up at the convent, but my father tried to assure them that he would manage somehow to take care of them himself, though I know that he was grateful for their prayers and kindness. And it was at the church on the hill that Matty was finally laid to rest, overlooking the deep valley of trees and undulating landscape running east towards the sea, at Mpopogolo.

The coast at Dar-es-Salaam, was intensely hot and sultry. The Commissioner's residence stood in its own grounds along the coast road, above the cliffs overlooking the Indian ocean. A spacious house, it had its own thatched rondavel which was used for VIPs and visitors. Both places had the customary whitewashed walls inside and out, and both were modestly furnished with pretty, chintz-covered furniture and matching curtains. How well I remember them, as we had been used to blinds at our house! Surrounded by its spacious lawns and gardens, fringed with waving palm trees, it would have seemed the most idyllic place on earth to stay for a few weeks, but each day was tinged with sadness and tears, and I was glad to have my big sister to cry and hold hands with as I came to depend on her more and more.

The Dawsons had two daughters, slightly older than us, who were very kind and generous with their time and spent endless hours with us, taking us down to the sandy beach to swim. It was peaceful, just watching the tide come and go, and the crabs run in and out of their burrows as the surf rolled over them. We would sometimes sit on the cliff tops and watch the high waves pound on to the volcanic rocks below, leaving the large caves and giant rock pools filled with sea water as the tide receded; and it was in one of these deep cavernous pools, that Mr. Dawson painstakingly taught both Joan and I to swim. The coastline was beautiful, with its extensive lengths of silver sand and overhanging cliffs of spiky, sharp-edged volcanic rock, pitted and gouged out over millions of years. The pools made the ideal home for hundreds of crabs and other sea creatures, and we wore plimsoles every time we went swimming, ever mindful of the spiked sea urchins which nestled in every crevice. Poor old Ayah; she was bitten by a snake in the garden during our stay in Dar, and had to be rushed to hospital not long before we returned to England. She recovered, but we never did see her again. With all that had happened, she must have been happy to see the back of us, I think.

Meanwhile, from what I understood, Joseph had been held in prison after being picked up on a minor burglary charge, which delayed our return home to England. Then there was the inquest. My father didn't tell us exactly what had upset him at the inquest. I remember he was very angry and upset and deeply offended by a remark which referred to Matty's code of dress – what it was we never knew. Whatever it was, there was some justice in the world, when the killer was eventually hanged in prison.

For years, I would often hear my father hum to himself or sing 'Waltzing Mathilda' while he was on his own in the workshop or bathroom. There was such melancholy in his voice which would bring a tear to my eye. Did he just like the tune or did the song remind him of my mother, Matty?

Before our return to England, two BOAC stewardesses were flown out from London to help on the flight back home, and Joan and I were given Martin and Mary, who were only a few months old, to hold on our knees and feed at meal times, which made us feel terribly responsible and grown up!

Chapter Two

We landed back in England that autumn of forty-eight, after a very long flight, to a host of waiting reporters; but all my father wanted to do was to get away from Southampton to Euston, and home to my grandparents with us as soon as possible and with the least amount of fuss. It proved to be difficult, and rather than wait to catch the train from Euston Station and be hounded most of the way by people asking questions, my father summoned two taxis to take us the whole way home.

"Where to, Sir?" the driver asked.

"Birmingham," said my father, noting the look of amazement on the drivers' faces.

They couldn't believe what they were actually being asked to do. All the luggage was piled into the first taxi, and we all piled into the second one. The drivers put blankets over our knees, as the weather was cold, and with the twins once again cradled in our arms, we were driven to our grandparents' home in Birmingham. Although the journey seemed to take hours, we were warm in the back seat of the taxi and, feeling very tired but still holding on to our twins, we fell asleep. We reached our destination by late evening in pitch black, and all I remember was being extremely tired and irritable at having to step out into the cold night air, then having to walk up the long cobbled lane (not wide enough for any car), and up the brick pathway to the front door of my grandparents' house.

Winter came in with a vengeance that year, or so it seemed. The large semi had three good-sized bedrooms upstairs, three rooms downstairs, and a kitchen, but no bathroom. Every room had a fire place, but only the fires in the three sitting rooms, were ever lit. The front room bay area was eventually fitted out with extra seating and became our sitting room; the middle room, with an extending table, became the main dining and play area. My grandparents certainly weren't short of furniture! Joan and I shared an old double bed in one of the upstairs bedrooms with an old kapok mattress which had to be turned each week and the lumps thumped out of it. The twins top and tailed in a single bed. In the freezing cold of the winter nights, icicles hung from the inside of the sash windows and, in our flimsy cotton nighties, we huddled together for every scrap of warmth we could get. There were no inside bathroom facilities, save a ceramic bowl and jug of water on a side table for hand washing. The toilet was outside next to the coal house, which meant a long walk down the flight of stairs, through the sitting rooms and out into the cold each visit; and at times it was so cold that even the water cistern froze.

Although, my father still had his job open to go back to, in reality he didn't want to return to Africa and was happy to stay in England, where he was at least assured of a roof over his head and a home for his children. Looking after us cannot have been easy at that time: rationing was on, there were the extra clothes and washing, and the responsibility of two tiny babies to be taken care of. It must have been an enormous undertaking for his parents as well. My grandmother was profoundly deaf, which meant that dialogue was kept to a minimum, and we always had to lean over and shout into her ear to make ourselves understood.

During our stay, some sort of routine was established at home, but as time went on there were difficulties, and there was talk of short-term fostering for Joan and me, until my father could focus on some sort of future for us all. With still a few months to go before the end of his leave, the Colonial Office and Mr. Dawson, his Commissioner, appealed to him to return to Africa and try to put the past behind him. Perhaps his eventual decision to return was, in part, thanks to his brother, David.

However, fate took a hand in the shape of a young, attractive, dark-haired nineteen-year old nurse. It so happened that my uncle David, a young RAF wartime tail-gunner on the Halifax bombers, was working at Castle Bromwich and met Betty, an attractive nurse from the local fever hospital, at a dance one evening. Right away, he thought that she would make an ideal partner for my father. So they were duly introduced to each other and after a brief courtship Betty and my father were married at the local registry office in February 1949, with my uncle and his pretty fiancée, Olivia, present. After a short honeymoon at the coast in Bournemouth, my father brought home his young wife to meet his children.

Dressed in our Sunday-best clothes, we were standing at the bottom of the lane when the car arrived, and were greeted with the words, "I want you to meet your new mummy".

Over the previous weeks, I had developed a lazy eye leaving me with a slight squint, and on top of all that I was getting over a bad bout of bronchitis which kept me barking all day long – I must have looked a sorry sight! I cannot imagine what would have been going through her mind when she saw me. A young woman with a ready-made family to look after! I am sure that it was enough to send her fleeing from the scene, gasping, "I think I've made an awful mistake!". But, God bless Betty, she stayed to take care of us; with her pleasant, sweet-smiling face and her kindness, we warmed to her right away. The following day, clutching her engagement ring money, she took Joan and me into town on the bus, and bought us some pretty new clothes and shoes.

As the date of our departure from England approached, both my parents felt it was prudent to see an ophthalmic surgeon about my eye problem before we left. And so I began a series of visits to the Birmingham Eye Hospital, which was known to have an excellent reputation, and was seen by an ophthalmic surgeon by the name of Mr. Churchill. Placing my chin on the ophthalmic apparatus I was asked to look into the gadgetry and try to put the lion in the cage; try as I did, I could never get that wretched animal to enter his cage! I would eventually need an operation to correct the astigmatism, I was told; meanwhile I was fitted with a horrible looking pair of spectacles (very fashionable fifty years later!) which I hated wearing.

Finally, when the time came for us to leave England, we waved our farewells to our grandparents at the garden gate, then left by taxi for the train station, and on to Southampton Water to catch the flying boat to Africa. This giant, high-powered, amphibious aircraft, conceived and designed not for the prosperous or privileged class, but to carry letters and parcels to all parts of the British Empire, had a hull instead of the usual bulk fuselage. An enormous, inspired combination of boat and wings which could fly over the oceans, come down on water and lie at anchor, then take off again from the water as majestically as a land-plane manoeuvred on firm ground, was always a rare and magnificent sight. Carefully planned to contribute to the comfort of fifteen or more passengers and five crew members, it even boasted a promenade deck. The Empire Flights, as they became known, followed the Nile route from Alexandria to Cairo, down to Lake Victoria, Naivasha, across to the east coast of Africa, and onwards to the Cape.

As we sped along the mile it took the flying boat to rise from the water, the surf hit the porthole windows at speed, and up we went, leaving the coast of Southampton behind us.

Once again a special stewardess dressed in her crisp, white blouse and dark navy suit, with BOAC insignia emblazoned on her cap, was assigned to help with Mary and Martin. She was kind and attentive, especially as a good many of us were feeling queasy from the droning noise of the engines (which could be deafening). I can remember that it was a great relief to touch down on the waters off the shores of Alexandria.

We disembarked on to a motor launch and were taken to stay at a suite in the Cecil Hotel, where the place seemed to buzz with activity. There were people everywhere, and the foyer entrance was crowded with light suited men, porters and baggage. We were shown to our room, overlooking the busy main street below, and we stayed put, playing and drawing in our books, taking our meals in the room for the duration of our stay, and while temperatures soared outside, we were cooled in our room by the two whirring overhead fans.

It was during our stay at this time that I remember my mother staying in the room to look after the twins, who were by now quite mobile, while Joan and I, accompanying my father, went off to meet our grandfather Darmanin – Matty's father. He was a tanned, short, stocky man with a handsome open face. We sat patiently in our comfortable chairs in the hotel lounge, together with a teddy bear each, a Christmas present from who else – Father Christmas – while the two men talked for what seemed like hours. I finally fell asleep and had to be woken up to say good-bye to him – unaware that it would be the last time we would see him. We were told a couple of years later that he died in Egypt.

Our stay at the hotel was short, only a couple of nights, so when we left the following day to go back on board the flying boat I was not looking forward to the journey one bit, the sound of the engine noise still ringing in my ears. The one part of the journey that I disliked in those days was the initial, overwhelming smell of stale hot air and aviation fuel as you entered the craft, which was enough to make you almost instinctively reach for the sick bag. However, the incredible views and sights in flight were an overwhelming compensation.

As we flew over Cairo and looked down on the magnificent pyramids at Giza, just eight miles out from the busy city, the air cooled and the sun threw light over the tall, golden dunes casting giant shadows across the ground. From the promenade deck the view below us was incredible as we sped over vast areas of desert, punctuated by small areas of canvas camps and dwellings dotted around palm tree covered oases. The wandering herds of camels and wildlife appeared as tiny moving dots.

We continued down the path of the River Nile, the water glistening and dotted with light sailing craft as it drifted in and out of view, until the late afternoon when the sun went down, and darkness came. When we landed at Khartoum to disembark and the cabin door opened, I felt the full force of the day's heat waft in to meet me: it almost took my breath away. All the passengers were ushered down a gangplank towards some uniformed customs men, who were sitting behind tables under a large enclosed tent, ready for our baggage check. I was delighted to see a table set out with glasses of orange juice; I was more than ready for a cool drink, but it was warm, and after taking a sip from the glass I felt my stomach churn.

When we re-entered the flying boat to sit down I was ill over everything, and my small contribution did little to enhance the atmosphere in the cabin, as my poor mother tried desperately to clean me up. During the late hours we were given blankets to keep us warm from the night chill, and I went to sleep.

We finally landed near the shores of Lake Victoria, where we completed our journey in the flying boat, and were taken to stay with friends near Kisumu for a few days. During our stay with them, we went swimming in the lake each day, until we were 'ambushed' one afternoon by a disgruntled hippo and forced to flee for our lives.

We flew on to Nairobi by Dakota aircraft and stayed at the Norfolk Hotel for another few days, which was pleasant. From Nairobi we all flew on to Moshi in the northern part of Tanganyika, where we were met at the airstrip by Mr. Dawson and another of his colleagues, who drove us to the Lion Cub Hotel, where we were required to stay for an unspecified duration while the house we were due to move into was nearing completion.

The hotel was on the outskirts of the town, not far from the prison and, like many of the local buildings, it had whitewashed walls and a red tiled roof. The stay gave my mother some time at least to acclimatise, and we did have some native help. The bedrooms were spacious and comfortable, and it must have been an immense relief for her to finally be able to unpack the load of clothes and nappies which had been piled into a dozen or so large heavy suitcases, and have them laundered by the hotel dhobi.

Louvered wooden shutters at the window kept any intruders out. Coir carpeting covered part of the red cardinal floors, and to my delight there were twin beds for Joan and me – a change from sharing, and Mary and Martin had a large cot each. Outside, the tall canopy of trees shaded the rooms from the force of the hot afternoon sun, and the bushes and garden made it an ideal place for a good game of hide and seek.

That week, one of us fell ill with chicken pox, followed by another, until we were all inflicted, which meant that we could no longer eat with others in the dining room or go anywhere other than our rooms. When Joan got bored with crayons and books, she found a more interesting way to entertain herself: with a pair a scissors she found lying in a bag, she began to cut up her bedspread – I thought it was a great game too and joined in. My parents were not amused, and we were both spanked.

Venturing outside into the open at any time of day invited hordes of flies, and before long we all had infected lesions on our legs and arms, which required medical attention. Sleeping at night was uncomfortable and the twins cried continuously from their discomfort, which meant a lot of weary hours for my mother.

One morning we were abruptly awakened by hysterical shouts coming from her bedroom. Directly above the headboard, she had spotted a scorpion crawling up the mosquito net, and my father was called upon to dispatch the beast at once! "Welcome to Africa," my father declared, but she wasn't in the least bit amused. After that experience, it became a compulsory ritual each night before retiring to bed, to walk around and check all the nets – the numerous holes in them hardly kept out the marauding mosquitoes, let alone scorpions!

My father had already begun his work at the Karanga Prison, which I understood was relatively new and run on the same concepts as the one at Kingolwira, and he became absorbed in his work with a great determination and hope for a new start, for the sake of my mother; however, it cannot have been easy to try and carry on, for it was still early days for him to forget all that had taken place a year earlier.

The Big House was nowhere near completion when we did finally move into it, but the bedrooms were completed and the walls painted. The sitting and dining rooms were almost finished. We had some furniture although the house was still waiting to be completely roofed leaving some areas open to the elements.

A tall, light-skinned, African man named Mohammed, and an attractive lady named Marion, had been taken on, as cook and Ayah. Mohammed came with excellent references from his previous employer at the hotel where he had worked for some years. He was in his mid-years, with aquiline features, and the shiniest bald head that I had ever seen in my life; and he appeared to possess something of a sense of humour. My mother, who had learned a few words of Swahili in the short time since her arrival, needed our help to understand Mohammed's Swahili; however, between all of us we managed to get some form of dialogue going. He seemed a pleasant enough person and, after acquainting himself with the layout of the kitchen, was eager to please and set to work right away.

There was a lot to be done at the Big House, and a few of the inmates from the prison, with an African warder in charge, were allocated to help with roofing and to fetch and carry.

Electricity and water had yet to be piped to the house, so in the meantime, oil burning 'tilly' lamps were prepared each evening before dusk, and hung in every room of the house for lighting. All the water for drinking and bathing had to be carried from the spring in the valley in large tin jerry cans, then boiled and filtered. At night the house was open to the black sky, and the bright lights from each lamp, attracted moths and all kinds of night bugs which flew around and about, cavorted and died. The outside lamps also attracted bats, which flew from the eaves to the trees and back again, and the small lizards scampered and scuttled across the ceilings to catch an insect or two. No one complained if a bug or two fell into their soup; you could hardly see anyway, and you just carried on with your meal!

My mother tried hard to settle down to her life in Africa, and she began to receive a few friendly visitors. But there were times when she felt utterly inadequate for not being able to grasp enough of the language to put across to the Africans, what she wanted them to do. This led to bouts of frustration and tears. My father cannot have been altogether truthful with her about the hardship he knew she would encounter; maybe he was unaware of the full extent of it himself! But it took all my mother's pioneering spirit to overcome the many problems, and there were many, many tears!

Before long, a tall concrete structure was built on the hill behind the servants' quarters to carry a huge water tank. All through the day, a pump chugged away, pulsating hundreds of gallons of fresh spring water from the valley below, along pipes and into the tank. When the house was finally finished, the walls were painted with the customary whitewash inside and out. Electricity was piped to the house about a year or so later; meanwhile the lamps were our only source of lighting everywhere.

The heavy vegetation around the house was cleared by the inmates, supervised by the ever watchful Askari (warder). Felled trees were sorted for logging and firewood, and removed by oxen-drawn cart. Many were the times that Joan, myself and the twins, would sit on the back of the cart for a short run down the road, and watch snakes slither across the freshly-cleared site. There was always a frenzy of excitement when anybody came across a snake in their path. It was more often than not, followed by a lot of animated arm waving, jumping about and feeble lashing out with sticks, sending the poor, half-dazed creature slithering off to safety. I rarely saw an African kill a snake – legends and superstition regarding these creatures were endless, and when we were young, the stories we were told struck terror into us.

One afternoon, I was looking through the window of the hallway as Mohammed walked by carrying an enormous bundle of sticks on his shoulder. From the bundle appeared an emerald green ribbon-like thing which began to dangle from the sticks. I suddenly realised that it must be a green mamba. Wasting no time, I shouted out loudly to him to drop the load, and as he did so, the snake reared at him, missing him by inches, then escaped back into the bundle of sticks. He finally extracted the snake from the wood, holding it coiled at the end a branch, moved it on to higher ground and let it go. As it disappeared into the grass, I asked him why he hadn't killed it? He explained that snakes were sacred relatives that had come back from the dead.

Snakes weren't the only hazard. Black centipedes were a constant menace. Entering the overflow pipe at night, they would fall into the bath and, unable to make their escape and being too large to be flushed down the outlet, they had to be removed carefully with pincers and disposed of. On one occasion, my father went to the lavatory, and it was customary for him to take a newspaper with him to read, but as he opened up the paper, a centipede fell out on to his lap, giving him the fright of his life – he later described the scene of the incident in great detail, which had us all laughing; however, these creatures were able to inflict a terrible bite.

Moshi, a German settlement and garrison town during the First World War, was a large town, situated at the foothills of Africa's tallest mountain Kilimanjaro. It had a pleasant, temperate climate and was the home of the Chagga people. A well-educated and religious people, due to instruction by the early missionaries, they had at their head a young leader, Chief Tom Marealle II. It was a reasonably prosperous area by most standards, producing and exporting some of the finest coffee in the world, grown on the foothills of the mountain. It had its churches, schools, and military army barracks of the King's African Rifles, as well as many government buildings and banks, and a busy, thriving market town.

While I attended the local primary school near the centre of town, Joan went off to boarding school in Arusha, some fifty-two miles away. My mother had come on well with her Swahili, and proved that she had excellent management skills too, instituting the planting of trees and flowering shrubs. A shamba (small vegetable garden), was created under the shade of the water tank and, with millions of years of untapped fertility in the soil, everything that was planted grew and thrived; with free labour to hand, the land around the house was levelled and areas grassed. Bougainvillaea, in its many shades of colours from cream to fuchsia, made up the hedges, and iris, African cannas, begonias and marigolds festooned the borders. Also planted were the avenue of young Poinciana trees, on either side of the approach road. Near the house, standing about a hundred feet high, were three of the tallest trees in Moshi which could be seen from great distances away. With their incredible size and dense foliage, they also served as a landmark for passing aircraft.

Within a short period of time, the prison had developed into a viable working farm, and eventually the use of yoked cattle to do the heavy work was replaced by a Ford tractor and trailer to help with the ploughing and moving of bagged grain and the like. The sisal, which grew in abundance, not only made protective boundary fencing, but, when harvested, its fibres were teased out into long strands to dry in the sun for making woven matting.

All inmates had their allocated daily duties. The Masai, being natural herdsmen, were tasked to look after the growing herd of cattle and other livestock; which meant that they took responsibility for dipping, rearing and slaughtering. After milking each morning these tall sinewy fellows would lead their charges out into the open prairie around the prison, and when Joan and I were home at half term, we often joined them on their long walks. Armed with our sticks, just like the Masai, we pretended to herd too and we enjoyed the company of these tall handsome-featured men with their incredible sense of fun and humour. The walks sometimes took hours in the sunshine, but we had to be back at the boma by early afternoon for the Masai to return to their cells for lock up.

When Mr. Lunn, his wife and son, Brian, came fresh from England to join us, they moved in to the Big House and my parents moved to a brand new house that had been built about half a mile away. Like my father, Mr. Lunn, who became my father's second-in-command, had left the Coldstream Guards and joined the Colonial Service. As a result the two families became good friends. Like all newcomers to new homes, the Lunns made a number of changes to the Big House, and a few additions too. They installed a small barrel with a series of tiny drill holes. This hive, placed in the tall tree above the house, was to encourage the bees which had the reputation of producing the 'tastiest honey in the world'; so they were told by their cook. I recall the glee on Mr. Lunn's face as we were all paraded out from the sitting room to marvel at this contraption placed about thirty feet high in the canopy.

There was a great amount of joy when my mother became pregnant with her first baby and in February 1951 my brother, Peter, was born at the local government hospital just a stone's throw from the centre of town. Joan was away at school at the time, but the twins and I were around to enjoy the immense excitement of his homecoming. My parents held a huge party for friends when he was christened six months later. His godparents, Mr. and Mrs. Tsoukas, were a lovely Greek couple with two pretty daughters. They owned a coffee plantation a few miles out of town on the undulating mountain slopes. I recall that they had the most beautifully manicured lawns and gardens which stretched as far as the eye could see, with ornate garden ornaments and bird baths. What stood out in my memory was the pack of unruly hounds, large and small. Their Alsatians knocked you over with their sheer weight and exuberance when they bounded over to greet you, which could be terrifying, and then they would run off and chase each other wildly in and out of the flower beds, causing damage and mayhem; often smartly followed by the angry gardener waving a stick and shouting and swearing abuse in Swahili!

In a short space of time after our arrival, we seemed to pick up every childhood ailment going around. The twins and I caught whooping cough from some friends' children who were staying with us for a while, and we wheezed and coughed our way through the days and nights. It must have been an awful time for my mother, who was forced to farm Peter out to stay with Mrs. Lunn for a short period of time to avoid him being affected in any way, while she tried to cope with the rest of us who were going through bad bouts of coughing fits that appeared to last an age.

That year, acquaintances of my parents came to stay with us from Tanga on the east coast with their young daughter, Molly, aged about six. During their visit, I had taken Molly under my wing and happily played with and looked after her. So I was more than delighted when her parents asked mine if it would be all right for me to join them at the coast for a break, as it was thought that I would make a good companion for Molly; apart from that, it was also suggested that the sea air would be good for my rehabilitation after the bad bout of whooping cough. I jumped at the idea and persuaded my parents to let me go, totally overjoyed at the prospect of being near the sea once more and having the opportunity of being able to go swimming every day, as their home was not far from the beach. Molly and I got on very well initially, despite the gap of a couple of years in our ages.

Tanga, situated roughly between Mombasa and Dar-es-Salaam on the east coast, had a large modernised port which was developed by the addition of a rail link built by the Germans in the late 1800s. Restored, it was put in to operation later to link Moshi and Tanga for the purpose of exporting mainly sisal, but also coffee and sugar. As the ships were being unloaded at the dockside, we could watch the dhows and other coastal craft traffic, perhaps on their way from the Persian Gulf and the Red Sea, coming and going, to and from the smaller ports on the southern coast of East Africa. I do not know whether Molly's parents had relatives or just friends who worked on board the ships, but on a couple of occasions we were taken out by launch across the waters to have tea in the ward room of the visiting Union Castle.

Tanga, the second largest port after Dar, was five degrees south of the Equator, hot, humid, with its shores around the harbour fringed with mangrove swamps, harbouring mosquitoes and water-snakes. Yet to us as children, it held its fascination. On the sand dunes and between the palm trees near the beach we often spotted vast numbers of long black millipedes which snaked their way along the sands, under the fallen palm leaves and over the dunes. They were a great source of entertainment and we could amuse ourselves for hours playing with them; barring their pathways with sticks, which caused them to roll on their sides into a tight circle, protecting their numerous little feet; they would play 'dead' for a few seconds, before going on their way again, and we always referred to them as 'Tanga trains'.

When Molly was due to start her first term at the Catholic School Convent, I was asked if I would like to accompany her, so I duly went along with whatever the family decided, always assuming that it was my parents' wish that I should do so. I recall very little about my time at the convent, except that I was very excited when we were all issued with small black slates and a slate pencil to write with on our first day. The convent was run by nuns in their crisp white wimples and long black habits, and there was always an air of unrivalled serenity as they walked about silently along the corridors with calm dignity. Their order made such an impact on me that I was so sure that when I grew up, I would follow in the footsteps of one of these kind people. Any running up and down the corridors was frowned upon and good manners were encouraged at all times. They were strict and stood for no nonsense, but they were also kind and always calm, and I loved it there.

Sadly, before the term had come to an end, my increasing discontent and impatience with Molly's behaviour and whining reached boiling point and on occasions we fell out. I was unhappy at constantly being responsible for her after school while her parents rested happily in their bedroom in the afternoons. Being responsible for her, as well as entertaining her, became irksome, and the playing inevitably ended with a punch-up and my getting into trouble.

Adding to my rapidly growing disquiet, I was most distraught, when I was made to have my waist-length, brown, curly hair cut short one day. I presume that it was supposed to make getting ready for school easier, but having worn it neatly plaited before, I was now faced with a head of thick, unmanageable hair. With the humidity of the air, it dried and frizzed, and no amount of combing would tidy it up. I cannot recall the numerous occasions that I was sent back to my room to re-comb it – with the added threat of going without my tea if I didn't get it right! My hair in fact became such an 'issue' that one day, I stayed in my room and flatly refused to leave it. I cried, refused to comb it and told them in no uncertain terms that I didn't want to eat with them any way – and I wanted to go back home to my mother! I can imagine the phone call to my parents after that. The next thing I knew was that my mother was coming to collect me to take me home.

Not everything was bad about my stay with them. I recall one very funny incident that took place one day. Molly and I had been invited to a friend's birthday party and all the children attending were invited to dress up for the occasion. Most of the children's parties we attended were lavish affairs. Molly decided that she wanted to go as a ballet dancer, and I thought that her idea was clever and wonderful and I, too, should like to go as a ballet dancer. Molly's mother was a good dress-maker, and began right away cutting out the fine pink and white satin and netting which would make the two small tutus. So there was great excitement each day when we returned from school to find that more sewing had been done until, finally completed, the two tutus were hung on two small hangers inside the bedroom door for all to see. When the time came around to get ready for the party, Molly was given first choice and plumped for the pink tutu. Then out of a shoe box appeared a pair of the prettiest pink satin ballet shoes that I had ever seen and after Molly had put them on she preened in front of the mirror, as I looked on delighting in her joy. She looked like a little fairy. I could hardly contain my wild excitement when it came to my turn to dress up and put on my ballet shoes. I put on the tutu and stood excitedly waiting for my little shoes to appear, when to my horror and dismay, a pair of black shiny Wellingtons were produced from inside the wardrobe. I didn't understand the significance at first: not for me the delicate little ballerina but – a circus act! I was mortified, as I so wanted to look as dainty as Molly – and it quite ruined my day, although I laughed about it years later.

I felt some sadness yet relief, at my final farewell to Tanga. I knew that I would miss the kindness of the nuns at the convent school, but I was happy to see my mother again. I ran to greet her with open arms as she got out of the car, and we cuddled. When she noticed that my hair had been cut and enquired as to why I had had it done, I fully intended to blurt out my feelings right then and there, but before I could utter a word to her, we were joined by company and no more was said.

Another incident which remained vivid was when a

meal was prepared for all of us on the veranda, in the afternoon on which we were due to leave. It would have been wholly unmemorable but for the sudden appearance of a six inch black centipede waving its scarlet antennae, and making its way hurriedly towards the table. Molly's father, with his knife and fork in his hand and by then half way through his meal, suddenly bent down and with a swipe of his knife, sliced the creature in half. For me, the incident might have been forgotten, but for the fact that he continued to eat his meal, using the same knife!

When we got home, Joan had arrived back from boarding school, and Mary and Martin, whom I hadn't seen for months, appeared much taller, while little Peter with his fair hair and beautiful features was delighting everyone with his infant antics. I was just immensely happy to be back home again and to see them all. In my absence, a Rhodesian Ridgeback dog had joined the family, lodging with us whilst the owners were on their six months' leave in England. He was a good companion for us and an alert guard dog, but had the annoying habit of running off down to the native villages about a mile outside the perimeter fence. Sometimes he would be gone for days, causing my parents many anxious hours of looking and calling out for him, only to see him return home covered in filthy mud and ticks after running through the undergrowth.

My parents entertained a fair amount and at home in Moshi 'open house' was often the order of the day and this could mean any day and at any time. Our native cook coped reasonably well with the many demands made upon him to produce interesting meals for dinner and 'bridge' evenings, and my mother was never unduly perturbed when the flour, sugar, tea and other produce mysteriously disappeared from the store cupboard: petty pilfering went on all the time – it was expected and wasn't regarded as stealing by the Africans, merely their due! Sugar and tea were very popular – so was the Scotch Whisky!

When my mother got herself a part-time job in town, she left Marion, our Ayah, to look after the twins and Peter, while Joan and I were at school. But during the school holidays, we took charge of the twins and often took them out with us, or kept an eye on them while they played around outside. Mary was a contented child, remaining absorbed with her toys and dolls, but Martin was highly adventurous, and if he wasn't falling out of trees, he was always getting himself into scrapes.

Outside the house by the side of the bathroom window, a barrel water-tank was housed over a kiln stove to heat the bath water; the open fire underneath the tank was kept on the go all through the day, and topped up with firewood by the native labour who were allocated to work at the house. As youngsters, we took advantage of this 'cooking' facility and cooked maize and red bananas in it until they were crisp and ready to eat. However, Martin, having observed us prodding around with the sticks in the fire to produce such delicacies, decided one day to have a go himself. While he poked and played in the fire, unnoticed and unsupervised by us, he inserted his hand in to the fire to retrieve his gourmet's delight, only to withdraw it immediately accompanied by howls, as a number of hot coals stuck fast to his delicate skin.

His loud screams and howls of pain drew our attention to what had happened and, fortunately, Mohammed rushed from the kitchen to his aid right away with some rock salt dissolved in water to soak his hand. Without a doubt his quick thinking averted what could have been a serious injury and we were most relieved that Martin was left with few blisters to have to explain away to my parents! On another occasion the twins came rushing into the house, crying, shaking their hands and jumping up and down. For moments we stared at these two little waifs, who looked quite comical, and couldn't see why they were carrying-on so. Giving no indication and totally preoccupied with making the noise, they left us to solve the problem for them. We peered down at their legs and feet and discovered that they were, in fact, being eaten alive through their socks by red safari ants, which were gradually creeping up their legs. Quickly and carefully we had to remove by fingertip, each hooked ant, one by one, to avoid the twins being bitten further; we then bathed them both in antiseptic solution.

With plenty of free time on school holidays, each morning we were able to accompany Marion on her jaunts to see her friends down at the warders' quarters. It was a place well out of bounds to us normally, but we figured that what my parents didn't know, didn't hurt! It was also out of bounds to Marion while we were in her charge – but we were not about to tell. The sheer excitement of doing something you were not allowed to was overwhelming. Peter's fair hair and skin made him a favourite with the warders' bibis (wives). He was never short of cuddles, being continually passed around from one set of loving arms to another. While the twins played happily with the local native children and chased the chickens, Joan and I got down to the serious business of learning how to mill maize into rough grain. Using an old bevelled-out tree trunk representing a mortar and introducing small handfuls of maize kernels a bit at a time, then pounding hard into them with a four foot pole as a pestle, we could produce coarse grain which when cooked turned into a thick porridge called 'posho'. When cooked and flavoured this was very pleasant to eat and on occasions we were even invited to sit and join the wives at their meals. We simply loved our jaunts down to see them. The women folk were extremely industrious; when they were not cultivating and digging in their shambas or collecting firewood, they were sweeping and cleaning the grounds around their houses. With chickens and children running around, they still made time for us. We learned a lot from them, as they taught us their craft of basket weaving: from long strands of dried grasses, we criss-crossed lengths of the stuff into weave, with inches more added, on every visit. Sitting amongst them, we whiled away the hours weaving, and as we got better and faster, we were able to add massive lengths of weave in a single sitting. Our Swahili improved too as we sat and listened intently to them swapping stories and laughing. When the weave was long enough to be sewn, we made our very own kikapu (basket).

During the balmy afternoons at home, we were allowed access to the kitchen at the back of the house, as long as we cleared and tidied up after ourselves. So many of our afternoons were spent experimenting with ingredients for recipes, and we turned out gourmet offerings to the twins. Joan always loved to cook – she was gifted. I spent time helping her make cakes and as we were never without tins of Nestlé's condensed milk at the house, we overdosed on home-made sweets. Her speciality was fudge, which she made by the tin-full. Whatever Joan was making, there were lots of leftovers – enough for the prisoners who were working around the house or nearby. There was an element of risk attached to doing this, but we always made sure that the warders were well out of sight for fear of getting caught – or we would have got them, and ourselves, into deep trouble and my father would have been furious if he had ever got wind of it at the time! However, it brought a smile to his face when we told him years later of what we used to get up to!

The servants' quarters were strictly out of bounds to all of us, mainly to respect the staff's privacy, and we did generally adhere to it. Mohammed always took the afternoon off after lunch and retired for a couple of hours to his room. Marion, who was always supposed to be on duty through the day looking after the twins and Peter, for some reason never seemed to be about, and took to disappearing around the back of the servants quarters. We never questioned her movements; why should we? But one afternoon we heard squeals of delight and laughter coming from Mohammed's room. We knew he was a family man. If I remember rightly, he had two wives and nine children. His wives and children lived miles away from Moshi and he saw them infrequently. Being curious and nosey to find out why there was such jollity, and urged on by my big sister to investigate the matter, I hastily pushed a box from the kitchen to the wall beside his room, looked through the partially opened shutters and peered into the darkness. I couldn't see anything at first, but what I had failed to realise was that whoever was there could see me, as the light was behind me. By the time my eyes had adjusted to the darkness, I beheld two figures in the nude, wrapped around each other. I quickly closed the shutters and ran off in haste to tell Joan. We were so busy falling about and laughing and sniggering, that we hadn't noticed the approach of Mohammed from the back of the house a few minutes later. He was furious, and grabbing my arm and holding it outstretched, he used his forefinger as a cane, bringing it down like a whiplash across my arm twice – which was extremely painful – but I suppose it was to serve as a warning against any further intrusion into his privacy. This was his favoured way of punishment, followed by tutting and shaking of his head. I knew right away that what I had done was wrong, and maybe I had deserved his punishment; the staff were the rule of law at all times when my parents were away from home. At the dinner table that evening, my mother noticing the welts, enquired as to how they got there, and I found myself making some feeble excuse in case I got myself in even more trouble.

After that little episode, Joan and I decided that we would give neither Mohammed or Marion any respite; we would not invade their privacy, but instead we would play tricks on them every time they disappeared into the back together. So whenever either of us walked near the kitchen – which was as often as possible – we would rattle the shutters, sending them both into blind rages. As children we feared nothing and trusted everyone, especially the servants, yet our ignorance almost led us up a sinister path to an unpleasant side of life.

One afternoon when my mother was away visiting friends, Joan was having her usual baking session, with me as her helper. Mohammed entered the kitchen and, walking towards us, he calmly unfastened his trousers fumbled around, and exposed himself to us. We were somewhat taken aback as we stared in disbelief, thinking at the least he was being rather naughty and at worst very rude, and we tried shyly to ignore him, and left. We both knew that what he had done was wrong, but at no time did we ever imagine that we were in any kind of danger, and we never told our parents. Also, at no time did we associate this with, or were ever aware of, any sexual connotation; in fact we had found the whole episode exceedingly funny and at bed time that night it became the topic of conversation. We laughed so much that we must have made enough noise to awaken the household, for our jollity was brought to an abrupt end with shouts of, "quiet you two!" coming from our parents' room. However, when Mohammed again repeated his actions about a fortnight later, it unnerved us so much that we kept well away from him and the kitchen boundary.

It was always the custom that whenever our parents left the house to attend official engagements or parties, an African warder would be asked to patrol the house outside the grounds until their return. There were other occasions too, which required both to attend: sometimes there were arguments or marital disputes at the warders' quarters which often got out of hand, and on more than one occasion a wife would arrive sobbing or bleeding and needing help to resolve a family dispute, which would mean both my parents leaving at unsocial hours to deal with difficult situations; another would be the escape of a prisoner from jail when the phone would ring, followed by the high-pitched sound of blown whistles, generally followed by a frenzy of activity which would alarm and cause fear in Joan and me.

Shortly after seven o'clock one night, the sky was dark but there was a full moon. The phone rang, and in the distance the warders' whistles could be heard. Leaving the cook and Ayah in charge of all of us, my parents got ready to leave the house. Before setting off by car for the prison, they both made sure that the lights were left on in the hall and the doors of the house securely locked behind them. We were given strict instructions and forbidden to let anyone enter the premises during their absence, and by about nine o'clock that evening, we had settled ourselves in our beds. So it came as a frightening shock when sometime after that there was a rattling of the back door handle. Terrified, and wondering who it could possibly be, I froze to the bed not daring to move. I whispered to Joan, "Who could it be? The escaped prisoner? Who?" Suddenly we recognised the voice of Mohammed. Choosing to ignore him, we kept quiet and still. He continued to rattle the door handle and bash the door until Joan, not able to stand the noise any longer and fearful that he would break in, left her bed, with me following on behind, and went to enquire what he wanted. We both peered out into the darkness and saw him standing on the steps looking rather dishevelled and very drunk. Wild with anger and frustration, he demanded that we open the door, and, as he continued to rattle the handle, we became increasingly worried and frightened as to what he would do. Choosing to ignore him, yet feeling anxious, we returned to our room. Moments later, to our great relief, we saw the car headlights light up the sky and approach up the drive. Mohammed had gone before the car reached home and my parents were none the wiser about what had occurred that evening in their absence as, for some misguided reason, we didn't wish to be responsible for him losing his job; we said nothing at all of that evening, but we were intensely relieved and happy when he was discharged a day or so later from his post – the reason being that my father found out that a good deal of his precious whisky had gone missing! I cannot recall what happened to Marion, the Ayah, but I do remember that she taught us a naughty song which I could not possibly repeat.

Chapter Three

The few years short respite after the end of the war in Europe gave people time to come to terms with the loss of loved ones and homes. Over those years many people, drawn together through adversity, tried to rebuild their shattered lives. The world was ripe for change and for some it couldn't come soon enough. So, the 1950s constituted a period of change from the rigours of war to an uneasy peace in the world; none more so than in Africa, where a wind of change was blowing throughout the continent. In Kenya, men had come home from the war to join their families and settle on the fertile lands of the Highlands and Aberdares. As more Europeans arrived to settle, so more and more land was cleared and allocated to them. The Africans saw this land as their own and demanded its restoration. When the Europeans resisted, the land question and the genuine struggle for freedom, became an issue. A great many of the Africans living in Kenya were from the Kikuyu tribe. Some moved into the mountains to form their own band of freedom fighters, enlisting the help of Jomo Kenyatta (a young British-trained lawyer) to help fight their cause.

All too soon, however, amid stories of oathing ceremonies and secret rituals that bound and instilled a savage discipline, came killings by armed gangs calling themselves the Mau Mau. The conflict led to the Government declaring a State of Emergency in October of 1952.

These were disturbing and frightening times for my parents too, not least because it became clear from many of the stories that reached us that even once-loyal and trusted staff could be intimidated to turn against you, as many in Kenya found out to their cost. The calm of the open prison, where inmates could once be seen going about their daily tasks, took on a whole new feel. A high grey stone wall was built with lookout towers at each corner, replacing the barbed wire fence, the purpose being to contain any dissent or riot within the jail, but also to be ready to accept any overflow of detainees from the now already filling detention camps in Kenya. The imposing façade of the prison building took on the look of a medieval castle standing in a rural garden.

At home, the rifles which were normally held secured were double-locked, and my father taught my mother how to shoot with the hand gun which he had bought her for her protection. She kept it close to hand during the day, and under her pillow when in bed.

When more and more stories of farmers and their families being hacked to death, and their animals being mutilated, reached us from Kenya, my parents decided that it would be prudent for my mother to return to England with all of the children at the end of the school term and that my father would follow in a few weeks after his tour of duty was up.

Levi, a native man from the local Chagga tribe, had taken on the dual role of cook and houseboy. He was very reliable, a quality which made him a valued member of staff; always neat in his appearance, he worked hard and took on many tasks, supervising the labour, even the gardens, and he seemed to enjoy his status as cook, houseboy and butler.

Before we could return home to England again, everything in the house had to be packed and crated up, then everything was stored and locked up in one of the bedrooms, to await our return in six months. It was compulsory that all end of tour leave had to be taken in the United Kingdom; the complete change to a cooler climate was considered not only to be beneficial but necessary.

Our flight home was not without its own mini-diplomatic incident. We arrived in Egypt at a time when there was rising nationalism in the country, and where Britain was seen as a symbol of alien domination and Arab powerlessness. All in all they did not like us much! Our standing in the Middle East was reaching an all-time low. And the portly playboy King Farouk was about to be ousted by Colonel Nasser and his Egyptian army officers in a bloodless coup. The Egyptian authorities seized any opportunity they could to make things difficult for any British person travelling through their country. Without warning just before takeoff, the aircraft door was opened and about four armed guards appeared and demanded that my mother and the five of us disembark. We left the aircraft and were marched across the hot tarmac at bayonet point to a building – there could hardly have been a sight more ludicrous! There, we were kept waiting in an office whilst my mother spoke with the Egyptian authorities – something to do with the passports, and something about Joan and I having been born in Alexandria. It was nothing serious, just another reason to cause as much aggravation as possible to the British! I never knew the whole story exactly. Meanwhile, the other passengers endured the heat of the midday sun in the aircraft, waiting for us to re-board. We were delayed for quite a while, and some sandwiches were brought for us to eat, which turned out to be very expensive indeed. It never failed to amuse me that despite my mother's ordeal at Cairo airport, her fury extended only to the price she had to pay for "those ghastly Egyptian sandwiches"!

We arrived home in England to a beautiful sunny afternoon and caught the steam train to Birmingham. Passing along the canals we looked out at the long barges heaped high with coal on their way to their destinations, and at other more colourful ones moored alongside the grassy banks. There were rows of neat terraced houses side by side, punctuated only by the ruins and rubble of a war not long passed. The smoke from the engine wafted in through the open carriage window and the dark, smoke-stained brickwork of the high station walls came into view, as the train pulled up to New Street Station. We caught a taxi home feeling very excited indeed. It was lovely to see our grandparents again. The twins were much older and Peter was meeting his grandparents for the first time. We sat down to a lovely tea which had been prepared for us, and there was a lot of excitement and chattering, for there was much catching-up to do. We went out for a walk around to the local park. Like the city, which was badly bombed, the residual bombing left its war scars nearby and there were still pot holes and craters around, with some of the corner houses reduced to piles of rubble. Despite all the hidden dangers which lurked around some of these derelict buildings, like magnets they drew many of the youngsters to climb and play, and we were no exception.

The roads were comparatively free of traffic and people on the whole were tolerant of children playing in the street. We often had a long skipping-rope held from one side of the road to the other with a dozen of us taking part. People everywhere appeared friendly and would stand in their doorways chatting to neighbours or watching the youngsters at play. Men would doff their hats at a passing funeral hearse as a mark of respect, and there was always a "Hello" no matter who you were.

We were all registered at Sommerville Road School about half a mile away from home. A large, red-bricked, Victorian building with a row of outside toilets and open coal sheds, its sloping tarmac playground with iron gates at the top of the slope, made it a fun area where a good number of us congregated at playtimes. In winter the slope made an ideal sliding area, so there was often a race after the bell, to get to the slope first. Through the school entrance door and into the passageway, were a row of small hand-basins. Nearby, stacked metal crates holding dozens of the silver topped, gill-sized bottles of milk, would wait to be collected by the class monitor. The spacious main hall with its high ceiling stood central to the classrooms which surrounded it. Throughout the school, there was wooden parquet flooring, and the tall cast iron radiators on each wall kept everywhere inside warm. Each classroom was furnished with double benched desks, each with their tiny white porcelain ink wells at the corner. There were often more than forty children to each classroom, and all faced the teacher and the blackboard. There was strict discipline and the cane was still in use. The prefects made sure that the rules were obeyed at all times and they were often difficult to pick out in the sea of uniforms, as they loitered near the cloakrooms and passageways for the unwary – the catching of a latecomer, entering school after whistle had blown, was a regular sight. Each classroom had a window which looked out into the hall, so for any misbehaviour, the favoured punishment was to make a pupil stand in the middle of the hall with their hands on their head, the punishment sometimes continuing through break time. There was no way to avoid being seen. Everyone, filing out of the classrooms and into the hall and cloakrooms to collect their hat and coat, pointed fingers and sniggered! An extremely humiliating experience indeed! And I talk from experience!

I remember that Christmas was a happy, fun time; after weeks of rehearsals of the nativity plays, each class performed its own play before the visiting audiences in the hall. Classrooms were decorated with homemade paper chains and lanterns and everyone's parents contributed a little something towards the Christmas tea parties, like cakes and jellies. There was carol singing and times of great cheer, and even the teachers joined in the fun and silly games that we all played.

Rationing was coming to an end and our local corner shops were beginning to fill with more interesting items of tinned, as well as fresh, produce. Milk was delivered by horse-drawn cart, which pulled into the lane every day. The grey mare on our round knew it was a 'pit stop' for her, and the kind milkman allowed us to give her the nose-bag containing oats for her to eat, whilst he delivered milk to the few houses in the lane. When the smart horse-drawn 'Hovis' cab pulled up, with its dark brown horse, to deliver bread to the local bakery, stroking or touching her was greeted with a scowl! I did enjoy going shopping to collect the fresh warm bread from the bakery, neatly bagged, but the temptation to nibble at least one of its four crusty corners was too much to resist. At home our meals were of simple fare. Before the advent of corn flakes and other cereals we began with a large bowl of porridge or bread and hot milk or tasty bacon dripping on toast. We all stayed to school lunches, which I have to confess I did enjoy. All the meals were wholesome fare of 'meat and two veg', followed by a sponge or pastry pudding with custard.

It's amazing how we can often recall the silly things we did as children. For instance, it was Joan's and my job to prepare afternoon tea for all the family, which was often bread, butter and jam, followed by fruit. It meant that the first one home got the laborious task of buttering the two sliced loaves – a job both of us hated. So if we saw each other walking along the street going home from school, tactics would come into play: we dawdled or hid from each other, but invariably we met at the gate to the house; the first one there, would wait for the other – neither of us wanting to make the first move through the gate. Only exasperated shouts of "hurry up you two" coming from the house would end the deadlock!

The winters were wonderful. The thick flurry of snow that fell would lie crystal clear on roads, gardens, hedges and tree branches, glistening in the sunlight, and it gave us hours of pleasure just playing in it and snowballing. Sadly though, by the following morning, the soot from the chimney fires would have fallen to the ground and darkened it.

Within weeks, I had begun my visits to the Birmingham Eye Hospital to see the surgeon, and Martin had now joined me, as he too had developed an astigmatism which needed attention. It was my parents' hope that we underwent our eye operations well before our return to Africa, so it was imperative that we were seen urgently, and if it meant pulling a few strings so be it. However, at the hospital, we queued for hours to be seen, moving along crowded pews awaiting our turn. Sometimes the process would take three or more hours. It was very tiring and wearing, following the same ritual week after week and meanwhile I missed many precious hours of school lessons. However, all the hassle and waiting eventually paid off, both of us finally had our operations, and we convalesced at a lovely retreat for about ten days until our eye patches were removed. I remember being bought a Parker fountain pen which I treasured, and was mortified at losing it a week later at school. At home my grandmother had helped to look after the younger members of the family while my mother was busy with hospital visits.

My grandmother was a highly intelligent, well-read lady with a wicked sense of fun – which I know she passed on to my father. A wonderful story-teller, she would have us glued to our seats, hanging on to her every word. As for most of her generation, physical hardship was commonplace, and like many of the young ladies of her generation she had entered service as a young woman and began her early years working as a maid at Warwick Castle, before she was married. Her married life brought her to a home in Small-Heath in Birmingham where her great passion was her garden where she would spend hours pottering. I recall that all the cool ashes from the fire grates of the day before were religiously collected and scattered on the garden and her roses always thrived and looked beautiful and were the envy of her neighbours.

We saw much less of my grandfather, because by the time we had risen for morning breakfast, he had already left for work. He was a tall man with incredible strength, which possibly came from the hard work that he did, but there was always a project on the go at home, and there was nothing that he couldn't do! He kept to a daily routine after work though; when he returned home he would change into his ordinary clothes, a collarless shirt with rolled up sleeves, a pullover or tank top jumper, and a pair of old trousers with a leather belt. To me, he was always like a comfortable jacket. A wonderful man with simple pleasures. He loved to go fishing and I remember digging in the garden for worms with my uncle; believe me, not any old worm would do – they had to be the right size and colour – I shudder at the mere sight of them now! He was also a man of routine. In the evening his job would be to fill and carry in the bucket of coal, then he would read the local newspaper, then sit down to his evening meal.

My grandparents' sitting room was modestly furnished – I think that we ended up with most of their furniture in our rooms – so they made do with a couple of chairs and dining table and a large storage cupboard in the corner. The focal point was the huge cast iron cooking range and fireplace with over-mantle, which took up two-thirds of the area of one wall and also doubled as an extra cooking space. The bevelled brass hearth surround was always kept highly polished, and in front of the hearth was a hand-made deep 'clippie' rug, which was hand woven from pieces of old fabric. My grandmother always had something on the go. She was either knitting socks for my grandfather or making rugs. The delightful smell of granny's baked bread or mutton stews often permeated throughout the whole of downstairs.

We had no washing machine at the house, just a boiler which was built into the corner of the kitchen, and with the five of us, it was hard work for my mother. She preferred to do the washing by hand in the long porcelain sink and, with only cold running water, kettles were constantly on the go; in the winter, her hands were, more often than not, chapped and sore.

Bath times were long drawn out affairs and had to be completed before my grandfather returned from work for his tea. My grandparents' sitting room doubled as the bathroom at least twice a week. The long zinc or tin bath would be brought in from its hanging place on the wall outside, and placed on the spread-out towels on the floor in front of the warm range. Again, kettles of boiled water were carried from the kitchen and poured into it; the five of us took it in turns to go first, while our clean clothes hung on the rail over the warm fire, ready to wear.

My father arrived home in England in February 1952 to the sad news of the King's death. Hourly, we listened intently to the news on the radio. We learned that the news had reached the Princess and Duke, while on holiday at 'Treetops' in Kenya. No one could have failed to be moved by the pictures on the front pages of the newspapers of the Queen Mother, or of the Princess coming down the steps of the aircraft on her return from Africa, and later on, the Queen Mother and the two princesses veiled in black at the funeral. Our hearts warmed to them and we became instant 'Royalists'.

At school – ironically, it was also my father's birthday – the pupils from every classroom were ushered into the assembly hall to listen to the radio broadcast of the funeral procession to Westminster Abbey. There was a profound sense of sadness, as the country went into mourning. Even the weather was cold, damp and foggy.

Next door to my grandparents lived an elderly deaf gentleman with his frail, deaf and dumb wife, and my grandmother always took a great deal of interest in their well-being, although she never interfered in their lives. Mr. and Mrs. Jones, the neighbours on the other side of them, were also generous and kind to them. The old lady always walked about the house with a small cushion perched on her head, held on by a ribbon tied under her chin. She looked quite comical to us, but there was a serious side to her attire: it gave her complete protection against walking into things and banging her head. When she wanted to attract my grandmother's attention, she would wave a long broom above the adjoining high fence. More often than not, it was us who saw her first.

Then my grandmother, would stand on a stool, lean over the fence, take hold of her hand and use the sign language to communicate with her – something she later taught us to do.

With all the warmth she had in her bones, I could not for the life of me reconcile her attitude with the neighbours on the other side of us. They were a German family, and my grandmother simply refused to speak to them. Yet they were the kindest people you could meet and, as children, I recall that we were regularly treated with comics and sweets which were pushed through the letter box for us; they were always kind and courteous to my mother; and, to cap it all, my father even went to school with their son when he was young. However, my grandmother had an intense dislike and mistrust of anything German and was not about to change her views and wouldn't be persuaded to change her views, which stayed with her always.

We left the shores of England once more in the spring of 1953, waving a tearful good-bye to my grandparents. We had had a long stay with them and, having had five children and their friends about the place, I think they would have missed us in time, but meanwhile they may have breathed a sigh of relief at our departure. I had mixed feelings about leaving; we had made a lot of friends, and a lot had also been achieved, not least Martin and I looking and feeling a lot better, having both had successful eye operations.

I think we flew out on one of the last flights by BOAC flying boat. On board was a diplomat from the embassy and his family on their way to Nigeria. Joan and I were seated near to them, and we were able to enjoy the company of their youngsters of about our age, and indulge in a few board games. We had become seasoned travellers, and by now I was well aware of the privilege of having the opportunity of meeting and knowing a people from another land, a privilege so seldom attained without the luxury of travel. I cannot remember where or when the family going to Nigeria disembarked; we had had a few hours of interesting and entertaining conversation with them. I know that when they left, I put aside my books and spread myself out over the empty seat beside me to sleep, trying to blot out the constant drone of the engines, until I was woken up by the stewardess and told to fasten my seat belt. I think we landed at Lake Naivasha, where we disembarked on to a launch and then changed on to another aircraft for a flight to Nairobi.

We stayed at the Norfolk Hotel again, now the traditional haunt of visiting celebrities. Joan and I were fascinated with the lifts and spent a great deal of our time riding up and down in them. No one appeared to mind when Joan asked, "Which floor do you want to stop at?" each time a native porter appeared with suitcases; they were very patient with her. Another time, she floated down the staircase, holding out her skirt, pretending to be the Queen, to the amusement of onlookers.

My mother took us into town to do some shopping for material for my new school uniform, and we were treated to afternoon tea at the New Stanley Hotel.

Flying out of Nairobi, we went over beautiful, undulating, green landscape with its incredible diversity of plantations, forest and savannah, with meandering rivers and deep forested gorges. It was good to be back, and within a couple of hours, we were flying over the Big House with the three tall trees, then came to land at the dirt airfield in Moshi. As we slowed to a stop I tried to remember how we had left the place many months earlier.

There was a cool breeze as we emerged from the aircraft and a fresh fragrance in the air from the short cloudburst that had fallen about an hour earlier. Moshi had had no rain for some time, the driver told us, so the rainfall had lifted everyone's spirits. Mr. Lunn was there to greet us with Mr. Shah, another Prison Officer. My parents, the twins and Peter went along in their cars, and Joan and I travelled in the front seat of the prison Bedford lorry with the driver and all the suitcases, where we had a good vantage point to see everything along the route home. The driver was in a jovial mood. I had to confess, it felt good to be in the warm climate again too.

We approached the old iron bridge over the Karanga River and as we clattered over the wooden planks, we looked down and saw some baboons chasing each other through the trees. Turning into the steep, hairpin bend, the driver put the lorry into a low gear and we slowly climbed the hill to the top. We passed the outside of the prison boundary with its row of sisal plants, and a small troop of vervet monkeys were making their way across the road in front of us, making for the prison – so nothing had really changed much there!

The entrance looked a little different from when I last saw it: suddenly the trees looked taller. The view of the mountain was obscured by clouds, but as we drove up to the house, the Poinciana trees which had been planted years earlier, were in full bloom with their dense red blossom and one white flower in each head; they looked stunning in the sunshine. Mrs. Lunn had prepared a nice tea for us, and she was delighted to see us back once more. By the time we had finished our tea and headed back to our own house, the yellow-golden sunset hastily beckoned the evening to a close. Levi greeted us and it was clear that he was happy to see us back again.

I had forgotten just how intoxicating the smell of DDT was. This polluting spray was liberally used to fumigate each room in the house at dusk and I admit to quite liking the smell. I slept soundly in my bed, unaware of and untroubled by mosquitoes that night, and awoke the following morning to a warm, bright, sunny start. As the clouds began to lift, the breathtaking view of the snow-capped peak of Kilimanjaro, standing majestically at 19,750 feet above sea level, could be seen from my bedroom window, and at that moment, I thought that I had to be one of the luckiest and most privileged people in the world.

The whole house was up early and after breakfast we took a walk around the gardens before preparing ourselves for the day's task of helping my mother to unpack the cases and crates. By lunchtime, Joan and I were exhausted with all the fetching and carrying, but at least we didn't have the added work of having to prepare the lunch, and we could sit down in the comfort of the dining room and be waited on.

The following day, armed with a clothes list, we were

taken into town to shop for school uniforms and to have the green material bought in Nairobi made up into dresses. I had a new, grey felt hat with a green satin band and badge which had to be sewn on, and the clothes list had seemed endless and, Oh dear! – all those name tapes. Joan had already endured boarding school for a couple of years, and I felt some trepidation as we left the house and got into the car to go to Arusha School to begin my first term as a boarder. My mother had supervised us as we had packed our own trunks and tuck boxes with all sorts of goodies, and she had constantly tried to reassure me that I wouldn't be the only new face that term, but somehow I wasn't reassured and everything felt so alien.

The children who attended the school, came from all parts of the provinces, north south, east and west. There was also a mixture of different nationalities, Dutch, South African, German, Italian and other European countries. On the journey, Joan sat silently on the back seat not saying a word, and I know that deep-down she hated going away to boarding school. As we drove along the almost straight tarmac road and Mount Meru came into view, I began to get butterflies in my stomach. Near Arusha the air was cooler and the vegetation denser. The pastoral Masai herded their cattle and goats not far away from where giraffe browsed unperturbed on the leaves of tall, flat-topped acacia trees and, in the distance, zebra and herds of antelope grazed.

We approached the centre of town, passed the clock tower, with Subzalis Garage on one side of the road and pulled into the school grounds with their enormous trees and colourful gardens. We passed Mr. Hampshere's house (the Headmaster) and drove up towards the attractive open-arched façade of the school front entrance, with its wide circular flower bed of flowering cannas and beautiful, large-headed, red, white and pink poppies. Already, we saw that a number of children had arrived and others were still arriving. As we got out of the car, and my mother drove away, Joan burst into tears. She was inconsolable, and even her friends who came over to greet her after her long absence from school, couldn't pacify her. Mrs. Forrester, our Matron and close family friend, came over to greet us. She was a middle-aged, tiny, neat little lady with tightly-curled hair and she wore spectacles. She put her arm around Joan's shoulder trying to reassure her, and together we walked into the school, followed close at heel by Matron's snub-nosed Pekinese dog. I tried hard not to show that I was upset too, and I received little comfort while Joan was so upset, but the fact that my big sister was crying made it difficult for me. I could not understand why she was so unhappy, and her friends approached me the following day to tell me how miserable she had been during the night, crying. I just couldn't believe she could be so sad – she had many friends at the school; there was Marie Ebnor who came from South Africa, and the De Beer twins Anna and Nellie – relatives of the famous diamond-mine dynasty, and others. Marie – otherwise known as 'Plebbs' – was perhaps her best friend, and poor me had yet to find one friend. After a day or so, she cheered up, and although I was a year younger than them, they let me join their close group and the five of us eventually became inseparable.

Although I was not the only newcomer to the school, I felt that I already had a head start on the rest as I had my sister there. Joan already knew the ropes and showed me around. The school was set in spacious grounds of giant eucalyptus trees, among others, and at the back of the school there were open playing fields, and a swimming pool. There were two houses, North which was the upstairs dormitory and South downstairs. The boys were billeted well away at the other end of the school. Each dormitory slept four to five girls in single beds and there was a partitioned wall separating the dormitory prefect from the rest of us. We had mosquito nets on each bed, and every morning we stripped our beds before going down to breakfast, and returned after breakfast to make them up before Matron's inspection; the whole place was run like a military barracks.

Along one end of the upstairs corridor was a small chapel, permanently dimly-lit and unlocked, reserved for quiet prayer time. At the other end of the building, Matron had her living area and study, and sometimes on a Sunday afternoon, a group of us would end up having tea with her in her study. The washrooms were along the corridor and the stairs were wide and curved, with a lovely walnut banister and hand rail. The layout downstairs was similar to upstairs, except it had the bathroom and boiler room which was permanently warm, so that any sports clothes or towels could be washed and hung over the pipes to dry. Outside the dormitory building was a deep, concrete, semicircular, thatched walkway to the main school. In the lawned grounds of the school an enormous Galapagos tortoise wandered around freely, grazing on leaves and flowers, and if we were playing nearby, we picked some of his favourite Hibiscus flower heads from the tops of the bushes, where he couldn't reach, and fed them to him. We were forbidden to take a ride on his back, but I know that most of us at some time did sneak a crafty ride when no one was looking!

Discipline in-house was strict; Matron was not averse to using the slipper. No one was allowed to leave the dormitory in the morning until the bell had been sounded from downstairs. The first up in the morning would strip their bed, stand ready with towel and toothbrush in hand at the door, ready to dash for the wash room; then dress and be ready to walk down for breakfast. There was fierce competition for the best turned-out dormitory, which was rewarded with the Queen's picture to hang in their room for the week, regarded as a privilege.

After school prep and before time for lights out, each dorm would take it in turns to dress up and act out a fable of their choice, which was immense fun. Matron would walk along the corridors turning out the lights as she passed each room, calling "Good night" as she did so; talking after lights-out was forbidden and getting caught doing so, meant the slipper! But it didn't stop the midnight feasts, with cake and sweets, which were smuggled into the dorm on occasions, being shunted along the floor to each other. In fact, part of the fun was seeing what you could get up to after lights-out without getting caught. For those who didn't go home at weekends, Saturdays were a real treat and began with a visit to collect your pocket money and a stroll to the tuck shop. It was also letters home day, which was supervised by the duty teacher. But we all especially enjoyed the afternoons, with the organised team games of hockey, cricket or rounders; there was much rivalry between the teams of the two houses. There were the organised paper chases too; we had at least one a term, which took us across fields and pathways, over the culvert bridge and rail viaduct across the river, where the local native women, in their colourful clothes and beads, could be seen doing their washing on the rocks or bathing their children at the rivers edge below us; they would watch and wave as we snaked in a long line above them. And, of course, how could one forget those Randolph Scott and Sonja Heine films every Saturday night?

The week leading up to the Queen's Coronation was exciting for us all. With news of the elaborate preparations for the crowning of the new queen at Westminster Abbey, we began our own celebrations, by decorating our rooms with flags and anything we could find which was red, white and blue.

In England many had already bought their first television set in readiness for the great day; a few of us listened intently to the commentary as it was relayed through the radio in Matron's study, and we were all given a souvenir mug as a reminder of the great occasion, with a special supper laid on afterwards.

The finale to the term was always the sports day, a time to show who was the best between the two houses. Joan and I were rivals in the swimming, and we had some excellent swimmers amongst the boys in north house. South house always did well with Joan and Anna and Nellie, who excelled at athletics, and south house invariably won on points in the end.

I loved boarding school, but I cannot remember learning a great deal while I was there. I saw lessons mostly as an intrusion into my playtime and I somehow floated through lessons on a cloud, blissfully unaware at the time that I had a form of dyslexia which made co-ordination and reading from the blackboard difficult. Sometimes I struggled with words and my writing was painfully slow, only to get to the end of my work and find the odd jumbled letters, but nobody got cross or impatient or even questioned it. Perhaps it was seen as best ignored, for I cannot remember any help coming my way, and like all children in a group, it is embarrassing to be singled out as needing help.

There was always the usual flurry and excitement of packing at the end of each term, with the noisy clattering of the trunks being shifted from under the stairwell to the dorms, which would continue throughout the day. I was always thrilled to see my parents pull up at the front entrance of the school to pick us up, but not more so than Joan.

Chapter Four

Each homecoming was tinged with added excitement as there was always some fresh project on the go or new renovations being carried out.

As I said, my father, who had always been a keen angler, fishing in the lakes and along the canal banks in Birmingham with his younger brother as a child, decided that fish ponds were what was really needed! When talking with a friend by the name of Mr. Gold, a balding, swarthy, slight-framed man, who always wore a dark French beret on his head and who shared the same passion and enthusiasm for fishing as himself, he sought his help in producing a feasibility study on the possibility of building fish ponds down at the prison. It would be an engineering challenge for them, and perhaps a change for the inmates from the endless hours spent stone-chipping aggregate for the railways and highways. It would certainly be another source of protein in the prisoners' diet.

Both men sat at the dining table and in the office working on plans and drawings. There would be no problem with manpower, and lower down the valley there was a natural fresh water spring, which could be harnessed; so, with permission from higher authority, the project was put into operation and the work began. The prisoners worked hard, and hundreds of tons of rock and earth were excavated and moved by small working-parties carrying and ferrying baskets of soil in lines, to build the retaining banks, until eventually the large open basins, each the size of a couple of football pitches, would make up the fishing ponds.

A long, concrete gully was built to carry the fresh water to fill these huge basins, and a concrete sluice with wooden trap-gate was installed to ensure that any overflow could escape and discharge into the banana plantation. The steep soil banks were grassed, and young 'tilapia' fry, which were considered to be fast growers, were introduced.

Over the following year, the grass became established, ducks and geese were introduced (with a wooden shed as their small home), and nearby the pawpaw trees, oranges, and other trees, began to bear fruit. All the hard work, which had taken many months, had turned the whole area into a mini paradise.

As children, we took full advantage of the fish ponds when we were not at school; we spent many hours fishing from the banks with our makeshift rods (carved out of branches), and lines and hooks, and for bait we used chopped luncheon meat. Most of the time, our wriggling catches were put back; it seemed that only the small fry ventured to the edge of the ponds. There were also the odd times when one of us would fall in, with cries of, "I knew that would happen" coming from the rest sitting on the banks, with leaden expressions; but we could swim. We had competition for our catches too – leaving the fish unattended in a bucket of water for any length of time invited the tall, stalking grey herons who took great delight in poaching them. A vast number of different birds, like the colourful kingfishers, hammercocks, white egrets and finches, which flew in, eventually made the fishponds their home.

Returning from our fishing trips, my father, who was blessed with quick wit, would ask whether we had managed to catch anything, to which the reply was more often "No." He would retort, "Blessed be the one who expects nothing, for he will not be disappointed." He could elevate his annoying phrases into an art form. I do remember, however, that he made no comment when I returned home one day having caught Martin fair and square on his top lip, which meant a long walk home with him still attached to the line and hook at the end of the rod. It was a funny sight. A pair of pliers had to be used to cut off the barb and extract the hook end. Of course, the rest of us thought the incident terribly funny, but Martin failed to see it that way!

Just when life was looking rosy, we received the awful news from my uncle in England, that my grandfather had died from cancer. "How could this be so?" I thought. We had only seen him over a year earlier and he had looked so well. If he had been ill then, he certainly didn't look it! I just couldn't believe that this wonderful man, my Granddad, who we loved so much, a strong man who could hammer a two inch nail into a piece of wood with one blow, was dead! To add to my father's misery, he wasn't given permission to return home to attend the funeral or to see his mother – something to do with the continuing state of emergency in Kenya! I well remember the forlorn look of sadness and sorrow on his face!

At the beginning of that term, we didn't get the customary lift to school by car. Joan and I travelled with friends by train. It was our first experience on a train abroad and we boarded with great excitement. The journey was slow, and as we stood to peer out of the open sash window, we were able to take in the smells and the beautiful scenery in style. We passed great open expanses of yellow savannah and thorn trees, and gazed at young children below, herding their goats and waving. There were open areas between each of the coaches, where we stood on the rattling iron grilles and looked through them to the rail line below, whizzing by under our feet, and as the train slowed down to cross a rail bridge viaduct, the native women and their children waved and shouted to us. The train was almost at a crawl and some of the youngsters in all forms of dress, came running up to the windows with their baskets full of oranges, lemons, bananas and other assorted fruit, and others held up their sweet maize cakes, which we bought to eat on the journey. It had been a wonderful experience, and by the time we reached our destination it was school teatime. There was always a plentiful supply of bread and butter on the tables – plates of it; so we hastily dipped into our tuck boxes for the Milo tin, or sugar or jam, to make our own special sandwiches!

At school, we were informed that some of the pupils would be going to Oldeani School, some ninety miles away from Arusha, for at least a term because of the overflow of the new intake of children at school. The pupils chosen to go would be from the older age group, mainly any twins or brothers and sisters, and there would be an equal ratio from the boys' section as well. When the list came out, of course, my name was not on it. Feeling dejected, I retired to my room and lay on the bed.

I had always been included in my sister's group; but now Joan, Marie, Nellie and Anna were leaving me behind, and I was forlorn. Fair enough, I was younger than the rest; but more important, my big sister was leaving me! Joan carried a great deal of clout amongst the pupils and, unbeknown to me, she went off to see Mrs. Forrest, who in turn consulted with the Headmaster.

The following day, when Joan and her delegation of friends, rushed over to tell me that I would be leaving with them, I was overjoyed. With all our bags packed and loaded into two large open station wagons, we departed with our drivers Mrs. Forrest and Mrs. Robinson on our long drive to Oldeani. Not far out of Arusha, the vehicles began to climb steadily through plantations and forest roads. The weather was warm and we made a couple of stops to walk about and have a picnic break. A few giraffes with their casual gait, loped across the road in front of us; but when a couple of lions were spotted some distance away, we were recalled to the confines of the car for fear of what might emerge from the bushes.

We arrived at Oldeani late in the afternoon in the aftermath of a heavy shower. The car laboured and whined and Mrs. Forrest had to drive carefully to avoid the deep potholes in the road, where the rain ran in rivulets down gullies and pathways on to the forest floor. A beautiful rainbow appeared across the sky and disappeared into the valley below us. By the time we had unloaded our luggage, we had left a thick trail of mud from the roadside, up to the steps and into the passageway leading to the dormitories.

After being allocated our beds and lockers and being

shown around, we were feeling weary, grubby and bedraggled, and so after tea we showered and turned in for the evening. That night I lay awake, listening to the different sounds that echoed around the building. The dormitories were spacious and Mrs. Robinson, who was to stay as Deputy Matron, had her own self-contained living quarters next to us. The dormitories were raised up from the ground, so that you got a panoramic view of the whole area from the paved veranda which had a wide flight of steps down to the ground; everywhere was green; it was totally wild country. The following morning, we awoke to a warm sun trying to break through the rising mist clouds, and the atmosphere felt damp as the dew hung heavy during the first part of the day. We attended our school lessons, and after school we were allowed plenty of free time to do what we wanted. The evenings were short, as darkness came early, so after tea we retired to our rooms to play, sew or read.

We soon got used to the constant night noises from the grunting warthogs and the laughing and chattering of the hyenas, outside our windows at night. A tall spear-carrying Masai native, dressed in his off-the-shoulder attire patrolled outside the dormitories each night. Some mornings there was clear evidence that the hyenas had in fact ventured on to the veranda as we slept. We could hardly blame our night carer for disappearing into the toilet for a sleep or to keep warm on occasions, as being at such a high altitude (we were only a few miles from the Ngorongoro crater), the vast high plateau was shrouded in heavy cloud mist, and the night air could turn bitterly cold.

Occasionally we were troubled by creepy-crawlies in the dormitories, mostly after a rain storm. Each morning we prudently gave our clothes and shoes a shake in case of something nasty hiding in them, especially after one of the boys had a bad experience with a scorpion in his shoes, and had been bitten.

The school food was pretty horrendous at Oldeani. The native cooks appeared to lack any culinary skills, and the constant complaints about the meals went unheeded. I almost dreaded meal times. The porridge sometimes contained weevils; the fried eggs which were served on occasions for breakfast tasted or smelled awful and sometimes, when you were happily tucking into your nice looking vegetables, your best friend would draw attention to the cooked critters in it!

We eagerly awaited letters each week from our parents, and we were kept in touch regularly with the twins' and Peter's progress. How they had spent a wonderful time on the Wallis's farm at 'Kibohehe'. Aunty Freda Wallis, a tall, handsome lady whom we all loved dearly, could organise wonderful, eventful children's parties and games, and I remember one year, her hiding a whole lot of Easter eggs among the bushes and flower gardens for us to hunt out. Our family had spent many hours with their children, who were almost the same ages as ourselves.

Not all news from home was good; one letter arrived to tell us that the Lunns had been attacked at the house by the swarm of bees from the barrel hive. Both were badly stung and as they managed to crawl indoors to summon help they were pursued by the angry swarm in to the house. Fortunately my mother was at home to help, but they were taken to hospital in a bad way, and the incident could have cost them their lives. Luckily their son Brian was away at school at the time.

When term came to its end we again packed our belongings and left Oldeani in a convoy of vehicles for the drive back to Arusha School. Although the ride was rough and bumpy, the journey was downhill most of the way and we could savour the magnificent views of the plains from the high plateau.

My parents' social life had gathered momentum in our absence. It appeared that there was little else to do in the long days after work except entertain or attend garden parties. My mother always arranged an enormous children's party for our homecoming; the balcony was festooned with balloons and all the trimmings, and the children of friends were driven in to attend. However, we rarely spent quality time with my parents on their own, without the constant interruptions from friendly callers to the house. They had many friends and acquaintances amongst the farming and local communities. My father spent a good deal of time with, perhaps his two best friends, Mr. Basciera, an avuncular Italian gentleman who owned a garage, and uncle Bernard Wallis, a burly good-looking man whose knowledge of animal husbandry and farming skills he valued as second to none. On the Wallis's plantation they kept horses and cattle and Auntie Freda often exhibited at the provincial agricultural shows. She had quite an influence over my mother who then began to take a great interest in the shows too, exhibiting flowers and vegetables. However, when she entered our cockerel in the 'birds' section and won first prize, her enthusiasm got the better of her and she became hooked!

I recall with great amusement a prize, liver-coloured, shorthorn bull named Ferdinand being purchased by the prison at one of the shows; Mr. Lunn was asked to take a vehicle and driver to collect the animal the following day from the farm where the purchase had been made. The bull was duly loaded into the back of the truck and tethered. The two men, duly satisfied with their harnessed load, got into the truck and drove off down the road. They had not gone far, when they looked through the rear window to the empty space behind them and noticed that the bull had vanished. Bemused, and no doubt extremely worried, they retraced their steps back along the road and spotted the animal, happily feeding from some nearby bushes. Just as they backed the vehicle to it, the bull took off into the wild with the two men, ropes in hand, following in hot pursuit. Each time they approached it, the animal took off again until they finally lost it and had to give up the chase. Sitting around the table having lunch, we were interrupted by a rather flustered Mr. Lunn who arrived looking very red and distraught. He beckoned my father into the hallway, and the conversation went something like this:

"You couldn't possibly lose an animal that size, for God's sake."

"Well we tied it up reasonably securely before we left, Basil."

"It obviously wasn't bloody good enough," continued my father. "I suggest you get back to where you last saw it, take more men with you and find it: and don't come back without it."

When my father got cross, he would pace up and down the room like a trapped animal in a cage, walking back and forth huffing to himself, and woe betide anyone uttering a word while this little performance was going on!

I felt sorry for Mr. Lunn; he hadn't meant for it to happen – he didn't expect it would happen. Ferdinand, a huge, prized, dark-coloured, magnificent animal, was eventually captured by the side of the main road, but not before he had drawn the attention of a number of onlookers who had stopped their cars nearby. Ferdinand had obviously fared none the worse for his ordeal and went on to sire a great number of strong calves. When, a couple of years later, he ran amok down at the boma and gored a couple of his minders, his fate was sealed, as he was deemed to be much too dangerous to handle or keep, and he was sent for slaughter. As children, our gruesome curiosity knew no bounds and we sneaked off down to the boma on the day of his sentence. Peeping above the wall we watched the grizzly scene unfold. With quiet ceremony, prayers were said by the Masai who were ready with their gourds to collect the blood. Poor Ferdinand, his bones were unceremoniously thrown out in to the open field in the baking sun where, before long, the skies filled with circling vultures that flew in to squabble and feast on his carcass, while his hide was strung up and hung out in the sun to dry. It seemed a poor end to such a magnificent beast, but the safety of the inmates was paramount.

Each fortnight required the ritual shopping trip into town to Moolji's grocery store for the 'big shop'. The Mooljis were a delightful Asian couple, who carried a comprehensive stock of merchandise in their store. Nothing was ever too much trouble to get in if it was unavailable at the time and, if there was a heavy amount of shopping that could not be carried on the day, the items could be delivered the following day. The store became another meeting place for the local residents to catch up on the gossip. These shopping trips could take hours, and whilst we waited around Mrs. Moolji would always hand us some sweets and ice-chilled Pepsis from her refrigerator. But my mother always parked the car at the front of the shop and sometimes the hot midday sun would bake the inside of the vehicle and we would have to leave the doors of the car open for a number of minutes before getting in to it for fear of getting scorched from the black leather upholstery. (Sadly, Mr. Moolji was to lose his life some years later, after an armed attack at his home.)

Getting home with the shopping was another story. Part of the 'fun' was the car-run up the steep hill over the old iron Karanga bridge. With a full load of shopping, plus children, the climb was fraught with difficulties and, more often than not, a hit and miss affair because if the correct momentum wasn't attained the first time, it meant the two biggest, that is, Joan and me, having to get out to help push the car up the slope, whilst my mother negotiated the first gear and released the handbrake at the correct time. There were occasions when one wrong move and both of us could quite easily have slipped beneath the back wheels. After a few scary attempts, my mother perfected the manoeuvre up the hill to loud cheers from her back-seat drivers!

Keeping food ant and bug free was a constant battle for everyone living in a tropical climate. Flour, bread and sugar were common targets, and the ants were even able to infiltrate tins with closed lids. The fine meshed cupboard standing in the kitchen was to some extent a deterrent, but it became necessary to sit the food-safe legs in small pots of paraffin, for these clever ants were able to sniff out any crumb left lying about, as Martin and Peter were about to learn to their cost when one night they decided to raid the food-safe and returned to their beds to share in the loot. While innocently discarding their empty packaging under their pillows, they left telltale crumbs in their beds before going off to sleep. To describe how resourceful these red 'safari' ants were, during the night, they had snaked up the side of the house, through the chimney stack, across the sitting room, through into the passageway and into the bedroom of the sleeping pair. In the early hours of the morning, we were all awakened by screams coming from their bedroom. When the light was switched on in their room, it revealed that the ants had moved over the nearest bed, which was Peter's, in a sweeping pincer movement, covering his bedding and him. It was an astonishing sight to behold, and the bedclothes had to be discarded outside. Perhaps the most incredible thing was that the next morning there was hardly a sign to say that the ants had ever been in the house.

We were brought up in the culture of wild and

domestic animals and from our early exposure, there was barely any other aspect of our lives which had been so consistent. Most of all, perhaps, there was that greatest of craving of any youngsters, an innate desire to possess them, to hold them and have them for ourselves, and in a way we were extremely lucky, for we experienced these pleasures in every way – we had it all. Our close association with them, however, often brought its heartaches and in many ways carried its own hazards!

When we were given two, three-month old, sandy-coloured Ridgeback puppies, we were delighted. They were completely different from one another in character and looks. The strong dominant one we named 'Bruce', with his white-tipped paws and a broad, white patch on his wide, handsome forehead. However, he didn't display the straight, long ridge down his back, just a short disrupted ridge. Strong willed and short tempered, yet with the heart of a lion, he was destined to be a good guard dog, but his one great fault was that he had a habit of chasing after bicycles and cars. His brother, 'Kim', was gentle, with a dark muzzle and a well-defined ridge on his back, which is the sign of the breed. They sometimes fought with each other at meal times, with Bruce being the main instigator, but on the whole they were close brothers. Fortnightly, the cattle were dipped down at the boma to remove parasites, and we regularly took the two dogs down to the area with us and put them through the dip first. They often accompanied us on our walks from the boma on the long cattle trail, but the flies and ticks were a constant nuisance, and we had to make sure that the dogs were free of them before returning home. It was during this period of time that we all became inflicted with horrid, boil-like, painful lesions on our arms and torsos and had to go to the hospital to have them lanced. To our horror they turned out to be the bot fly maggot, often associated with cattle, which had laid their eggs under our skin: the whole episode filled us with utter revulsion. The lesions seemed to take an age to heal and, furthermore, we were discouraged from venturing out for walks amongst the herd in the end.

For a number of miles around the prison perimeter, there was still a lot of unspoilt, green forest-cover which was a natural habitat for wild deer and their predators alike. The odd injured or lost fawn would be brought to the house for my mother to restore to health but, sadly, many were in a poor state when they arrived at the house, and would die soon after. But she did have some success with others which she nurtured back to health until they could be released. Meanwhile, they were kept in the pen with the chickens and ducks.

We had occasional glimpses through binoculars of two cheetahs, that would sit on top of the termite mound some distance from the house, basking in the sun. And not too far away at the Karanga Gorge, there were many sightings of leopards, which were partial to a meal of dog as well as baboon. The presence of a leopard in the area near the river, didn't deter the movement of the troop of baboons who lived among the trees there. It didn't stop them from venturing out into the open and becoming a menace either as, each day, they left the gorge and crossed into the prison grounds making daylight raids into the maize field, pulling down and destroying the stalks as they reached for the ripe cobs. They went through the crop, leaving swathes of ruined areas in their wake; they didn't discriminate either - any crop was a target. The troop sentinels posted about the tall candelabra trees, would bark warnings of these interlopers, or any other danger, and the only way to move them on was to fire a volley of rifle shots over the field, but those that didn't heed the warning were shot.

While the Mau Mau conflict raged on in Kenya, many troops flew out from England to help the local police deal with the detainees, and to boost the morale amongst the European population. Meanwhile in Tanganyika, my parents remained cautious about the situation going on in Kenya, and we were relatively untouched and untroubled by what was going on over the border.

Mr. Lunn, who had recently returned from home leave in England with his family, took over from my father who had come to the end of his tour, and once again there was the usual flurry of packing and crating to be done, with everything again stored and locked in the rooms, while Levi stayed on to take care of the house for the duration of my parents home leave.

We flew home by BOAC Hermes aircraft and arrived in England in the evening to cold, damp weather. After a night stop at a hotel in Sutton Gardens in London, we caught the train home to Birmingham.

It was good to see my grandmother, now a widow, but she looked so much older, and had visibly aged since I had last seen her a couple of years earlier. The sparkle had gone out of her eyes, and it was obvious to everyone that the light had gone out of her life. The house would never feel the same again without Granddad! She often appeared withdrawn and would leave the house, sometimes for the whole day, without saying where she was going, which worried my mother; and when she was home, she would sit for ages just gazing into the open fire while warming her outstretched hands and, with her little white mob cap on her head, she cut a lonely figure. One day she returned home in terrible distress after falling off the platform step of a moving tram. The tram had begun to moved off before she had stepped down on to the pavement, and it had dragged her along for a number of feet before anyone had noticed her plight. But she refused to be taken to hospital, and the experience quite traumatised her.

Once again, when we came over to England, we were expected to carry on with our schooling where we had left off, which was often traumatic for me, but in the meantime we spent hours of our time playing in the local park just a stone's throw from the house. The bomb craters had all been filled and were gone, and a new ground surface with new play area equipment had been installed. It was a godsend to us, although it meant a walk around the block to gain access into the play area. Trying to climb the fence to take a short cut, meant instant rebuke from the park keeper; in those days anyone who wore a uniform had authority and you did as you were told! The railings extended beyond the lane to our house, and it was easy for my mother to attract our attention through them, to call us home.

In the evenings after tea the young ones went off to bed and Joan and I would sit and either knit or sew in front of the warm fire. We listened to 'The Archers' on the radio; in fact, the radio was rarely turned off. We cried, just as many did, when 'Grace Archer' died in a barn fire at Ambridge! The newspapers even carried stories of people sending flowers to the BBC. We listened intently to the news coverage, with blow-by-blow accounts of conflicts around the world – Indo-China, Algeria, and, of course, Kenya, as well as other places. We loved to listen to all the cricket matches and especially the fight for 'The Ashes' – my mother was an avid cricket fan. We listened to the heavyweight fights, the weekly adventures of Francis Durbridge's Paul Temple was a must, and we even listened avidly to the shipping forecasts and gale warnings – learning all the strange names of the different places. We swooned to Johnny Ray and Frankie Laine, and jived to Bill Haley.

When one day news arrived from Moshi to say that Levi had been in hospital for a while after being badly injured at the house, my parents were very upset and worried for him. Apparently he had gone to investigate a break-in at our house. Thinking there was only one robber, he proceeded to tackle the man, only to be set upon by his accomplice with a panga (long machete) cutting off part of his ear, and leaving him for dead. Meanwhile, the men had prised open the nailed down crates, and ransacked the lot, leaving the premises with as much as they could carry. Poor Levi, injured and bleeding, managed to crawl to the phone to call for help. Among the valuable items stolen were my father's suits and precious cine films that he had taken of the animals in the Ngorongoro Crater and Lake Manyara; films that he would never, ever be able to replace.

Confirmation of a new tour and short working spell at the prison headquarters in Dar-es-Salaam reached my parents during their leave, and plans were worked out for Joan and me to stay in England for a few months to continue our education until the move back to Moshi later on.

As it wasn't possible for us to live with my grandmother at the time, it was decided to ask my mother's parents if they would take us for the short duration to live with them. So Joan and I found ourselves at a new location and a brand new school once again.

My mother's mother – Nana, as we knew her - lived in a large, six-bedroomed house in a fashionable area of the famous silk town of Macclesfield. My mother, who was the eldest of Nana's children, never knew who her real father was or, if she did know, she certainly didn't say; but there was talk amongst many that she was the daughter of noble folk. It was said that Nana had worked as a cook for some wealthy landowners as a young woman, and when she became pregnant she had left their employ and moved into the large house. In the early years, few people ever talked of their backgrounds or past relationships; there was always a veil of secrecy attached to any minor indiscretion, and any skeletons were firmly shut in the cupboard! Certainly no one ever enquired into anyone's business – to do so was considered intrusive in the extreme and at worst, downright bad manners! Suffice to say, that if my mother did know her real father's identity, she would take his secret to her grave. My mother was brought up by relatives who had a farm high up on the hills at Leek in Staffordshire and, from what I understood, had had a hard life until she was old enough to leave the farm to go into nursing. Meanwhile, Nana married a humble, hardworking farm hand, and they had eight children together. She was a small, neat and tidy woman, whose spectacles always hung at the end of her nose (I always felt that I wanted to push them back on to her nose for her); a woman who scurried about like a ferret everywhere she went, who had to have almost everything done in a hurry, and who tutted furiously if anyone ever got in her way.

My parents flew out to Dar-es-Salaam with Mary, Martin and Peter, and I can remember feeling desperately hurt at being left behind. My father began work at the Prison Headquarters while my mother took a part-time job at the Inland Revenue building in the town. Joan and I always looked forward to news from home, and in turn we wrote to our parents each week, giving them our news, which wasn't half as interesting as theirs!

We were of similar ages to some of Nana's children and we all got on well and attended the same school. The two oldest sons worked on the railways as foot-plate men on the steam express engines. They could tell wonderful tales of their journeys each day, up and down the length and breadth of the country, and the names and numbers of the express engines that they had travelled on that day. They, like their father were 'grafters', with a great deal of enthusiasm and love for their trade. They would leave for work at all times of the day or night, in their uniforms, with their packed lunches and enamel tea urns; returning home with black faces and hands, from hours of shovelling coal. Both of them went on to become train drivers, and then eventually reached management level in the rail industry, exchanging their uniforms for the traditional white shirt and suit.

The oldest of the sons were as industrious as some of the younger ones were a problem! The boys indulged in truancy whenever possible, and got themselves into all sorts of scrapes.

Joan and I had a great deal of time for Granddad though; a tall, but hunched, man with short, dark, unruly hair. He left in the early hours of each morning to work on a farm, carrying his leather-booted, wooden clogs, which he would put on at the door before leaving, mindful of waking anyone. He slept in his own room, perhaps because of the unsocial hours of his work, while Nana slept at the opposite end of the house. He was a mild-mannered man most times. However, he wasn't averse to handing out corporal punishment to his younger sons with a leather belt, to bring them into line. I found the occasional punishment meted out to them harsh and distressing, and Nana's attitude towards her husband behind his back served only to undermine his authority with them: it certainly did little to engender the respect that he so thoroughly deserved. She was an overbearing woman, with strange notions, like, it wasn't necessary for girls to go to school as long as they could cook and keep house! Although I have to confess that I could perhaps share a good deal of those sentiments now!

Both Joan and I were relieved to get away to school each morning. We were sometimes exhausted with housework. We had both experienced a great deal of disruption in our schooling, and I, especially, needed all the academic motivation I could get. Nana refused to accept that we had homework to do, and passed off the idea as unnecessary and a complete waste of time. In fact she would not allow us to bring homework home if she felt that it would interfere with the daily routine of housework, or take up time badly needed to do more 'useful' things.

When Joan and I were asked to compete in athletics or recreational sports or represent the school in any way, she became uncompromising and spiteful. It became dreadfully embarrassing to be captain of the netball or athletics team, and not be allowed permission to get away for matches or sports events. We made various excuses, but when we ran out of them we just decided to defy her and go anyway. On our return, we would face a barrage of questions and the inevitable retribution from her. Of course, it cannot have been easy for her to have a house full of adolescents, but there was never any let-up in the hard work. Walking long distances to school each day took its toll on our foot wear. Her punishment for our not toeing the line, was to refuse to buy us any new plimsolls. At one stage at school I had to ask a dear friend if I could borrow her new, white footwear to enter a sports competition, and then return them to her before she could take part too. Fortunately, we didn't enter the same sports!

In our frustration, Joan wrote to my parents in Dar-es-Salaam and we wondered why there was no reply from home, until one day, Joan saw that the letters were being intercepted at the letter box by her and the friendly postman. When Joan confronted her about the affair, she was instantly rebuked for such an accusation.

After the letter incident, it seemed that our stay had become untenable. Certainly we didn't wish to stay with her any longer than we had to. Our freedom was to come with the good news from my parents in Dar that my mother was returning to England soon, because she was expecting a baby. We were, of course, delighted on both counts and it meant that she would be coming to take us back home to Birmingham. We were ecstatic to see her and eager to find out everything about the family. She had, in fact, received our last letter to her, detailing the problems we were facing in living where we were, but would only refer to the subject obliquely, though she did make some passing reference to our complaints. However, at the time of receiving our letter she was already making plans to return to have the baby in England and would be able to deal with the situation at first hand. In the event and by mutual consent, we all drew a veil over Nana and our stay; labouring on about her, would have been futile.

It was good to see my grandmother again. She had genuinely missed us. The run-up to Christmas was sheer joy too, despite the cold, frosty weather. My uncle and aunt came over for tea. It was uplifting to hear the laughter once more coming from the front room, and Auntie Olivia going into raptures as she jived to Johnny Ray. A trip to John Lewis to take the little ones to see Father Christmas was a fantastic treat, as the store always put on a magnificent show of automata, coloured lights and trimmings, which sent us into raptures of delight. We bought toys, drawing books and coloured crayons. While the grown-ups enjoyed themselves in the front room, we hung balloons everywhere and whooped it up in the living room, playing hide and seek in the dark and running from room to room while my grandmother showed great tolerance; or maybe it was the fact that she couldn't hear us. Despite her deafness though, she could feel any vibration if we were too rowdy. We tinkered on the piano – none of us could play it – and sang carols, and stuffed ourselves with cake, jellies and toffee apples.

Maybe the merriment of that afternoon caught up with my mother, because it was on Christmas Eve that Joan was awakened in the early hours of the morning to go down the road to a telephone box and ring for an ambulance. Poor Joan, she recalls how, with just a blanket over her shoulders – there was no time to get dressed – she ran out into the cold night air to the telephone box, which seemed miles away at the time. When the ambulance arrived, my mother had managed to get herself dressed and downstairs with help from my grandmother.

Baby John arrived on Boxing Day 1955, at the hospital in Marston Green in Birmingham. A photograph of him, held by a cheerful black nurse, his tiny face wrapped up in a blanket, appeared in the newspapers the following day, together with others, heralding the hospital's new arrivals.

We were delighted with his homecoming, and this tiny, fluffy black-haired baby, wrapped up like a tight parcel, was passed to each of us in turn to hold. He was a contented baby who received plenty of love and affection from us all, and was never short of volunteers to help push him around in his pram.

That winter was one of the coldest and most uncomfortable times that I was ever to experience. Long-speared icicles hung from the guttering and the water pipes and the outside toilet cistern froze. The raging fires in the grates at home, had little effect on the biting frost around. There was some compensation perhaps as, when walking to school, we could skate and slide on relatively car-free roads. The fires were maintained throughout the days and nights during the cold spell and we went through a lot of coal, with the local coal men making a delivery to the house on a fortnightly basis. My grandmother did make me laugh though; she insisted that the bags were strictly counted in to the coal house, which she observed from the window at a discreet distance. She had always been satisfied about the honesty of the men, until she learned from Mrs. Jones, next door but one, that they were sometimes fiddling the ration, pretending to empty the whole bag, when that was not the case. With the coal fires came the dreaded 'smog', of course, and we sometimes walked home from school with the air pollution filling our lungs.

By the spring, my mother began to fret as the letters from my father in Africa became less frequent. She put a brave face on things and continued her daily chores. Life went on, with few changes. Being in our teens brought slightly more freedom and privileges, and we had the opportunity of going to the cinema, but were still expected to pull our weight around the house before going off to school, especially with a new baby around. My mother rarely got out with Joan and me, not wanting to leave my deaf grandmother with the responsibility of looking after the four youngsters. However, on a rare occasion Joan and I were taken to see *South Pacific*, starring Mary Martin and Ezio Pinza, at the Birmingham Hippodrome. The whole performance was a thrilling and wonderful treat and it was to ignite my enthusiasm and love of the theatre, especially musicals and dance. On another occasion, my mother sneaked us into the cinema to see the film of the H G Wells novel *The War of the Worlds* which had an 'A' certificate. I remember sitting in my seat as the usherette walked by, and waiting for her to tap me on the shoulder to ask my age.

That year Donald Campbell broke the water speed record, and I remember Joan and I being very saddened by news of the death of James Dean in a car accident – all the papers carried the story – they were full of it. For a while, for us anyway, the problems in the world were forgotten.

The following year, 1956, Mr. Churchill had resigned as our Prime Minister and was replaced by Mr. Anthony Eden. Africa seemed so very far away, and we listened to news of the country which was experiencing further turbulent times. The Sudan had become an Independent Republic. The French had withdrawn from Morocco and Gamal Nasser had become President of Egypt, and only a few months later would close the Suez Canal, further infuriating the British government.

In Kenya, the emergency had almost come to an end with the capture of the Mau Mau terrorist leader Dedan

Kimathi, but not before many European farmers and their families had been massacred, with thousands of loyal Kikuyu and servants hacked to death by their own kind, while endless heads of cattle were left to die on the farms from hamstring and other unpleasant mutilations.

At home, fashion and music flourished and moved ahead. Wearing our flared skirts and sugar-nylon petticoats and stiletto heels, Joan and I attended our first big school dance. I remember the thrill of being allowed to wear a faint trace of lipstick – wow! We rocked and rolled to long playing records and the sounds of Bill Haley and Elvis Presley, and drank pop, but we had to be back in the house by nine! We began to walk out with friends, but were expected to take the little ones with us for long walks, with John gurgling happily in his pram – thank heavens, he was too young to tell tales then! We sometimes met with friends in one of the local parks and sat around and swapped tales.

Poor Alice, she wasn't like us; we didn't much care for her either. She was a person, perhaps in her late twenties, with learning difficulties. Her greatest love, was a small well-worn tennis ball, which she would bounce up and down, with little co-ordination. Somehow our presence in the park, drew her like a magnet and each time we arrived, she would happily rush over to join us. She wore her long hair in bunches tied up with ribbons on either side of her head, and her thick brown stockings hung in wrinkles around her open-sandled feet. We tormented her by catching the ball when she bounced it our way and throwing it to each other, while she tried desperately to retrieve it, sending her running off squealing like a piglet in sheer frustration. I often thought years later, about how unkind children can sometimes be. It had been very unkind to trick her like that.

When my father returned to England, we rented our first television and at the time there were only a few programmes shown at certain times of the day. But I remember watching the first episode of 'Emergency Ward 10' and 'Coronation Street', and the stars who would become household names. Strangely enough my sister Joan found herself living opposite Pat Phoenix's home in Cheshire some years later.

My father spent time with the boys, setting up a model railway. John was now at a more interesting stage; he toddled around and enjoyed getting into mischief. For some time there was an air of peace at home. Joan and I walked out with boyfriends, Tony Ford (otherwise known as 'Ant') and Peter Walton, who was Ant's friend. We laughed a lot and had a wonderful time. With their racing cycles, which they both kept in gleaming condition, they would meet us occasionally from the school gate to walk home. A few 'Teddy Boys' hung around the street corners in those days. Wearing their long fashionable jackets and crêpe-soled shoes, they preened and coifed their hair, hoping to impress the local talent. My grandmother cursed their very existence and warned us of the dire consequences of associating with any of them. To begin with, we found them slightly intimidating and kept our distance, but we soon realised that they were good fun to be with and quite harmless – simply 'posers' of their day!

I began a shorthand and typing course one evening a

week after school with a couple of friends. The course, for the hour, cost half a crown. Squirreling tuppence from the gas meter money, meant that I could purchase six aniseed balls, which I kept for Peter and me when he met me after evening class and we walked home together.

I was content and settled at home in my well-ordered routine when it was time to pack up once more and leave for Africa. I had mixed emotions. I had become quite settled in Birmingham and liked Marlborough Road School and the feeling of unhappiness at leaving all my friends that I had made, and especially Peter, was emotionally overwhelming. However, the choice was not mine to make. We exchanged letters for about a year then, like most distant relationships, the letters became fewer until they finally stopped.

Chapter Five

As the aircraft flew over Kilimanjaro towards Moshi, I looked down on to the landscape, my face pressed against the window. The sun was hot and the wings of the aircraft glistened, flashing intense light back at me. Below, neatly outlined rivers snaked in and out of sight between undulating hills, and we recognised the tiny green fields on the slopes as coffee plantations, and through a mass of forested green, small cleared patches of farm buildings and native settlements were visible. It was then that I felt a tingle of excitement and anticipation at seeing old friends once more and moving back to live in the Big House!

Mr. Manly, the new Commissioner of Prisons, who had arranged to meet us at the airstrip, was late, and when he finally arrived, looking somewhat shaken, he apologised for not being there for us, and went on to say that on his way to meet us, he could not avoid hitting a horse which ran into the path of his car. The horse, which had escaped from the Larson Riding Stables nearby, was injured and, sadly, had to be destroyed. The front of the car was badly damaged and had to be towed away to a garage. So we waited around the airstrip for some time for other transport to arrive to collect us. One Land Rover and a truck for the luggage duly arrived to get us home.

In our absence, the house had undergone a face lift, the walls had been repainted and a few changes made here and there. Even the inside looked different, yet it was comforting to be in it once more. After an early evening meal, we unpacked enough of the suitcases to allow a change of clothing for the following day, then retired early to bed while my parents sat up into the night talking.

A neat, good-looking African man, named John, was interviewed the following day (Big John as he eventually became known to us all – in view of brother John). He began work as the new cook and houseboy. Having lived locally and been to the mission school, he spoke good English and came highly recommended by his brother, who was one of the prison warders. He was married with a young son, and my mother was happy to encourage both his wife and son to move into the servants' quarters with him, which eventually they did.

It was about this time that some men who had been apprehended in town on some felonious charge, attracted more than the usual attention when they were brought before my father to begin their sentence. On closer inspection, he had noticed that they were wearing familiar looking suits – HIS suits! The suits had been part of the contents of the packed crates which had been stolen during the break in at our house some months earlier, at the time that Levi was left injured. (Levi eventually recovered from his injuries and later went to work at a hotel out of the town.) I remember my father fuming and being extremely indignant over the fact that not only were these men wearing his suits, but they had the audacity and cheek to cut off the bloody trouser legs! As he put it.

Joan began a new job working at the chemist store at the front entrance of the commerce building in the centre of Moshi town. I was still of school age and had about six months to go before completing my education, but for some reason, I was given the choice of going back to Arusha School or beginning work in a book shop which was owned by some friends of my parents. I think that in the end, my decision to take them up on their offer was solely based on my parents' financial situation at that time. They were now faced with trying to educate four of us at boarding school, and the fees and uniforms were going to be very expensive. As it turned out, not returning to school was to be the best decision of my life and I had no reason to ever regret it!

So I began work in the family-run business which was in the centre of the main commerce building complex and not far from where Joan was. The Twiga bookshop was the largest of the only two bookshops in the town, the other being the Lutheran bookshop next door. Apart from the extensive range of books, and paperbacks, we also kept a comprehensive range of government office and school equipment, as well as many of the foreign language periodicals. My immediate task each morning was to ensure that the English and local newspapers were named and delivered by the young delivery boy to the customers in the district and work places. It was a varied and interesting job, and anyone and everyone who lived in or around the area, would at some stage come in to the bookshop.

It also became another meeting place to catch up on the local gossip and meet friends. After working there for a while, it was obvious from some of the folks' more outrageous behaviour that this was more than just a meeting place, but a cover for some secret assignations and other goings-on.

There were many interesting people who came to Moshi – the real home of the local Chagga, a proud, good-looking and well-educated people, who were inspired by their young Chief, Tom Marealle II, a dignified man of immense personality who my parents got to know well, and talked of with great fondness.

Each working day at the bookshop was different, and you never knew who you would see or meet in the course of a day's work. I felt so privileged to meet many fascinating people from all walks of life. Some new up-and-coming African world leaders met and attended conferences in the district. A book written by the Police Chief, Ian Henderson, called *The Hunt for Kimathi* – the story of the capture of a Mau Mau leader – a new book on our shelves at the time, caught the eye of a young, good-looking politician, Mr. Tom Mboya, who went on to purchase a copy. There were countless visitors to the region: Prince Aly Khan and his actress wife, Rita Hayworth, were frequent visitors to the local Asian community. Many of the actors, actresses and camera crews who were filming in the area stayed at the two major local hotels and dropped in each day for their newspapers. From wildlife photographers and ornithologists, to climbers and servicemen on leave from their bases in Aden, each day would bring a variety of fascinating, colourful and interesting people. Joan later told me that she kept the autograph book, which was given to her by Mrs. Forrest, near at hand and had managed to obtain autographs from a number of well-known names, John Wayne, Robert Taylor, and many more. Anthony Newly was always funny and a breath of fresh air when he came in to our premises, and so was the American actor, Orlando Martins – with his incredible infectious laugh and big grin. They were among some of the many stars and actors who were working on films being made in Arusha and Moshi. One of the films entitled *Adamson of Africa*, was done on location in Moshi and Mombasa, but when the film in question went on general release, the title-change to *Killers of Kilimanjaro* caused much anger and outrage amongst some of the local people. Numerous films had been made over the years in and around the area, as the climate and the locations were exquisite, making it an ideal place for scenery and wildlife.

When my father was asked to appear in a bit part of a film I was thrilled; it was not the first time that he had been asked. My joy soon turned to disappointment when he spent time deliberating whether to or whether not to, finally declining the offer. Betty Williams, a local artist, was commissioned to paint a background scene for the same film, while two of my friends had minor stand-in roles.

It was on an ordinary, hot afternoon on an ordinary working day, that a young khaki-uniformed policeman entered the doors of the bookshop. He browsed amongst the paperbacks and magazines and was later joined by a couple of his colleagues. All of them were with the new intake at the Police Training School in Moshi, and were based at the old, vacated King's African Rifle barracks. He walked over and asked me for a particular Kiswahili

Dictionary and I was glad to show him to the area where we had a varied selection of a foreign language books and brochures. I had not taken much notice of him really, as he spent some time choosing a few books that he wanted. He walked to the counter, paid for them, then, with a pleasant smile, he thanked me, and then I did notice his handsome face. He dallied a while and then he and his colleagues left together, and I didn't give any of them much thought after that.

By the mid-1950s, Tanganyika was slowly preparing itself for self-rule, and already there was a lot of feeling of uncertainty amongst the Europeans, and one could rarely pick up a daily newspaper without seeing the word 'Uhuru' glaring more than half a dozen times from its front pages, or eavesdrop on someone's conversation without hearing the same word repeated time and time again. 'Uhuru' meant freedom to the African, but the concept of freedom, was interpreted differently by the black man and the white man.

Having learned the rudiments of shorthand and typing at night school in Birmingham, secretarial work was not my ambition in life, but merely a means to an end. I think that my father's vision for me was a secretarial course, followed by a good, steady job – perhaps as a means to finding a husband – but that was not my ambition at all. What I really wanted was to eventually do nursing, in Nairobi or wherever, if and when it became possible. Meanwhile I had resolved to continue to teach myself to RSA certificate standard and try to see if I could get a secretarial job locally. So, armed with an old typewriter, a tape recorder, and my father's encouragement – I was woken up each morning at about 5.45 before he left for work at six o'clock for 'unlock' – a time when I was able to put in a good couple of hours of study before breakfast. I found it was pleasing to work during those quiet, early hours of the morning, still dark and cool, with only the noise of the birds to keep me company, as I sat at the dining room table till sun-up. When light came, I would clear my work away so that Big John could set the table for breakfast and, by the time my father had returned home, the sun would already be highlighting the gleaming whiteness of the snow capped mountain in front of us.

For some odd reason my parents offered to look after a young, black Labrador puppy, named Buster, for friends who were on leave in England. We had already acquired a Siamese cat given to us by some wildlife film people. We didn't really want it – my father, in particular, was not overly fond of cats, but we took it in just the same. Buster was a sloppy, gangly animal, and totally out of control. He was finally banned from the house and had to join Bruce and Kim in the kennels outside, after continually jumping up on the furniture, but not before he had knocked over coffee tables and spilled drinks. The animal was a menace! On the whole he was a good natured creature, but a poor excuse for a guard dog! He caused utter chaos and my parents despaired of his antics at times. He became the bane of Big John's life, and even the cat gave him a wide berth. The Siamese cat had three kittens, which she used to move around the garden, well-hidden from the dogs, but what happened to them in the end, we never did get to know – we suspected that Buster was involved somewhere along the line!

At about eight each morning, we would all sit down around the long dining table to enjoy our breakfast of pawpaw and fruit juice or, as my father preferred, fried bacon, egg and fresh cooked tomato, picked from the garden that morning. After breakfast, we would then leave together for town, where Joan and I would be dropped off for work.

One morning a lorry pulled up outside the house to a squeal of brakes and Big John came to us to say that Bruce, our inquisitive, brave little Ridgeback had been run over – his desire to chase vehicles eventually cost him his life. The driver couldn't be blamed: shocked and upset, he pleaded that he couldn't avoid hitting the dog as he ran towards the side of the vehicle. Bruce was buried deep in the field far out of sight of the house, and poor Kim, loped and pined for days at the loss of his brother, and even Buster's silly antics couldn't cheer him up.

A large shed with a corrugated iron roof was converted into a workshop, and my father spent many hours at the weekends with 'Bakari', a habitual petty offender with some engineering skills, in the hopes of rehabilitating him, and steering him into more worthwhile pursuits. Bakari was in and out of prison like a yo-yo. In fact, like many other inmates, he enjoyed the well ordered life of the place, and liked to come back to the 'Kingi Georgei Hotel', where he knew that he would be provided with somewhere to sleep and regular meals. Each time he re-offended, he would end up at the house, with my father saying, "Oh, not you again Bakari!" "Oh yes Sir," would come the reply from Bakari, his broad smile showing a set of gleaming white teeth. He was a personable man, a real character, and a quick learner, and once he had been shown how to do something, he could be relied upon and trusted to carry out any amount of work in the garage, from stripping down engines, to turning the lathe, to making any part of equipment that needed replacing. Martin, Peter and young John pottered about the workshop with Bakari during the hours after school, turning out boats and planes with oddments of wood, and my parents didn't ever turn a hair; they knew that the boys would be completely safe in his hands.

My father was, on the whole, a reasonably patient man, but there were certain things that would occasionally cause him to lose his cool – mainly involving the workshop. He was a stickler for neatness when it involved his precious work tools, and was well aware of the dangers of having untidy work areas. He was always adamant that each tool had to be cleaned and placed in its allocated spot above the work bench after use – every tool had its place, and woe betide if the item he was reaching for was not there when it was needed. His philosophy was also "Can't – means Shan't," and girls in his view were equally as capable as boys and vice-versa. I recall having been bought a pattern and some pink satin once and, with my father looking on in horror, I butchered yards of the material in a vain attempt at making a ball gown. He ranted and raved at my ghastly mistakes until he could stand the sight no longer and snatched the pattern and material away and made up the dress for me, with the words, "You see – with a little effort and care, anything can be achieved!".

Showing great patience at other times, he taught us all how to use the right tools for the right job. I was a reasonably quick learner in this field and enjoyed anything to do with engineering, mainly because I had a keen eye and understood the theory, design and workings of most things. However, everything I ever learned and much of what I know now, I owe solely to my father and will always be eternally grateful to him. Suffice to say, that my knowledge has always stood me in good stead over the years and saved the family a great deal in time and money.

He was not always so serious when working; there was often a lighter side to him even when he was in the workshop. When Mr. Basciera brought a couple of Italian racing motorcycles and a Lambretta to the house, the engines were stripped down by the two men, then cleaned, and the motorcycles repaired and restored as good as new. It was then quite a funny sight to see the two of them mount the bikes and ride round and round the house like a couple of teenagers. Like his own father, there was nothing that my father couldn't put his hand to or make. Perhaps one of his best inventions was a four-pronged mixer he made for my mother from a small motor. It could certainly have been the forerunner to the electric mixer that I use today. The only problem was that we feasted on Victoria sponges for weeks until the novelty wore off!

My father was enormous fun to be with, but sometimes his 'fun' bordered on the reckless. I can remember that he once made a go-cart trailer with a plank and four old pram wheels, which he tied to the back of a bicycle, and then insisted that all of us children sit on the contraption, whilst he rode the bicycle, pulling us behind him. We all squeezed on to this so-called go-cart with Joan steering, to, "Right we're off," as he took off down the incline towards the fishponds at a rate of knots. As we gathered speed, the ride felt exhilarating and we convulsed into peals of laughter, until Joan found steering in a straight line at speed quite impossible. As he cycled on, he failed to notice that one by one we had fallen off the trailer on to the sharp gravel road. It was not until he finally came to a stop at the bottom of the hill, laughter bursting his sides, that he looked back to see his six crying children, scattered along the road behind him. When he returned to the house, my mother was furious, accusing him of 'irresponsible, childish behaviour', as she attended to the tears, cuts and bruises and torn clothes.

One of the funniest times I can remember with him was when, dressed in his uniform, he took me out as his pillion passenger on the back of the Lambretta. We rode around the fish ponds a couple of times, passing some of the inmates who were working in a gang. The noise from the bike had quite obviously disturbed the flock of grazing geese nearby, because the second time we passed by them, the gaggle took off towards us, flapping their wings and making a terrible noise. The next time we took a detour, deciding not to go anywhere near the geese. Rounding a bend, we found ourselves ambushed by them on another part of the pond embankment and, taking evasive action to avoid the birds in full flight with open beaks and flapping wings coming towards us, my father lost control and the bike skidded up the bank, throwing us both, unceremoniously, to the ground. The whole scene was utterly undignified and must have looked like a bit part from a Stan Stennet movie. Of course all the gang of onlookers fell about, seeing the 'Boss' sprawled on the grass verge.

Getting up very early in the morning for work meant that it was a long day for me, and I looked forward to meeting Joan for a sandwich lunch and a midday coffee, upstairs in the Kilimanjaro Native Co-operative Union (KNCU) building's refreshment hall, before work in the afternoon. We exchanged stories of the interesting folk we had seen that day, or talked about our arrangements for going out with friends. One afternoon before returning to work we were happily talking and I accidentally walked into the path of Roy Rogers, plus guitar, coming out of the lift on the ground floor. I apologised as it was my fault, but he insisted it was his – a true gentleman.

We always looked forward to Wilfrid and Norbert Veit returning from Gordonstoun Boarding School in Scotland to their parents' coffee farm on the hills, because they were always immense fun to be with. I was particularly fond of Wilfrid, with his handsome smile and crazy ideas, who would often enjoy racing around the vast areas of plantation in his open jeep. Always full of ideas of what to do or where to go, there was never a dull moment with either of them. We enjoyed a day's picnicking at the waterfalls at Marangu. They regularly had a house full of friends from school who came to stay with them for the holidays. Dr. and Mrs. Veit were especially lovely folk. Having fled from Germany during the rise of Hitler and fascism, they had happily made their home in Africa. When war came, Dr. and Mrs. Veit who would otherwise have been interned by the British, were relocated and allowed to keep the farm and run it. Mrs. Veit was a fun lady, young at heart and exceedingly generous and kind, inviting us to her home on a number of occasions to parties, to swim or play badminton. They were memorable, heady, carefree days which I shall always treasure.

We spent a memorable day's safari at Tsavo. Very early one morning, Wilfrid and Norbert, plus Mum to chaperone, pitched up outside our house in their farm lorry, complete with wooden side battens, to pick Joan and I up to go for a game drive to Tsavo. We sat on some seats in the back of the truck, our knees covered with blankets against the usual early morning chill.

Continuing our drive along the road through Old Moshi to Himo, following the Voi to Mombasa road, we reached Tsavo as the sun was coming up. Pausing at the palm-fringed river bank we had a stroll around, being careful not to venture too far from the safety of the lorry, and stopped for some light refreshment. We then drove on to Mzima Springs, sat on benches in an underwater chamber, and peered through the glass windows to watch the hippos and the shoals of barbell fish swim by.

By ten in the morning it was hot. Tsavo is more arid than the Serengeti, and at that time the grass everywhere was sparse and bleached from the sun. There were a few scattered giant baobab trees and thorn trees and a liberal scattering of huge, red termite mounds, but the red soil was delicate and dry and looked incapable of sustaining any kind of life at all, and by then the rainy season was already well overdue.

We stood up on the truck, looking out on to the river ahead as the hippos grunted and wheezed, their ears and nostrils barely visible above the churned up discoloured water. In the distance a couple of huge crocodiles basked in the sun, and a solitary turtle sat precariously on a floating log to hitch a lift, while a flock of brilliant white egrets congregated along the grassy verges of the river bank.

At midday we sat down under the cover of some thorn trees to eat our picnic lunch and, as we did so, a small troop of curious monkeys advanced, uncertainly, to drink some distance from us, but our slightest move sent them scampering back into the safety of the nearby trees, barking protests at the invasion of their haunts. A large herd of elephants lumbered by in the distance, occasionally glancing towards us, and pausing to pick up mounds of earth in their trunks to scatter over themselves as they strolled to the far bank to drink; they were accompanied by the opportunist white egrets riding on their backs. A number of small flocks of grey helmeted guinea fowl scratched and foraged in the dry dust and scurried off at our approach. We stayed on the back of the lorry for some time, watching a regal secretary bird trying to pick away at a small reptile it had just caught, and were so engrossed that we had not noticed the approach of a rhino from the other side until the beast was upon us. Suddenly, all hell broke loose as she charged at us, striking the rear wheel-arch with such force that it lifted the back of the vehicle a foot or more into the air, sending us sprawling and tumbling in the back, and Wilfrid off the tailgate. Before we could compose ourselves, she struck again. We were all shaken and slightly bruised and my heart was pounding as Wilfrid quickly managed to scramble back on board before she was ready to come at us again. The lorry moved off but she continued to chase us, snorting with fury and eventually disappearing behind a cloud of dust as our vehicle gathered momentum. A warthog family ran across the road in front of us with their tails held stiffly in the air, the little ones following on behind, carrying their little aerials too. From the moment the sun advanced high into the sky, the awesome heat penetrated the sun baked earth, and the entangled growth of thorn and mopani scrub along our route wilted and curled, so that only their faint shadows were cast on the powdery dry red earth. As we drove on to Taveta and walked to the top of the hills to look down on the view below us, the atmosphere of the afternoon heat concentrated the sounds of the buzzing insects.

Feeling pretty tired from our early morning start, we headed for home. Along the road, we passed the occasional group of native women dressed in their brightly coloured traditional dress, walking along carrying large bundles of thatching material and sticks on their heads. We passed a few conical shaped native dwellings and outhouses discreetly hidden between scattered plots of banana and sugarcane. A number of herds of goats grazed amongst the wild gorse bushes watched over by their very young herdsmen. As we neared the domed splendour of Kilimanjaro, towering above the more rugged, craggy outline of Mawenzi, a cool breeze had sprung up, and the restless zebra and gazelle along the route prepared themselves for the night to come. By the time we reached home, the sight of the gathering rain clouds in the distance promised a welcome relief from the weeks of drought.

The long, hot spell had plagued us all with millions of locusts at the 'hopper' stage. These pests, blown south from the Sahara, lingered for weeks, devouring grass, shrubs and crops alike, until they finally paired off. They jumped about clumsily, knocking into things, and many was the time that I had to extract them from the front of my dress, or from between my petticoat and skirt, and pick them out of my hair. They crept up trees and hung in great numbers on the tall grasses until whatever they were clinging to became so heavy they fell ungainly to the ground. Only the marabou storks found them remotely palatable, and they flew into the fields in their hundreds to gorge themselves on them, as the smaller birds gave way.

Extreme weather conditions were not common to the area. Moshi had a pleasant, comfortable climate, but on one occasion the area felt the full force of nature in the raw. The rain came and came – it poured down in torrents. Four and half inches of rain fell in nine hours to be exact. The water level in the fish ponds rose rapidly. Despite the sluice gates being open, the immense pressure exerted on the walls of the banks caused them to give way and the volume of water leaving, cut huge channels through the banana and maize plantation, uprooting trees and hedges. Rocks, roots and debris from the field and ponds were carried beyond the perimeter fence in a giant mud slide, finally petering out on the fields across the main Moshi to Arusha road. The mudslide rose to over two metres high in the middle, and hundreds of acres of planted crops were ruined. A number of early morning commuters to work were caught in the mudslide, but mercifully no one was injured. Along the road lay rocks and bushes and amongst them, tons of trapped fish. Some of the local natives arrived on the scene and carried off kikapu full of fish to take home to their families. Eventually bulldozers were brought in from town to help with the clearing up operation.

All the ponds inevitably had to be drained, making a huge task, and the scavengers, like the monitor lizards, were quick to seize the opportunity to reach the isolated duck shed, get to the ducks' nests, and steal their eggs. The purple herons and hammercocks searched between the mud pockets looking for trapped fish, and hundreds of smaller birds dipped into puddles to bathe; the banks simply seethed with insects and butterflies.

We often took a walk down to the fish ponds to watch how the work was progressing, but one evening Buster joined us and proceeded to cause havoc among the ducks, chasing them along the banks and across into the centre of the deep quagmire. No amount of desperate shouting to bring him to heel would stop his endless pursuit. When he was eventually brought to heel, wagging his tail with glee, a number of ducks lay lifeless and covered in mud as others, exhausted and flapping wildly, fared little better, as we scrambled to retrieve them from the mess. Suffice to say that my father was so incensed at the carnage, that Buster was grounded for a long time.

To add to the misery following the downpour, for a couple of weeks at least, the whole area in and around the prison grounds was invaded by inch long caterpillars or 'army worm' as they were known. This seething mass of caterpillars, began their life nestled under rocks and stones, until finally emerging in their millions – green ones, black and white ones – crawling over the fields, lawns and drives. They crawled up the side of the house, falling into heaps, crawling and writhing over each other; it was like the unfolding of a horror movie. You could not walk anywhere without encountering these ghastly creatures which sent shudders up the spine, then, suddenly, one day they had gone.

At home, my parents continued entertaining, and my mother certainly knew how to do things in style. Joan and I were expected to help take care of the guests and to join in the festivities, but also help with the organisation and preparation beforehand.

At every large gathering, the staff always turned out in their immaculate white 'Kanzus', with coloured cummerbunds, caps and white gloves. All preparations for meals would begin the day before, and any ducks or chickens that were required, were caught and prepared at the back of the servants quarters. Most of the fresh vegetables came from the shamba and were soaked in potassium permanganate for a while, a useful sterilising agent to clean anything and everything, from vegetables to wounds and cuts, but its only drawback was that the violet-coloured solution could leave your hands stained brown for hours after use.

After these dinners, everyone would retire to the veranda for a coffee or a smoke. The music blared, while the sitting room carpet would be rolled back to the wall, and a faint dusting of powder applied to the floor ready for the dancing; dancing which went on for hours and hours as the whisky and coffee flowed. Behind the scenes, the ever-efficient staff busied themselves with the clearing and washing of the dishes, while from the kitchen the pans were removed to the back yard where they were scoured on the ground, with handfuls of ash from the day's fire, and warm water. All the linen would be counted and sent for laundering, returned the following afternoon crisply starched, counted and stored away, ready for the next dinner function.

Whether it was dinner evenings for a dozen people, official parties, cocktail parties or children's parties, there was always an excuse for get-togethers and everyone was afforded the same lavish treatment. I remember inviting a couple of young airmen, who were on their leave from Aden, to the house to join us for a meal on one of these occasions. An hour before midnight, a military Land Rover arrived at the front door and disgorged a rabble of a dozen young servicemen – all looking a good deal the worse for wear and demanding to know where the party was. My father, being the consummate host, invited them in to partake of dinner and as much coffee as they wanted. After their meal, they disappeared back into their vehicle, having helped themselves to a few beers, drove a short distance away from the house, then continued with their own noisy party in the back of the Land Rover, which went on into the early hours of the following morning. Thank you boys! Inevitably, I was advised not to issue invitations willy-nilly to young military men without prior warning of how many would be likely to turn up.

Where there was food, there were monkeys, and down in the valley gorge the vervet troop were on the move. Being creatures of habit, by about four o'clock in the afternoon they would hastily make their way along the avenue of trees towards the house, then come and sit on the branches overlooking the kitchen. Bobbing their heads from side to side, they would wait patiently, trying to get a better look through the window at Big John cooking. Their neat, black faces with wide, brown eyes would look down at us as they sat holding their tiny pink-faced offspring. They knew that somewhere around that kitchen lay the promise of free food. They were an incredible source of amusement to us. When Big John left the kitchen to collect firewood for the stove, they would hesitate and wait until the coast was clear, then make a dash into the kitchen, grab whatever food they could carry, then quickly scamper back up into the trees holding on to their booty in their dextrous little fingers. Not all their raids were successful though. Big John sometimes returned unexpectedly to catch them red-handed. There would be a silent pause for a few moments – followed by shouts and swearing – followed by the sound of pans and lids and kitchen utensils, then monkeys would flee in all directions.

Despite their frightfully amusing antics, they were always vulnerable to attacks from the many eagles and brown kites which circled overhead. However, the predatory birds did seem to prefer easier prey, like the young chickens and ducklings from the huge run behind the house. Any approach from kites would send the chickens and ducks running to safety, but those that were not quite quick enough would huddle together in the corner of their pen squawking in terror, as the birds swooped, picked up their quarry, and flew off. Their quick, ferocious manoeuvres would be over in seconds. Fortunately, most of the time they were foiled in their attempts as there was nearly always someone around the house or garden to chase the birds away, but we did lose a few young ducks and chickens that way.

One such attack on the vervet troop by the birds left a stunned baby lying on the ground after its mother had been snatched and he had fallen from her grasp. I picked him up; he was no bigger than the palm of my hand, and as I held him, his tiny tail hung limply between my fingers. I tried to feed him some milk from a doll's pipette, but he died later that day. This poor little creature had lost his mother, and I wondered if his feelings were so very different from ours after losing a parent. The troop were eventually moved away, but one of the vervets remained in the vicinity, and became a great favourite of the twins, Peter, and John. They named him 'Chippy', and he often appeared when they returned home from school in the afternoons. The youngsters would spend hours being entertained by his wild antics in the back garden. In time however, when the twins and Peter eventually departed for boarding school, the once friendly cheeky little monkey became a nuisance and began nipping the heels of every passer-by. Even I was caught unawares on a couple of occasions whilst out walking. When he later became aggressive and dangerous my father, sadly, was forced to shoot him.

A couple of weeks before John's third birthday he was bought a new red tricycle. After breakfast we all congregated on the front balcony to watch his little face light up as he saw his present. With so many onlookers, he was a bit shy, and turned to look at us; then, smiling, ran to investigate it. He checked the wheels, but was more fascinated with the bell, giggling each time he rang it. He was shown how to pedal and we waited, all urging him to get moving, but he simply climbed off and ran back to my mother, who then gently took his hand and led him back to the tricycle and put him back on the seat. "Go on, John," she encouraged. "Have another go – we are all watching you."

"I can't," he said, "It hurts me." At first she thought that he was just shy because we had all been watching him. "We'll leave him to go on when he's good and ready," she said. Throughout the afternoon, we watched as he clambered on and off the tricycle, showing little interest in doing anything more than ringing the bell.

During the night he was restless and cried out a few times, so my mother took him into her bed. It was obvious from his temperature that he was sickening for something. She tried to get him to drink but he kept fighting the cup away. The doctor was called as his temperature rose further, and he began to complain that his legs were hurting. The doctor couldn't understand the problem; there were no spots or anything obvious. Over the following few days, John's temperature had reduced slightly, but he was poorly and restless through the nights, and was still in obvious pain, drawing his legs up to his chest. My mother was exhausted and at her wits end, when an awful thought struck her. Maybe she was witnessing the symptoms that she had witnessed some years ago as a young nurse in Birmingham: had John got polio?

She rang the hospital and the doctor came right away. Short of knowing what else it could be, he agreed with her diagnosis and suggested giving John an injection. She refused, saying that if it was polio, what good would an injection be? Polio was still a killer, and she insisted that John should stay at home to be looked after by her. My mother immediately instituted an intense regime of nursing care which meant that every couple of hours throughout the day and night, the bath was filled almost to the brim with tepid water. Handfuls of rock salt was added to the water, and John was immersed into it. Her plan was to mobilise and exercise his legs as much as possible and for this nursing task, she enlisted Joan's help, and they took turns to exercise his legs in the water, as he cried out in pain each time he was moved. By the end of the week, his temperature had fallen to normal but the pain persisted. By the second week, there was visible wasting and stiffness of the muscles in his legs, and he was refusing to bear his own weight, until finally he was unable to stand at all. While all this was going on, the twins and Peter were at school and unaware of the terrible drama being played out at home.

My mother had become utterly exhausted and each afternoon she retired to her bed, taking John with her for a sleep, staying with him constantly. One afternoon, she felt it safe to leave him to sleep on his own, and left the room to make herself some tea, then retired to the comfort of an armchair in the sitting room to read for a while. When she went back to check him later, what greeted her on her return to the room sent shivers up her spine. Looking straight at her was John, brandishing the fully loaded hand gun which she had always kept hidden under her pillow in case of trouble. He had been happily playing with it and, of course, when he saw her, he thought it great fun to point the gun straight at her. She closed the door quickly and shouted for my father, who rushed outside to the window to try and distract him, whilst she entered the bedroom and removed the gun from his hand. It was a delicate operation and the incident shook her up so much, that she refused to have any firearms in the house ever again.

Joan and I continued at our work places. Soon word spread that John had polio and I became aware that my continued presence at the shop was causing some alarm. I was assured by the lady who owned the shop, an ex nursing sister herself, that I was a hazard to nobody. Despite the ignorance surrounding the virus I wasn't happy with the situation myself and quite understood the fear of others of the unknown. As it was, my parents decided that we should all take a long break and as I was due some leave from work, it would be better for everyone's sake if it was taken at the earliest time possible. Arrangements were set in motion for a holiday at the coast in Dar-es-Salaam, combined with an appointment where John could be seen by a specialist. It was felt that the humid air and the sea would be of great benefit to him, as well as to the rest of us. Without any further delay, my parents packed up and left by car to drive to the coast, leaving me to finish work and follow on a week later by train.

As if by some turn of fate, and with only a few days to go before I was to leave for the coast, the young policeman I had seen a few months earlier came into the shop and this time I did notice him, as I stared unashamedly for a long time at his handsome profile under his blue peaked police hat, his tanned arms and strong tanned legs; he looked a beautiful picture, and it was then that I secretly fell in love with him. I was just fifteen. I simply had to make a point of saying hello. Instead, he introduced himself first, as John Thackeray. When I told him my name, he enquired as to whether I was related to Senior Superintendent Davis who had lectured to his police intake. "I'm his daughter," I said proudly. He then asked if I was going to the police ball the following week and would I like to accompany him. How I would have loved to. For some reason I stopped short of blurting out my age to him but declined his invitation, saying that I was leaving on a short break to the coast almost immediately. Well, I had given him my reason, but suddenly, somehow, a trip to the coast didn't seem so appealing. I didn't want to leave Moshi, for in my heart I would have loved to have gone to the ball with him. However, I knew that my parents would not have approved anyway, solely on the grounds of my age. That evening, I began to feel thoroughly downcast and an irrational, overwhelming urge to get away from home altogether filled my mind, so much so that, on that very evening, I wrote a letter applying to go to nurse in Nairobi.

As if matters couldn't get worse, a day or so later, two young scruffy native youths entered the bookshop. Their intention, unbeknown to me, was theft. They spent some time browsing, and I carried on with my work as usual, doing what I had to do. Before long, I noticed that a few items had gone missing from one of the shelves and, as I looked around me, I noticed one of the men stuffing something up into his jacket. When I approached and questioned him, his guilty friend took off through one door, and he tried to make for the other. I gave chase and caught the end of his flapping jacket and as I tugged, he turned on me with his fists, and landed a brilliant right hook to my jaw. In the ungainly scrabble, the contents of his coat fell clattering to the ground. Mr. Russell, the proprietor, came rushing out of his office, having heard the commotion, and apprehended the youth until the police arrived, as I stood there with blood running down my face and dress.

A week into their stay in Dar, my father received a phone call with the good news of his promotion, followed by a letter of congratulations from Mr. Maudling, the then Home Secretary. Under any other circumstances he would have been overjoyed. Of course, he was happy about it; he certainly needed all the good news that he could get at that time.

Mr. and Mrs. Forder, obligingly saw me on to the train from Moshi that evening for my journey to Korogwe and then Morogoro. I was the only white face to board the train that evening, and sat in the empty compartment feeling quite anxious and very lonely, and I had little time to enjoy the passing scenery as darkness fell quickly on the slow-moving train. I was forced to close the latched shutter, as the dimly lit overhead light invited all the moths and night bugs; in the end, I was forced to turn the light off and sit in complete darkness. The train chugged slowly along, reaching Korogwe in the early hours of the following morning, where I disembarked and walked into a building where I was handed a cup of tea in a rather grubby teacup and saucer. The air was heavy and warm and I opened my bag and shook off the few ants which had sniffed their way into it, and sat eating my sandwiches alone. I called at the nearby kiosk, where a number of crates stood piled high with fizzy drinks, and purchased a couple of bottles of Pepsi whilst I waited to continue my journey. After about half an hour, I was approached by an Asian gentleman porter, who told me that the train was terminating at Korogwe, and went on to say that the next leg of the journey would have to be taken by bus. I hurriedly joined the end of a queue of Africans who were ready to board the waiting bus and, looking about me, wondered how on earth we would all manage to fit in. My presence caused some stirring in the line and they all looked to me to get on first, but I gestured that I would wait my turn. However, fit in we did, everyone squeezed in together. There were mothers with tiny infants on their backs and older members of families carrying toddlers and parcels. There were suitcases and bags of clothing in all shapes and sizes, followed by crates and boxes. Other larger pieces of luggage were unceremoniously thrown up into the luggage rack, on the top of the bus.

By the time we were ready to set off, the rain had come down in a steady downpour. We continued our journey on to Morogoro with the bus swaying and groaning under its heavy load, and making slow progress as it negotiated the slippery, muddy, waterlogged surface of the road, until the vehicle finally groaned to a stop with a profusion of steam coming from under the bonnet. We sat in our seats whilst the driver got out to look at the engine, followed by a few of his front seat passengers, each taking turns to peep into the engine and chipping in with his opinion on what needed doing next. Ultimately, we all had to disembark into the mire. Wanting to show that I was equally informed about what the problem was, I suggested that we try to push the vehicle out of the really muddy area, to a place where the problem could be sorted out; after all, there were enough of us to lend a hand. My idea was received with great enthusiasm, and a good deal of hilarity broke out as I put my shoulder to the back and beckoned some of the others to do the same. Some just stood back and looked on in astonishment; others went into a huddle for a conference. At one stage the bus, with its flimsy luggage rack, threatened to disgorge its load of boxes and baskets filled with chickens and other livestock on to us. The natives thought it was great fun when I emerged, grubby, with mud splattered on my face and clothes. After some minor tinkering with the engine by the driver and his growing band of helpers, we continued on our journey and by the end of it I was among many friends.

With a cloth, and a bottle of the Pepsi, I was able to clean myself up, before arriving in Morogoro where my father was waiting to pick me up. "No need to ask if you had a good journey," he quipped, to which I had instant sense of humour failure! I was relieved and happy that the journey was over as I was hot and extremely sticky, and by the time we reached Dar the sun was at its height.

My parents were staying at the residence at Oyster Bay, overlooking the beautiful long sandy beach, and as we drove along Ocean Road all the memories of the place and wonderful smell of the sea during our many trips when we were children came back to me.

The following day, I joined the family to take John to the specialist, whose clinic overlooked the ships in the busy harbour bay. John needed to be carried everywhere, and in the clinic the specialist asked that two of us hold John's hands as he tried to coax him to walk along the straight white line marked across the concrete floor. John was reluctant to stand at all; and each visit brought more despair and tears as his progress, if any, was imperceptible and there was the mention of callipers for him. My mother began to wonder if he would ever walk again without some form of aids on his legs, but she was not about to give up on her young son just yet.

Each day, Joan and I carried him down to the beach, where he sat quite happily on the warm sand and chuckled as the surf washed over him. In the heat of the afternoons, we took to our rooms to keep out of the sun and John would happily sit playing, or drawing in his books, whilst listening to his 'Noddy' records being played over and over again, until he became word perfect with every one of them.

While we were resting on our beds one day, John slid down from his bed and crawled over to the bed end. We watched, not daring to say a word. Without prompting, he lifted himself on to his feet and stood for a few moments unaided, then sat down again. We just looked at each other and didn't utter a word, as he sat on the floor beside the bed. We pretended to ignore him. Then again he lifted himself up and stood for quite a while, finally letting go of the bedpost. We shouted for my parents, who flew into our room wondering what on earth was up. "Show mummy what you can do John," we urged. He then picked himself up again, stood unsupported at the bedside and took his first couple of steps. Tears filled her eyes. "Look mummy, I can walk," he said. We all ran over to him, tears streaming down our faces with joy, everybody telling him what a clever boy he was!

The specialist was amazed at the progress, and despite the noticeable wastage of his leg muscles, his progress had been nothing short of miraculous, thanks to the early nursing care and complete faith that my mother had had, that her son would recover and one day walk again. (I am happy to report that this six foot four inches tall man is now a DCI in the Police Force: how proud she would have been.)

Once he was able to stand up and support himself,

there was no holding him back; he enjoyed his days by the sea and we were able to leave Dar-es-Salaam a great deal happier than when we arrived.

With my father driving and me alongside in a brand new Volkswagen car, which he had picked up from the docks earlier for a friend in Moshi, we finally left the coast and headed back for home. My mother, Joan and John followed behind in the Austin. Along the Dar-es-Salaam road, we drove over the unmanned rail level crossing. Looking behind him, my father caught sight of a train speeding towards the crossing, which would soon be in my mother's path. He felt that she would not see it in time, until it was upon her. He stopped the car and waved frantically for her to stop. Luckily, she had seen the train just in the nick of time and was able to pull up moments before it rolled on in front of her; altogether it was a terrifying moment for us as we could only look on and wait.

When we reached the outskirts of Morogoro, my father pointed to the hill where Matty was buried and as I looked up, all I could recall seeing were trees. My father had not spoken of Matty since that fateful day in October of 1948 and we were always afraid to bring up the subject with either of my parents, fearing that it would cause much hurt; but there were many questions that I would have liked to have asked about her. I had my opportunity and, sadly, I let it pass – if only. We arrived home late in the evening after a whole day of travelling, a few frayed nerves and my first introduction to map reading.

A few days later after our return home from Dar,

Bakari was passing by the kitchen and saw that John was poking around inside the outlet drain with a long stick. He walked over to enquire what he was doing, whereupon Bakari was invited to look at the 'fish' that he had caught. On closer inspection, he saw a coiled black mamba about to strike. Immediately grabbing John by his shirt and uttering a few expletives, he hoisted him in the air with lightning reaction. The commotion brought my mother to the scene. The instant reaction saved John from certain death as, once bitten, the venom acts instantly, attacking the nervous system, and at that time there was no anti-venom against the species. When Bakari was finally released from prison he went to work for Mr. Basciera and was very happy indeed. I would have liked to have thought that it was to end with 'happy ever after', but news reached us in England some three years later that Bakari had been killed in a road accident when the vehicle he was travelling in overturned. A felon and a rogue he may have been, but he had a heart of pure gold and our family had a lot to thank him for. I can still see his beaming smile now!

**My father, Basil,
in the uniform of the
Coldstream Guard**

**My mother, Mathilda
(Matty)**

My father and my dear mother, Betty

The Big House, Moshi

Kilimanjaro ~ the view from the Big House

My Father outside the house at Kilgolwira: 1948

My parents, Joan and Me 1948

Coast at Dar Es Salaam

Poppet the dog, me and my sister, Joan, and our father
at Kingolwira

Homebound ~ the view taken from the launch of the Flying Boat

Prisoners at work ~ note no walls

Karanga Prison, Moshi, 1950s

Water tank and vegetable shamba (garden)

Martin, John, Mary, Peter and me relaxing in front of the house at Moshi

Joan with Masai villagers

Our engagement

Our Wedding Day

142

Police Training School Moshi Tanganyika, 1959

John on Gillmans Point Mount Kilimanjaro, 1959

My Father 1959 in Moshi

**Top: Temple Hill Officers Mess, Royal Air Force Changi 1964
Middle: Changi Swimming Club
Below: Our Landscaped lawns facing towards the Lloyd Leas
married quarters.**

RAF Watton, Norfolk

**Christening of Richard, four months old, with his Godparents,
Flt Lt Rod Donnelly and Judy, and Sqn Ldr Eric Denson and
Shirley, with their daughter, Kirston**

Richard, Peter and John Elliott, 1970

(Left) John Elliott and his wife Claire (Middle) Richard and Nathan (Right) Peter and fiancée Katherine

**John was privileged to do two Guards of Honour
for the Queen Mother at Leeming**

My sister Joan's children Richard, Victoria and Stuart taking a break from house renovations in Liskeard, 1986

Richard, preparing to go to Kenya, 1987

Nathan through 12 years . . .

. . . just like his
Gt Grandfather,
Grandfather
and father,
always a firm
supporter of
Newcastle
United Football
Club.

Ngorongoro Crater

Karanga Bridge

John relaxing in the garden

**Back row: John Basil, Morris, Peter, Rowena and Jacquline.
Front: Mrs Celestine, the Regional Prison Officer's wife,
Martin, Mary, Joan, Brian and me.**

Chapter Six

I was more than delighted when, waiting for me at home, I found a reply to my letter about nursing in Nairobi, informing me of an interview date. However, little did I realise that having written to the Matron without my parents' consent, instantly incurred their displeasure. But at the time I hadn't thought anything would come of it anyway, and my age would be a major factor. But I always wanted to go nursing and felt that this was all about individual choice – I didn't wish to be pushed into secretarial work, which is what they had both got in mind for me, as it wasn't something I intended to pursue as a career. After some persuasion, they decided that I should go for the interview; more as a courtesy really.

A month later, as my mother and I left home in the early hours of the morning, in complete darkness, to drive the two hundred and twenty miles to Nairobi, we were both in buoyant mood. We had not anticipated such bitter cold when we left and by the time we had motored a few miles, we were both regretting not having brought our jumpers with us. There was no heating in the car and our feet and hands were frozen. The driving conditions were difficult as the heavy dew hung in the chilled air and the beam of the headlights shone back at us in the gloom. We spoke little as it took my mother's total concentration just keeping on the road and trying to miss the herds of zebra and gazelle which ran across in front of us. Some would hesitate, mesmerised by the headlights, and we just had to be patient until they passed because a peep from the horn would send them scattering in every direction.

We continued on the tarmac road out of Arusha, stopping for a short while to have a warm drink from our flasks, and carried on in the dark to the border post at Namanga. By dawn, the warm sunshine had quickly dispersed the dew, and we gathered speed as the road ahead became clearer. Herds of giraffe browsed unperturbed on the thorn trees by the side of the road and a variety of smaller animals mingled with them; it was such a pleasing sight to behold, and I felt in a particularly happy mood.

Our arrival at Namanga, the border post between Tanganyika's northern province and Kenya, meant a short stop whilst the car was fumigated against any tsetse fly. A few young inquisitive native children appeared from all directions with beaming faces, curious to see what we were carrying, and to look at all the different vehicles which were now gathering at the border post. They ran off happily when my mother handed them a bag of sweets which we carried with us for the journey; it was more a gesture to keep them away from trying to push their hands into the slightly opened window and reaching inside. We still had a number of miles to cover before reaching Nairobi and, as we left the safety of the tarmac north of Namanga, my mother put her foot down on the accelerator and sped over the corrugated, dusty, murram road, finally arriving in Nairobi with time to spare.

We passed through some beautiful areas on the fringes of the city, but when we reached the centre the traffic was heavy. Certainly it wasn't what we expected, or what we were used to. There were cars and lorries tearing around everywhere, so we simply followed the flow. By the time we had gone around a roundabout three or more times, looking for the spot to turn off, we were both nervous wrecks. The city was busy, with smartly dressed, white-shirted, native commuters, striding purposefully down the pavements to their offices mingling with native shoppers in their bright coloured saris and dresses. The whole place buzzed with activity. We had passed by some beautiful, large whitewashed mansions and avenues of cool violet jacaranda trees on the outskirts, then driven round and round, until we were hopelessly lost, neither of us knowing where we were. We finally pulled into a safe spot to stop and ask directions to the hospital, and arrived at our destination on time, albeit a trifle harassed.

Matron greeted us both with a warm smile, and invited us into her study, where the interview began almost immediately. I felt that I was giving all the right answers from the look on Matron's face. There was a pause as she looked at my letter, "Well, I think you will do just fine," she said, and asked if we would like to take a look around. I felt so proud of myself, as if I had grown a couple of inches in height. We were shown into various rooms and passageways, and on a veranda was an amusing sight of a neat row of tiny tots, all seated on their potties.

We went back to the office, where the real business was to be discussed. "Well Mrs. Davis," Matron began. "We ask the parents to pay towards the uniforms and training." I watched as the expression on my mother's face altered, and my heart sank. "Perhaps you could let me know by letter when you could begin," she went on. "Joyce is working at the moment, and it will be necessary to give some notice," my mother replied quickly. "I quite understand," said Matron, rising from her seat. "Well, I look forward to seeing you, Joyce," she continued. We all shook hands once more and parted.

As we left, the sun was almost at its height and the inside of the car was like a furnace. Finding our way through the traffic was easier, and I hoped that we could take our time. Not a word passed between us, and I interpreted my mother's silence as an impatience to get away through the traffic. However, her continued silence as we reached open road from the outskirts of the city puzzled me. I broke the silence by saying that I thought my interview went well, and I couldn't wait to come to Nairobi. "You won't be going this year," exclaimed my mother. "And as for uniforms, I can't see your father wishing to pay out for uniforms for you; and besides, he wouldn't want you skivvying, because that is really all you would be doing!" I sat in silence and turned away to look through my side of the window as tears rolled down my face, my hopes shattered. How could she possibly be so negative? Why had we journeyed all this way, just for her to tell me I couldn't go. I was brought up to respect my parents' authority and wishes with unquestioning loyalty, because I loved them dearly and tried so hard to please, but I was heartbroken at her decision. I consoled myself with the fact that I would just have to wait and be patient; after all, she hadn't ruled out my going the following year!

The outskirts of Nairobi, with its diverse landscape of desert-like regions and open savannah plains, contrasted immensely with the beautiful pastel colours of the town. Yet only a couple of miles or so from the centre, wild animals grazed happily and freely.

Our homeward trip began pleasantly enough, until we were forced off the road and into a steep ditch by two heavily-laden, oncoming lorries. The vehicles passed us doing quite a speed, throwing up stones, debris and dust. It was fully packed with Kenya African National Union (KANU) supporters standing in the back, carrying posters, shouting Uhuru, and gesturing with the 'V' sign as they went. When the dust finally settled, we got out to survey the damage. How we had managed to stay upright in the ditch, I will never know: three wheels were firmly on the road and the rear was left suspended in the air. I was surprised that the car didn't tip over. There was slight pitting on the bonnet from the stones but apart from that there was no other visible damage.

We pushed and steered the car, with all the strength we could muster, back on to the road and carried on. A few miles from the border, my mother began to have problems with the steering. On inspection, she noticed that we had a puncture. We scouted around looking for flat stones, amongst the many boulders which were strewn about, to rest the jack on, but almost every one we turned over revealed light-coloured scorpions nestling underneath them, so we sifted gingerly through the few we had picked. We managed to change the wheel. Then, right out in the middle of nowhere, with the sun beating down on us, we again had to stop, as another of the tyres began to deflate. Having no spare on board, we could do little else but continue the drive at a slow pace, with both of us becoming more and more anxious. In front and behind us lay miles of undulating rough road and on either side, wild plain. We continued on gingerly, stopping every ten minutes or so to allow the engine to cool down. Meanwhile the tyre was getting hot and showing signs of wear; in fact, it was melting! It was futile waiting for another motorist to come by, and with the darkness only a couple of hours away we didn't even want to contemplate having to spend the night in that hostile environment, waiting to be rescued. Each time we reached the brow of a hill, my mother turned the engine off and we free-wheeled down the other side. Gliding slowly over one of the hills with the car now in a bad state, and ourselves not faring much better, we limped towards an assortment of untidy, dusty, old wooden shacks with rusting corrugated iron roofs. A number of dented, rusting, old jerrycans and old tyres lay scattered around, and not much else. Strange to think that we hadn't even noticed it on our trip up. At first, we could not believe our luck, but our joy soon turned to despair, when we could see no signs of life. After taking a look around we returned to the car and prepared ourselves for a night stop there, with half a bottle of Pepsi between us. It was clear from the state of the car that we could go no further. How odd that even a dilapidated old shack, a token of human habitation, could be of such comfort in our time of sheer desolation.

About half an hour later, from way off, across the long grass strode an elderly grey haired African followed by a younger man. We were overjoyed to see them and asked if they knew how we could get a new wheel and some water. It turned out that they owned the 'garage'. The young man, who we took to be the elder's son, unlocked the creaking wooden door, which looked as if it had been attacked by termites – and I'm sure that one hefty push would have seen it keel over. He entered the shack, returning with some tools which he used to remove the wheel, and then proceeded to roll it round to the back. Instantly, he went to work banging and hammering. Fortunately, we spoke enough Swahili to make ourselves understood and we were told that we had been lucky to pull up by his 'garage' when we did, as their place was manned for only a couple of hours a day and in fact they were on their way up the hill to their home when they saw us pull up.

The old man, wrinkled with age and baked by the sun, stretched out his dark leathery arm, plucked two bottles of warm drinks from a small crate, and beckoned us to take them: a far cry from the treatment we had received earlier that afternoon from some of the Africans. This was kindness being shown from one human being to another! The young man rolled the wheel back to the car and put it on. My mother thanked him and paid for the repair. She held out some money to pay for the drinks, but the old man declined. "Hakuna matata," no problem, he said. She insisted, as she took the old man's arm gently and pressed the money into the palm of his hand. He bowed his head, and smiled with such gratitude that you would have thought that we were doing him a favour, instead of the other way around!

At the border, we went through the usual formalities, before continuing on. Our faces and clothes were red from the dust of the journey, and we felt hot and uncomfortable, but it was good to be back on the smooth surface of a tarmac road once more, despite the fierce shimmering haze which rose up from its black surface.

We were making good progress along the road, when we were suddenly confronted by two spear waving Masai. With their red-coloured, plaited hair, and their short dark-coloured wrapovers modestly covering their nakedness, they ran towards the car waving their spears and beckoning us to stop. As they were standing in the middle of the road, my mother had no choice but to stop. I felt terrified. What now? She couldn't go passed them. Without a word, both men jumped into the back seat, straddled their spears across their knees and tapped her sharply on the shoulder to move off. Despite the open windows, the stench in the car permeated the atmosphere, up our nostrils and became almost unbearable. After about twenty miles, with nothing except an empty savannah landscape to the horizon, one of them again tapped her on the shoulder to stop. My heart was pounding – what now? What had they got in store for us? Would we ever see home again? A myriad of awful thoughts rushed through my mind. But they simply opened the door, and loped off, spears in hand, across the yellow savannah and into the haze, without glancing back or uttering a word. I should have felt ashamed at thinking such awful thoughts, but with their warrior-like appearance, and the then political climate of change, I had felt a terrible foreboding.

We were both relieved and happy when Mount Meru came into sight and stopped for a while on the road from Arusha, mainly to give the car an airing from the smell of cow dung that still persisted after the departure of the men. The variety of rich colours of ochre, oranges and gold that had lit the skies in the hour before sunset descended slowly behind the hills, and a warm, fresh evening breeze blew across the plains, with a hint of the faint smell of burning grass. By the time we reached home it was dark.

After my weeks of enforced leave from work, I was glad to be back again at the bookshop, albeit only for about a month.

All my earlier hard work on shorthand and typing had finally paid off – anyway, my parents got their wish! I took up a post as the Principal's secretary, at the Government-run Trade School in Moshi. One consolation for me was that it didn't entail travelling a great distance. The school was a short ride from the prison's side entrance, along the main road, and I could use the Lambretta to come and go each day.

The school was for young African students, studying all the different trades, from mechanical engineering, to electrical engineering, to woodworking, plumbing and blacksmithing – every conceivable trade was taught. The students who attended came from all over the country and ranged from local youngsters to ministers' sons. The school was the venue for some very important conferences, and it was even afforded a royal visit by Princess Margaret at one time.

The senior tutorial staff were mainly European and all

were highly skilled in their own fields, with young African staff under them as their deputies. The tutors, staff and their families lived in the very elegant government houses provided on the premises.

The Principal and his wife were acquaintances of my parents, so I found myself in a good position when applying for the post of secretary. The work was reasonably demanding, involving taking minutes at school meetings and conferences, but the bulk of the work was routine letters, with the Bursar taking on most of the responsibility for the daily running of the school. My appointment was really only on a temporary basis, until my father's end of tour. There was already talk of the European staff being replaced by their black colleagues after independence, but really no one knew what was going to happen. When a scandal hit the school, resulting in the expulsion of a few of the boys, the matter was considered too indelicate and unsavoury for my ears and, for a while anyway, I was excluded from the meetings which then took place behind closed doors. In those days, the secretary was still treated like a lady.

The view from my office window was marvellous. The room itself was light and airy, and I could fling the windows open each morning and let in all the smells and sounds of Africa. Each morning I looked out over a natural, unspoiled part of the school grounds containing trees, thorn bushes and bougainvillaea; and when the wind blew across the front of the building the fragrant scent of the frangipani trees was overwhelmingly lovely. Choosing to stay at work during the lunch hour paid dividends; I could have my sandwiches and then take a stroll around the grounds, or sit near the window, and feed and watch the beautiful variety of coloured birds fly in and out of the thorn hedges. Weaver birds had built their nests in a tall acacia tree only feet away from the open window, and their chirping and singing went on all through the day. Some prettily-coloured bee eaters were regular visitors to the bougainvillaea bushes, and the rustle of dry leaves on the ground gave away the presence of lizards hiding amongst them to any of the small, predatory birds in the vicinity. A variety of insects, butterflies and bees fluttered around the scented heads of the flowers, and waves of tiny, noisy, red-beaked quelia birds often paused to rest before flying off again to other pastures.

Our family spent the occasional weekend on game drives into the National Parks, which was always an incredible experience, and there were few restrictions on where you could roam in your car then. But by the late fifties, the Serengeti, which had been home to nearly all the world's best known wild animals, fell prey to the ravages of indiscriminate poaching. While humans made inroads into the animals' natural habitats, water holes and grazing areas, the Government re-evaluated the whole strategy of tourism and eventually boundaries were formed and the National Parks came under direct Government control which could only be altered by law. No one was allowed to live in the parks except the game wardens and staff who were employed to cover the lodges and the camps. The measures introduced did restrict access to certain places by vehicles, but it still didn't spoil the spectacle and sheer thrill of seeing wild game in their natural state.

My father so wanted to make a last trip to the Ngorongoro Crater before he was due to leave. One of Africa's wonder spots, it lies within the Serengeti National Park. The crater, exactly as its name implies, is an ancient, extinct volcano surrounded by high grass and scrub walls of about two thousand feet, and was always a popular place with visitors and conservationists alike. It was still a reserve in the fifties, which meant that it was scheduled at a future date to preserve wild life, whilst the local, pastoral Masai were allowed to graze their cattle in and around the area. But few knew of its humble beginnings. There had always been a track up to the rim, possibly originally made by elephants, then maintained by the local inhabitants and their animals, and years later developed into a single-track road which snaked through deep ravines and forest floor. Most of the early excavation and construction work was undertaken by labour from the prison. A favourite place for most tourists, it was always certainly my father's favourite place for a visit. So determined was he to make one more sojourn before his tour ended, that we left by car one morning as dawn was breaking and drove there, steadily climbing through small banana shambas and native villages. The road was wet with heavy mist as we wound our way up between steep banks, at a snail's pace. When we reached a particularly steep part and the car began to slide about, three of us got out. There we were, left floundering between steep banks on either side of us, with my father steering and us pushing. Eventually, after a struggle, we were able to gather some momentum, but it was hard work. Snorts from nearby alerted us to a lone buffalo standing on the embankment almost above us. He eyed us menacingly, displaying huge curved horns and shaking his head. We didn't stand around to wonder, but hastily scrambled back into the car, and my father put his foot down hard on the accelerator. If the animal had wanted, it could have been upon us in an instant, and the results didn't bear thinking about. I remember my father telling us that years earlier, when the road was newly built, he took my mother to spend a weekend visiting the crater. As they were driving up the hill almost at the top of the rim, their path was blocked by a feeding elephant which took an instant dislike to their presence and began flapping its ears and waving its trunk in a menacing fashion. With no room to turn the car around, he was forced to reverse back the way he had come for about a mile, with the animal hot on their heels, before it gave up the chase and disappeared into the bush; but it put the wind up both of them!

We reached the lodge hundreds of feet up and were shown to our rooms and settled in. It was basic but extremely comfortable. There were a couple of bedrooms, a bathroom and sitting room and there was a welcome log fire burning in the grate. Sadly, the rain began to come down at a steady pace, and we had to abandon our plans to go with a driver and four-wheel drive to the crater floor the following morning. As the crow flies, the drive down looked no distance at all, but in fact it could take anything between two and a half to three hours, and in the months of the rainy season the road was dangerous and completely impassable by any vehicle. After sorting out the sleeping arrangements, we retired to the sitting area where we just talked and listened to stories of my father recalling the time he spent with Dr. Bernhard Grzimek and his son Michael, the German father and son scientists who worked around the area. Sadly, Michael was killed in his light aircraft at the beginning of that year. A commemorative plaque was set into some rocks on the rim, above the place he had loved so much. We talked until it was dark and time to retire to our beds, and during the night, while we lay safely in our beds, we listened to the noises of the animals, the distant roar of lion and the patter of feet and chatter of hyena outside our windows.

We awoke the following day to brilliant sunshine, and drove to the Lake Manyara Hotel. Situated on the great Rift Valley rim, the new hotel looked out over the escarpment to the valley below with its shimmering lake of rosy flamingos. There was talk at the time of Manyara being made into a national park since native hunters and poachers, corrupted by the ever-widening influence of western trade goods, were killing off game in the area. An outbreak of rinderpest – a virulent infectious viral disease of ruminants – had also left the buffalo herds depleted for quite a while.

We arrived home in the late afternoon to the onset of a rain shower. The skies darkened with clouds of millions of flying ants leaving their termite nests. There was a scramble, as always, to close all the windows and doors and turn out the lights, but despite all these measures, the ants managed to fall down the chimney or enter through the gap under the door. Within minutes of landing, they snapped off their wings and began to look for a mate, first in twos and then joining up with others. As they crawled around the sitting room carpet, the whole place resembled a miniature busy rail station at rush hour, with endless rolling stock. They eventually dispersed down holes and crevices, or were washed away by the rain. Whatever, the dogs had a field day as they chased and snacked on them. I recalled that years earlier, Ayah, who found them to be a great delicacy, would hook them out of the ground with a twig and eat them – she even tried to persuade us to have a go, but I'm afraid that we couldn't oblige.

At the beginning of the new year, my parents were going through a particularly difficult and rocky patch in their lives. My mother had learned a lot about life in Africa. Kenya may have had its 'Happy Valley' crowd amongst its European fraternity, and without a doubt Moshi certainly had its 'Happy Mountain' crowd! There wasn't much that went on in the community without people either gossiping or knowing. Malice was a pleasant pastime for women with nothing to do!

My father's good looks and undoubted charm drew the attention of some ladies, including a well-known film actress. The telephone ringing and a voice not speaking at the other end brought tension and accusation. Rumour or not, he would, without a shadow of a doubt, have been an excellent catch for any woman. A charismatic character with a great personality, he was an amusing after-dinner speaker and, I was told, a wonderful dancer. I suppose there was bound to be talk. To my mother he was everything she ever wanted and she loved him, but her insecurity and the wagging tongues brought her a great deal of misery and much hurt. Disillusioned with the endless round of parties, unsubstantiated rumours of affairs, and interminable arguments at home, she began to withdraw from the limelight and focussed more on a quieter time with close friends.

She sometimes took off on the Lambretta on her own or with young John to visit the Goodes, a sprightly elderly couple who lived near by in Shanty Town, where she knew she would always have a warm welcome. Mr. Goode was an old soldier from the Boer war. They had an unusual house; it was a conical-shaped, thatched home and the inside was tastefully furnished with Victorian furniture and delicate china ornaments. They were both very keen gardeners, and it didn't matter what time of the day it was; they could always be found pottering around their gardens and tending their roses, wearing their khaki topee hats on their heads. Everywhere you looked in and around their garden had colour in abundance – it was like a little piece of England at the height of an English summer. The ducks had their watering pool, and the chickens ran around freely. I remember the very first time that I went to their home for tea. I was about nine years old then and I wore a pretty white flowered dress, which was new. Mr. Goode had complained endlessly about the Egyptian geese that flew in to their garden from the outlying areas, for a dip in the duck pond. He hadn't minded at first, but they would chase off his own ducks each time and were now becoming such a problem that they even intimidated the dogs.

Watching these geese fly in one day, I decided that I

would see them off, but when I stamped my foot at them, they made a run at me. I never knew how aggressive they could be and as a result I stepped back from them a few paces and lost my footing, falling backwards into the slimy pond. I emerged, covered from top to toe in dirty water. Instead of my mother having to take me back home, I cleaned up, and Mrs. Goode found me the smallest pair of shorts and T-shirt to put on, so I could stay for tea. They both cared a lot for my parents, but they were particularly wonderful to my mother, who they treated like a daughter, and she appeared content and happy in their company.

One day I received a telephone call at my office at the Trade School from Bill Aucott, The Chief Instructor at the Police Training School, who wished to speak to the Principal. (Bill also worked with John Thackeray – not only were they colleagues at the Police Training School, but they had both served in the Royal Air Force Regiment together in Oman many years earlier). After Bill had spoken to the Principal, he handed the telephone over to John, who spoke to me. The call was out of the blue, to say that he was back in Moshi after being away in the Southern province for a few months, and would I like to meet him for dinner. I did not know what to say, the call was so unexpected, and I must have sounded vague and quite dumb. The call was brief, but I merely said that I couldn't meet him, because I was seeing someone else at the time, but I hoped that he would ask me perhaps on another occasion. All I kept thinking was, if only he had asked me earlier – much earlier. It's extraordinary how often these two words haunt me.

However, I began to take more than a fleeting interest in John. There was very little you could do in Moshi without somebody knowing and, of course, there was always someone willing to divulge snippets of information on his whereabouts, what he was up to, and what he had done; and I was always willing to listen, although I was not always happy with what I heard. I know that he became very popular due to his piano playing, and even played a tune for Louis Armstrong on piano when he came to Moshi; he had joined the local drama group and received rave reviews in the local paper; and his rendition of Elvis Presley's 'Blue Suede Shoes' was a 'wow' at the Moshi Club with everyone. He certainly wasn't dull – far from it! I knew that the ladies liked him and I confess to a hint of jealousy, when I heard that he was seeing someone.

I continued to see Doug from time to time when he wasn't away on business, but being young, very immature and unworldly, I was content to be just good friends. I wasn't prepared to get into a physical relationship, although he was a pleasant enough person; a very nice man in fact, but a serious sort of man, and I certainly wasn't ready for, or desirous of, any form of serious relationship with him. One day, looking through some photographs with him, I came upon a photo of a girl whom I recognised as a school bully from my time at Arusha school, years earlier. The mere mention of her name was an anathema to me. The fact that he had had a relationship with her, left me with a slight sour taste. That aside, I did long for some fun in my life, and I certainly was not having much fun. I suspect that the telephone call from John had a lot to do with the way I felt! Just the sound of his voice stirred me, and I wanted desperately to find a way out of the relationship I was in. I didn't want to hurt him but I just desired to be free. For weeks I masked this ridiculous charade, as my thoughts were forever elsewhere. In truth, I think I was making us both miserable and he deserved better. The difficulties at home with my mother feeling so low didn't help, and had an immediate knock-on effect on Joan and I. We rarely found ourselves venturing into town except when there was an invitation to a function and, even then, restrictions were eventually imposed on us both because of the furore at home. It was easier to stay in most evenings rather than be stressed out with the whys and wherefores.

Although my father was based in Moshi, I understood that he was responsible for other prisons in the province, so when news came of an attack by a lion, which killed a warder at Maweni prison, he was once again away from home. The lion had earlier attacked a man from the Tanga shipping company, when he was cycling along the road with his son. The boy managed to escape and ran off to get help. The animal was eventually cornered and shot. Any trips away from home by my father for any lengthy duration, became a source of aggravation and self-doubt for my mother, and it made life doubly difficult and uncomfortable at home. We knew the background causes of her anxiety and, despite all the pretence, I am sure that my mother, being the proud lady that she was, would have found the source of her unhappiness a trifle distasteful to discuss openly with us. However, finally deciding that she had had enough, she made up her mind that she would leave for England at the end of the school term and take the youngsters home with her, leaving us to finish our work and follow on later with my father.

Tanganyika had been preparing itself for self-rule for sometime, and the colonial administration under its Governor, Sir Richard Turnbull, was well aware of the dangers of holding back the tide of change and the aspirations of its people, having seen the Mau Mau uprising in neighbouring Kenya. By the end of 1959 many people had sold or were selling their farms and moving to Europe and other countries, in anticipation of problem times to come, and an uncertain future. Most had lived in their homes for generations, from childhood, and in turn had brought up their own children in them. Some were sad to go; others felt intimidated and were happy to leave. Those who didn't sell their farms early, saw their land hastily being devalued.

In town there was an air of impending gloom as 'Uhuru' gathered momentum. Even at the Trade School, there was a show of defiance and arrogance towards the European staff by some of the Africans, and even I was not excluded from the 'treatment'; something we had not experienced before. However, not all the Africans were happy to see the Europeans leave. Some spoke openly of their fears and worries for their future. No one seemed to know what the real outcome would be, and many pinned all their hopes in one man 'Mzee' Julius Nyerere.

We had been used to electric storms in the tropics and in fact we had had some dramatic ones in the past, with trees felled in an instant and feeding animals burned to a cinder. But there was nothing quite like the storm that came late one afternoon before the rains. I arrived home from work and went to lie down to read on my bed. Suddenly, the skies darkened, and there was thunder in the distance. I had no mind to turn on the bedside light; in fact I quite liked the sound of thunder! It was quite exhilarating just watching the lightning spark and flash in the sky. I lay there watching and listening as the storm got closer, counting the seconds to the next clap of thunder until the storm was overhead. Suddenly, without any warning, through the open meshed window above my bed came a bolt of lightning. Silently it came over the top of me, snaking like a gnarled outstretched arm, through the door and into the passageway and continued towards the electric junction box just feet away. Its fingers sparkled and danced over the area, causing a blue haze to envelop the box, then just as silently as it had come, it recoiled its way back over me, through the window, and disappeared. It was all over in a few dazzling seconds. Moments later, there was a high-pitched crackling sound and then a deafeningly loud bang, and I knew instinctively that something dreadful had happened. I sat up and looked out of the window, and in the greyness, there was not a light to be seen anywhere, and all was silent. I called out to my mother to see if she was alright and was relieved when she replied. A while later, lanterns burned and shouts were heard coming from the prison. That evening, my father returned home looking distressed and shaken. The lightning storm had struck the prison, killing a couple of the inmates and injuring others who were sitting under a shelter eating their meal. The scene was utter carnage; he said it was horrifying. Having to identify the men was another thing. As he gently removed one man's cap, to my father's horror, his scalp came off with it. I recall his words to my mother. "Why?" he asked. "They were only there for minor offences, and they ended up facing the death penalty!" It rained heavily that evening, and by sun up the following morning there was a smell of freshness in the air and a beautiful rainbow in the sky, but it could not erase the memories of the horrendous savagery of the previous day.

My friendship with Doug was more or less over after he took me on a very boring fishing trip up into the mountain one Saturday. Despite all his kindness, I felt that our relationship, or friendship I should say, had run its course. We stopped at the club one evening after a visit to the cinema. There, at the bar in the club, drink in hand, was John talking to his friends. I couldn't believe the timing, and my heart began to race. I pretended at first not to notice him. There was soft music playing and a few people on the floor, dancing, as I walked by and sat down. I looked over to him and he smiled, and I smiled back. Moments later, while Doug and I were sitting drinking, he came over to our table and approached Doug for his permission to dance with me. While Doug hesitated, and before he could utter a word, I had leapt to my feet like a hussy and said, "I would love to!". How forward of me, but suddenly I didn't give a damn. All I cared about was that John was holding me in his arms and I felt wonderfully alive! He held me close as we danced and talked. He was three-quarters through his tour and leaving the following day to go to the southern province for a few weeks on police work, and when I told him that I would be leaving Moshi for good within the next couple of weeks, he promised to write to me in England. Walking me back to my chair, I could see that Doug was not amused; in fact, he was furious with me: he sat silently and we barely spoke to each other. After finishing his drink, he calmly rose to his feet and beckoned to take me home. We hardly talked, except when he asked me if I liked John – what could I say? As he dropped me at the front door I could not kiss him and I knew that I would not be seeing him again.

At the house, the packing and crating began again in earnest and my mother sold all the toys, clothing and shoes, and some furniture. All her dresses, some of which were evening dresses, were spread out on a table outside the back of the house. Some items she sold to the warders' wives, but some of the children's smaller items, she happily handed to the local native bibis. The household items were quickly snapped up and carried off in loads, perched precariously on heads. There were some tears from the staff as they said good-bye to her and the younger children, and some openly voiced their concern as to whether they would ever get another job. There was a great deal of sadness at her departure as Big John said his farewell. He had a lot to thank her for, not least when she helped to deliver his second child, a little girl.

There was the final flurry of small farewell suppers then my mother flew back home to England with the younger members of the family, with perhaps a great number of very mixed emotions. Few friends gathered at the airport to say their farewells, as many had already left the country for far-flung places.

Chapter Seven

I said my final farewells to my friends and colleagues at the Moshi Trade School, knowing that a number of them would be leaving Africa soon and going home to England or emigrating to far-flung parts of the globe. It was a strange feeling to be leaving home for good – but really it was not my home and never would be.

My father and I flew out from Moshi while Joan stayed with friends for an extra few weeks and would fly home at a later date. On the day we left, there was only a handful of people who saw us off from the airport. Before entering the aircraft, I closed my eyes momentarily and breathed in deeply the last smell of the place. The sun glared above us as we flew low over the Big House on the way to Nairobi.

We stayed overnight at the Norfolk and went out to supper with friends on the outskirts of town, returning late to the hotel to the laughter and chatter of the departing wedding-party revellers. Up at dawn, and already the sun was shining as we sat down to breakfast while the happy, cheerful, immaculately turned-out staff buzzed around tending to everyone's needs. Why couldn't I have felt the same?

As we taxied along the runway at Nairobi on our final leg for England, I was upset and tearful at leaving Africa for the last time, and it was difficult to conceal my feelings, as I sat back in my seat in the aircraft. I had time to reflect on my last few months and what might have been. I cursed myself for refusing a date with John, on an evening when my mother was particularly down at heart.

I never got the chance to explain or finally say good-bye to him and I doubted whether he would ever write. So many doubts, so many 'if onlys'; but it was now in the past and all too late! I had glimpsed John momentarily on the way to the airport, when he drove past us in his black open-top Morgan, but he was gone in a flash. I felt thoroughly miserable, and so mentally fatigued that I put my head down to try and sleep.

Flying over the continent on our way towards Rome, we encountered turbulence and I was brought abruptly to attention when hearing raised voices. Startled, I sat bolt upright. Passengers opposite to me left their seats and leaned over to take a look through my window at one of the motionless propellers on the starboard side. The stewardess called to fasten seat belts, and the pilot came on the speaker to try to reassure his nervous passengers that everything was in hand, and a further few minutes ticked by before he explained to everyone that he was feathering the engine and we were quite safe. As the pilot nursed the aircraft across the skies, all chatter turned to quiet contemplation. My father sat composed throughout as I, on the other hand, sat wracked with fear, which left me utterly exhausted until we finally landed. At Rome, we were delayed for a number of hours awaiting the arrival of a replacement engine from the UK. As I walked up the steps on our return to the aircraft, I was seized with an almost uncontrollable reluctance to re-enter through its door. The rest of the journey was without incident and as we came in to land, I was thankful the journey was over and I didn't mind that the weather was overcast and drizzling as we disembarked. I should have realised that I had nothing to fear except fear itself.

Having been away for over two and half years, I returned to a different England, where children were growing up in the security and contentment of a post war boom, where there was little unemployment, and where we were cushioned in the security of a welfare state. At home, we clung on to the strict old-fashioned values of family life and felt comforted and watched over.

My mother, together with my four younger brothers and sister, had moved into a four-bedroomed, detached, Tudor-style house in the suburbs of Macclesfield. It was a nice looking house, with an acre of wooded, rather ragged, scrappy land to the rear, incorporating a mixture of overgrown shrubs and weeds, and a selection of untidy gnarled fruit trees. Wasting no time at all we were each tasked to help in clearing the garden, which included some heavy digging. Then there was the laying down of slabs, and cement mixing for a new patio. Those that were taking time out, were tasked with tea making. It was hard, manual work but we all pitched in and had a laugh.

The immediate priority was to find a job, and that presented no difficulty at all; jobs were two a penny at the time. Saying that, nothing could be taken for granted. It was just as easy to be sacked with a week's notice, with no reason given, in those days! I had an interview on the Monday and began work on the Wednesday, as a shorthand typist and receptionist at a new electrical showroom. My three directors were well-to-do gentlemen: a solicitor and a couple of gents in the media. So, occasionally I found myself 'temping' in the solicitor's office. At other times, I helped in another new showroom which opened near the Oxford Road Station approach in Manchester, opposite the Palace Theatre where we hired televisions and other equipment to visiting celebrities who were appearing at the time. My wage packet wasn't brilliant, and I was expected to find, and pay, my own way when working away from home. I worked Mondays to Saturdays and had Wednesday afternoons off, which I treasured as it was the only real quality time that I had with my mother, and to do other things. As the businesses expanded and we became busier, my work schedule gradually increased. I enjoyed the job, and the reps and staff were, on the whole, a nice bunch of people.

I perceived a rapid change in the country over the following year. Because of the wider access to television, there was a greater influence from across the Atlantic in both music and fashion. We watched how the Americans did things, then followed suit. At seventeen you couldn't drink or vote, but you could die for your country!

Joan came back from Africa and began work in the town at the National Insurance Office. We settled down at home to a comfortable, albeit rather laid-back, quiet way of life, with television and all other modern conveniences at our disposal.

My father returned to Africa again for the last time – alone. This time his work took him to Mwanza, on the shores of Lake Victoria, to complete the delicate negotiations of hand-over to the incoming new establishment.

Part of both Joan's and my wage packets from work had gone on the purchase of brand new Raleigh cycles, and each weekend we experienced the joys of biking around the local, picturesque areas of the Cheshire countryside, through Prestbury, Poynton, Wilmslow and Alderley Edge. We once even cycled to Stockport and back, happily weaving our way through the traffic on the main roads without a care in the world. When Martin had a narrow escape from death after falling off his cycle in front of a moving bus – giving us all a nasty fright – it rather curtailed our long jaunts away from home. Even our daily cycles to and from work were fraught with danger from the build-up of daily commuter traffic, which was particularly hazardous on foggy days. Joan, on her way to work one day, was hit by a passing motorist. Luckily a policeman who had been standing across the road had seen the accident and she was taken to hospital with cuts and concussion. After a few stitches and an overnight stay, she was discharged, only to be readmitted for further observation days later because she kept vomiting.

Work at the showrooms became more demanding despite extra staff being taken on and I found myself not only the receptionist, but sales girl and general tea lady for the growing band of gentlemen. Being the only female at the showroom, I quickly got used to the minor harassment and oh-so-friendly male banter, which was rather tiresome at times. My precious Wednesday afternoons were finally absorbed into a normal, busy, working day, and after work it was preparation for evening meals and more work. We must have had the cleanest house in the country. After a while, I felt that the routine was stifling any ambitions that I might have had, and I appeared permanently fatigued.

After feeling unwell for a couple of weeks, I took myself off to see the doctor and, after careful examination, he informed me that I had shingles. I then endured a fortnight of sheer misery, and the tablets I was given did little to alleviate the awful burning pain and discomfort I was in.

While resting at home, I gave serious thought to a change in career – if I was going to do anything with my life, I had to do it now. So I took the plunge and wrote to the local careers' office, applying to join the WRNS, and sat back to wait for a reply which I received a fortnight later, with a date for an interview and medical – it was all so quick. On the day of the interview, I felt horribly nervous as I entered the portals of a tall, grey-stone building in Manchester, and began to wonder what I was letting myself in for. The medical went well and I joined a few other young hopefuls as we sat down to a couple of timed written tests, finally attending an interview board in the afternoon. As I caught my train home, I felt a great sense of relief and joy, that at least I had taken my first step to a possible new career – and it felt good.

About a week later, I received a hand-written letter, with a Newcastle post mark. I did not recognise the writing and wondered who it could be from; I knew no one from the north-east. I hastily opened it, more as a matter of curiosity than anything. It was from John. He was a man of his word after all. I rushed upstairs, and read it over and over again, it was short and to the point. He was back in England on leave, was about to tour with the Tanganyika 'Twiga' cricket team, and asked if he could come to see me after the tour was over. I didn't know what to think as I ran downstairs to tell my mother. Suddenly life at work didn't seem so bad after all. I wrote back to him immediately, saying that I would be delighted to see him and looked forward to our meeting.

When the day of his arrival came, I went to meet him and stood on the platform waiting for the train to pull in. I tried to remember what he looked like, and even began to rehearse what I would say when I greeted him off the train. As the train came to a stop and the doors of the carriages opened, I looked up and down the platform and watched a number of people climb down and walk away. For a wild moment I thought he hadn't come. Then, suddenly, I saw this beautiful, handsome, tanned man with a black blazer and grey flannels, walking towards me, smiling. He kissed me, and I felt shy and girlie, yet wonderfully happy to see him. Carrying a heavy bulging holdall, with a couple of cricket bat handles protruding from the top, in one hand and a suitcase in the other, we made our way home. Everything I had rehearsed earlier, what I would say to him, suddenly flew out of the window. It no longer seemed important – he was here with me.

Unaware that my father had left England to return to Africa, he offered to book himself into a hotel. However, I was glad when my mother assured him that it would be alright to stay with us, provided that he didn't mind sleeping on a camp bed in the sitting room.

The youngsters were intrigued with the cricket bats and wanted to play. With my father gone, here was another grown up to play with them and, all in all, he created a most favourable impression with everyone, especially my mother, which was all that really mattered to me.

That evening we stayed in and talked and talked, mostly about Moshi and friends, and there were no awkward silences; I felt comfortable in his company and I followed my mother's strict instructions to be in bed by midnight. The following evening we caught a train into Manchester, and took in a meal, and a film at the Odeon. We talked a lot that evening, mostly about everyday things, and John continued to skirt round the real reason for coming to see me. The weekend came, and we walked out in the afternoon to the local park. He was wonderfully romantic, sat me down on a seat, and bent down on one knee and proposed. I remember sniggering with some embarrassment because he looked quite funny, kneeling on the grass in front of me, trying so hard to be serious. I didn't take in what he had said, until he asked me again.

Later on, we arranged a long-distance phone call to my father in Africa, waited for a couple of hours before the call was finally put through, and then spent ages talking to him oblivious of the clock ticking away. It was wonderful to hear his voice from so far away, and he was equally happy to hear our news. In the same evening, we spoke to John's parents, and I felt so nervous and apprehensive, but warmed to their gentle Geordie voices. I think they were caught rather on the hop by John though – he hadn't mentioned anything about getting engaged before he left home.

Days later, I received a reply from the Navy, with an

acceptance form to fill in and a date and place to report for duty. I couldn't believe the timing – in my euphoria, I had forgotten to even mention the possibility of my joining the services to John. I returned my reply almost right away, declining their offer, then began to wonder if I had burned both my bridges – suppose in the end he was to change his mind about me? As I got to know him better, I abandoned my negative thoughts and remained happy to carry on my present employment until we could be married, and more than delighted at the prospect of returning to Africa with him. There I was, happy to marry this beautiful man, yet I knew so very little about him, except that he was born and brought up in Newcastle-upon-Tyne and his parents were Geordies with some Scottish ancestry.

While he was on his six-months home leave from the Colonial Service, he went north to his parents and spent a week with the Newcastle City Police; he was well looked after by them. Sergeant Geoff Hepworth took him around the various departments acquainting him with the different aspects of police work in the Northumbrian force. He then embarked on a three-month course in London, at the School of Oriental and African Studies, hoping to improve his Swahili. On one of his first long weekend breaks to the north, I joined him at his parents' home and we all went out for a celebration dinner at the Turk's Head in the city centre. It was to be my first meeting with his parents and I was a bit nervous, yet I wanted so much to make a good impression on them. After being shown to our table to sit down to eat, I caught the leg of the table with my knee, sending the contents of my wine glass cascading over the clean, white tablecloth. I had tried so hard to impress; instead, I sat down with my knee throbbing with pain, trying not to grimace and feeling foolish and rather awkward. John, in his usual calm manner, made light of it and tried his best to put me at ease; and his parents were wonderful.

I spent a lovely few days in Newcastle, meeting John's family; his grandmother, Lilly Robinson, who was a most amusing lady, who loved the theatre and could recite Gilbert and Sullivan verse for verse; then there was auntie Minnie, who loved to play cards, and uncle John Makepeace.

The weather was warm and sunny, and I was shown around the beautiful Northumbrian coast, and Seahouses, and we had great fun at the Spanish City at Whitley Bay, riding the roller coaster like a couple of kids. As we walked along the small bay at Tynemouth, we paused, and I wanted that time to go on for ever.

My stay had been short and I said good-bye to John, who was leaving to return to his course in London from one platform, whilst I left from an adjoining platform, for home. As we went our separate ways, I felt content and overdosed on happiness, as I entered the train and sat down, because I knew he loved me. The sun was shining brightly into the compartment, and as I rested my hand against the glass, the facets of my engagement ring danced rays across the window. As I looked up, a well-dressed lady across from me smiled, as if she could read my thoughts, and I smiled back.

I looked forward to the odd weekends, when John was able to get to Macclesfield and we could be together again. The younger members of my family revelled in his sojourns, he fitted in so well with the family and once again the house and garden buzzed with fun, noise and laughter. Hours of time were spent playing football and cricket in the back garden, but when Peter struck a cricket ball through the plate glass window in the sitting room, all ball games in the garden were banned. However, these weekend breaks were all too brief, with endless hours taken up travelling to and from London. Then came my tearful farewells and the lonely walk home alone. I stayed in most evenings, and once a week there was always Robert Conrad and "Hawaiian Eye" to look forward to.

The 1960s brought anxious times, yet they were exciting and dramatic years for us all. We felt the pace of life quicken and alter. Television became an incredibly informative tool, for world events as well as general entertainment. We watched the birth of space travel, the emergence of Black Nationalism and Civil Rights in the United States. In fact, television now made up much of our entertainment. With new innovations in fashion and design, the drab, heavy greys and browns of the post war years gave way to brighter and lighter colourful fashions. Larger stores emerged, embracing fashions for the thinner figure, and while some tried to emulate the stick-insects like Twiggy and other well known models, stores began catering for the would-be trendy, though some of us were still the shapely generation of 'breasts and bottoms'. I was proud of my nineteen-inch waist and yet some of us still managed to look like miniatures of our parents! I left the house each morning for work, wearing a smart suit and white gloves, and I secretly smiled to myself as I savoured the admiring glances from passers-by.

The local corner grocery shops gradually gave way to supermarkets, and the small garages around gave way to forecourts.

At home, we were a content, homely, middle-class family. We all looked forward to letters and photos from my father in Mwanza. He wrote long letters about the lovely weather, the places he had to go to, and about boating and fishing with friends on Lake Victoria; and the odd skirmishes he had with hippos. When a letter arrived to say that he had been in hospital with bilharzia, my mother was at her wits' end. She knew nothing about the disease and, dipping into some of her old medical books, she read: a mainly tropical disease – a worm parasite or (blood fluke) which is carried by snails, and commonly found in African rivers and lakes, and causes bleeding from the bladder. He must have been well aware of the risks he was taking, boating and wading in the lake. Many people did so with no ill effect and, of course, he didn't think that it would happen to him! My mother fretted for days waiting for further news of his progress. She got more and more anxious and worried when his letters became less frequent.

As Tanganyika reached independence, many of the European and Asian families, wishing to stay on in the new Tanzania, were asked to accept citizenship or leave. My father toyed with the option, but my mother was not keen to uproot the family and go to live out in Africa permanently; she didn't care much for the lifestyle; she cared less for the heat; and there may have been other factors. Whatever – she was staying put!

My father finally returned home to England to live, feeling good and looking tanned and well, But being home was not to be such an easy time for him, as he had been away from the country for many years. A lot had changed, and trying to find employment in a similar field was to prove a very difficult and frustrating task. When he was short-listed for a prison governor's post in the UK, and failed to get the position, he was disappointed. He wasn't entirely satisfied with the reason given at the time, that he had no experience in English prisons!

John had the opportunity to catch up with my father and discuss the future; that he would expect to take me back to Africa after we were married. He could only give John his own views and advice as he saw it, of course, but it would ultimately be John's decision whether to go back or stay in England.

As soon as his course in London came to an end, John wasted no time and paid a quick visit to the RAF Regiment depot at Catterick, meeting up with a few friends who he hadn't seen since his days in Aden. Squadron Leader John Harnetty was one of the Regiment instructors at the depot, an officer John knew well and liked, and after talking to him, John was persuaded to think about returning to the Regiment, although I'm not sure that he really needed much persuading.

He had loved his time in the service, and had travelled widely in the Middle East and Cyprus, serving with 58 Rifle Squadron at El Hamra and 62 Rifle Squadron, and 65 Field Squadron at Padgate, which became his first

Flight Commander's post, and 63 Independent LAA Squadron. Always the proverbial optimist, he had an open mind to opportunities and was always prepared to listen and take risks. After grammar school, he had originally hoped to embark on a career in teaching and in fact he did spend a short time as a student teacher, in a school in the poorer area of Byker in Newcastle, while waiting to go to Durham to read history under Trevellyn. But like many young men at that time, his life was to change course, when he was called up for National Service.

His move to rejoin the Royal Air Force Regiment, took me of course, completely by surprise. He telephoned me one day at my work saying that he had had a favourable interview with the RAF at Hendon, had written to the Crown Office in London to resign from the Colonial Police, and was about to go to London to have his uniform measured and made for the RAF. I suddenly found myself engaged to a Police Officer and was now about to marry a Regiment Officer. However, though surprised, I was nonetheless happy about his decision, and he began his new career as a Flying Officer at Transport Command at Upavon in Wiltshire, and took up his duty under Squadron Leader John Spencer.

At home, my father continued to job-hunt, and as the days ticked by, he spent hours working in the garden shed, which he had again turned into a workshop, surrounded by all his precious old tools. Martin and Peter often joined him in his projects, turning wood on the lathes and cutting on band saws to make oddments. The old Hornby train set was hauled out of its packaging and reassembled with stations and accessories. Martin generally took charge of the running, while Peter and John were allowed to recover the trains that came off the rails, and to use the signals on special occasions. Life at home became increasingly fraught due to the fact that my father wondered when he would receive his Tanganyika pension. But all the niggling little problems which caused him aggravation, and which in turn had a knock on effect on us all, were finally resolved. He received his 'Golden Bowler' payment and a small Government pension, and peace and contentment prevailed once more.

My mother was now expecting my youngest brother Robert, which we were delighted about, but in the midst of all this, my wedding plans went ahead painfully slowly, and I had little say in the matter – talk about father of the bride! John was always able to cheer me up, though. We laughed a lot and it was great to have his love and support when I most needed it, and in turn he was happy and enthusiastic about his work which was a great comfort to me.

After a year's engagement, hours of travelling up and down the country to see each other, walkabouts and coffees in Manchester, we were married at the pretty parish church in Henbury, near Macclesfield on 26th July 1962. It was a wonderfully happy day. The sun shone and the weather was warm. My sisters Joan and Mary, and my friend, Hilda, were my bridesmaids, and they looked a picture in their pink and blue satin dresses, with posies of sweet peas; I carried a bouquet of red roses. The wedding was a modest, leisurely affair for relatives and friends – mostly friends of my parents. But, like best laid plans, something has to go wrong. The photographer failed to turn up at the church for the photo shoot. However, there were no problems as far as my father was concerned, only solutions, and as he had had the foresight to bring his cine camera, he took a short film outside the church. We waited for quite a time to see if the photographer would arrive, but with our timings being critical for the reception we decided eventually to leave for the hotel. Half way through the reception, a message arrived at our table to say that the photographer had arrived. Sure enough, this red-faced, flustered, bag of wind had indeed arrived, full of apologies. Leaving the ballroom, we all filed out to the front, and my veil caught on something and was almost ripped off. Outside, we were pushed and pulled into silly poses, and were expected to pay for the privilege – it was an awful experience. Quite frankly the best photos were the ones taken by friends outside the church!

We honeymooned at the lovely spa town of Buxton in Derbyshire for a couple of days. Those sunny July days were very beautiful in Buxton, with its bright, colourful pavilion gardens and theatre. We went along to see 'Salad Days', a show starring a very young energetic not-so-well-known Michael Crawford. The following evening the film we went to see ran on longer than we had expected, and we had to dash back to the hotel before they shut us out, because John had forgotten to ask for a key! We had a great deal of fun in those days, and it was wonderful to wake up in the morning with the person I loved lying beside me. We set off to London for a further two days. As John showed me around, I was rather curious to find out how he knew the place so well. He began to tell me that for a time after national service, he had spent some time playing the piano around some of the night clubs in the city. However, the pay was poor and, after running out of money, he returned home to his parents who were delighted to see him, although they took a dim view to his new-found occupation, insisting that he find a decent career. While he lived at home pondering on his future, he bombed around Newcastle, and his mother became increasingly disgruntled at being taken for granted and the home being used as a hotel. So one day, he returned home to find his bags packed and put outside the front door. He later admitted to being a trifle ashamed at his inconsiderate behaviour at the time, and remarked that it had been a salutary lesson which he would never forget! So that's how he knew London so well! He did, however, take his parents' advice and get himself a decent job.

Having had a taste of service life, developing a liking for the warm climate, and also realising that he wasn't going to make a living at piano playing, he embarked on a career overseas. He joined the Tanganyika Police, and sailed on the 'SS Kenya' to Mombasa in 1957, to begin his Police Course in Moshi.

He said that it was a whole new experience, working with the Africans. He got on well with them and quickly made his mark, introducing much of the RAF Regiment skills he had been taught to the depot – he was responsible for training all new recruits. Dealing with the local natives was a new challenge to him. In addition to the normal run of robberies, assaults and burglaries, there was a great number of cases of petty crime, pilfering and receiving stolen property, the detection of which, John observed, the African Askari (police constable) seemed to have an uncanny knack for. He recalled organising a party of them to go with him to a village where, he was told, some goats had been stolen. A general playing around with beads and pips by the local witch doctor, was enough to reveal where the animals were hidden, leading to the apprehension of the culprits. A lot of police work was taken up with investigating other petty crimes involving over-consumption of pombi (the local brew fermented from red banana or potato – in fact it could be made from almost anything). There was the added problem of various types of drugs which were smoked or chewed. There were countless funny sides to some of the stories and experiences that, he told me, he had had during his police work which took him all around the provinces.

One among many of his ambitions of a lifetime was to climb Mount Kilimanjaro, which he achieved during an outward bound course. During his tour in Moshi, apart from his time studying, he put in a lot of hours burning the candle at both ends, partying, and he also had a keen eye for the ladies. In my heart I think he would have been happy to settle down to life in Africa and, rather like ourselves, he had envisaged a more leisurely timetable towards independence. So when he left Africa to go on home leave and play cricket with the Twiga cricket team at the end of 1961, he certainly was expecting to return – the next time with me.

After our brief honeymoon, we moved into a hotel

room in Pewsey in Wiltshire and John returned to work at Transport Command. He had not been in the Air Force long enough to warrant leave, but his Squadron Leader kindly saw that we had some time together. Looking for somewhere to live or rent after we were married, was a problem neither of us anticipated. He had not accrued the 'points' needed for a married quarter on camp, so for the first few weeks, our home was in an upstairs hotel room in the village pub. As John commuted to work each morning, I stayed in my room, knitting and listening to a small radio or going for long walks into the village, but I needed to do more.

Each weekend, I joined him at the cricket field with a number of his friends at the pretty, picturesque, nearby village of Eastern Royal. He had joined the cricket team after his arrival at Upavon, with another colleague from work. Eastern Royal Cricket Club was tucked neatly behind a row of beautiful thatched houses, with wonderful rose gardens. In one part of the field stood a large oak tree. Sadly, I cannot remember how many runs were awarded when a ball hit the tree. The team were a cheerful group of people, including a couple of the officers from the station at Upavon, a retired Colonel and his sons, a couple of stable lads from Sir Gordon Richards' stables, a pub landlord, and a long distance lorry driver, to mention a few. There were only a couple of wives and girlfriends who attended, and we ended up taking down the scores, making sandwiches and preparing afternoon tea for the players. My initiation into these proceedings was learning how to take down the scores and understand the umpires arm waving. It had been fun to play in the back garden at home, but this was serious stuff! At the end of the matches, I often made my way home, whilst 'play' continued with some serious drinking at Andy's pub, the 'Three Horse Shoes' in the village. When we finally had our own place, a couple of car loads of these noisy buddies of John's would pitch up at the cottage with him in the late hours, a little tipsy and very friendly, wanting coffee and bacon and egg sandwiches.

Meanwhile, I embarked on a secretarial post in Marlborough, working for a building firm, which was challenging and busy, on a princely pay packet of five pounds a week – but at least going to work was a respite from the boredom of the quiet hotel room.

By the time John had to attend a Fire Course at Catterick in 1961, I was expecting our first baby, so while he was away, I moved into a single room in a hotel in Marlborough to be nearer to work. The room was small, with basic furniture, but at least I avoided the long bus journey and it was only a short walk to work each day. I suffered dreadfully from morning sickness, couldn't face eating a cooked breakfast, and balked at the taste and smell of coffee or tea. I gorged on bread and butter, and I longed so much for the taste of fresh pawpaw and mango – all the lovely exotic tastes I could remember – but they were all a dream away, as no exotic fruits were available in the shops in England at the time. A jar of honey, which I purchased to try to soothe my cravings, made a poor substitute.

A hotel room again, different though it might have been, was lonelier than ever. I missed John terribly when he was away. I always thought I was well prepared for my life as a service wife and, of course, I would get used to the separations, but I have to confess that I was ill-prepared, despite my upbringing, and I hated him going away and never really ever got used to it in all the years of our marriage; but it is a painful reality that all service families had to get used to! I was fortunate enough to be able to work because I was off-base at the time. After the course, John returned to a busier than ever schedule at Transport Command.

Abroad, the American administration who had been plunged into crisis following the Bay of Pigs fiasco in Cuba in April 1961, continued to fall out with the Cubans and Russians. There was rising mutual mistrust in the world between East and West, and the political map of Europe was changing. The East German government closed its borders with the West and erected the Berlin Wall which divided the city. As tension mounted at home and abroad, and as the military stations in England were put on alert, the missile crisis in October brought us almost to the brink of war.

I saw very little of John at that time; all he would say to me, was to expect him when I saw him. There was no real comfort in his words and each time he left for work, I wondered if I would ever see him again. Not even he knew where he would be or what he would be doing at any time.

When the missiles on their way to Cuba were turned back to Russia and as tension slowly eased, there was a great feeling of relief at home, and life for us got back to some form of normality. We moved into a rented place near Devizes, but it was a long drive for John. Meanwhile the mess at RAF Upavon threw an enormous cocktail party for all serving personnel and a few local dignitaries; friends we hadn't seen in a long time were there and the evening was very relaxed. I was in the company of Air Vice-Marshal Stapleton and his wife, and we talked about everything. When the problem of housing and quarters was raised, I told her about the difficulties that we ourselves were facing, and that it would be months before we would be eligible for quarters on camp. I shall always remember her with fond memories – what a lovely lady. She just said, "Leave it to me," and disappeared. When she returned to me, she said that Mr. and Mrs. Soames, who were great friends of theirs, had a cottage in the local area which they sometimes 'let'. John was a lowly Flying Officer at the time, and he felt that we couldn't aspire to Churchillian rent, except for a short period of time. But after some deliberation, we decided to take it on. It was well above what we could afford, but if it meant living frugally, we would do just that. As long as we had each other and could be together, that was all that mattered.

We moved into the cottage with our few laden suitcases, radio and little else. The cottage was homely and in an idyllic spot in a part of North Newnton, about three miles away from the station. It looked a pretty picture, nestled in behind tall, thick, privet hedge on two sides, with an archway entry through to the front door. The thatched roof with its chimney stack, small Georgian-paned windows and a rustic, oak, latched front door, gave it a unique feel. The back of the cottage had been renovated by the family, with a modern kitchen and bathroom, and wide picture windows overlooking a raised lawn and open farmland beyond. Only metres away, stood an old, grey-stoned Norman church with a brook running behind it. Over a narrow, rickety bridge across another small brook, and surrounded by acres of cattle pastures, were our only near neighbours, a kindly middle-aged couple. He was the foreman and cattle hand who worked on the local farm.

My five pounds per week pay packet from work was enough to buy my weekly bus fare of fourteen shilling to go to and from Marlborough, while the rest was spent on the weekly food basket.

We were in an ideal place for our first real summer together, and we had a wonderful time. Although we were isolated, we were happy to enjoy the seclusion of the place and each other. The postage-stamp sized garden lawn at the front was visited daily by small flocks of partridge, milling about looking for food and they got used to us putting out bread for them. A mobile grocery van stopped near to the house about once a week, so I was able to buy fresh produce, and the local butcher delivered meat and fish. My very first attempt at cooking a Sunday roast to try and impress my new husband, was a complete and utter disaster. Not understanding the workings of the electric oven – we had always been used to gas before – I left the succulent piece of topside of beef, bought for the princely sum of thirteen shillings – a fortune at the time – incinerating on a high heat for about four hours. Certainly, it couldn't have looked less like a Sunday roast and I choked at having to bin it, while my poor husband sat down to tender vegetables instead!

Getting to work each day from the house, meant a walk of about half a mile to the main road to catch the bus, and I would return each evening at about six. It was always a race to see who could get back to the cottage first to get the fire on and have the kettle on the boil. I always felt overdosed on happiness, with a warm glow inside me, whenever I saw the distant light on in the cottage as I walked up the road, and my walking pace quickened in anticipation of getting home.

The winter of 1962 came in with a vengeance. Even as the cooler weather approached, we had great difficulty in keeping the cottage warm, despite the electric radiators being on. Burning a wood fire in the open, inglenook fireplace grate, seemed to have little effect, as the heat was drawn straight up the chimney. Our electricity bills soared, and I took to wearing my heavy coat around the house on occasions at the weekends – talk about orphan Annie. The chill winds whistled around us unceasingly and on Christmas Eve we awoke to frozen water pipes and snow, which had blown in from under the gap at the front door, half an inch thick across about eighteen inches of the carpet. Each blast of wind blew flurries of snow everywhere around us. The electric cables in the village couldn't cope with the weight of the snow and finally the electricity around the whole area went off.

John struggled to get to work through heavy snow that day, hitching a lift from the main road, and I sat and warmed myself over a couple of lighted candles. I managed to collect enough snow to fill a saucepan to boil over some candle heat for a cup of tea, and when my neighbours came over to see how we were coping, they took pity on me. They too were without electricity, but their home had a fireplace in every room, and they had running water. So John and I were invited to spend the following day with them and their family. My biggest fear at the house, was the possibility of burst water pipes and flooding in a thaw! The snows continued with drifts piling upon drifts, until buses and traffic were unable to operate.

When my mother rang a few days later, happily the electricity had been restored, and the pipes defrosted with only one minor leak. I couldn't tell her how miserable and cold we had felt during the nights, for fear of making her miserable for us. Outside the cottage, the scenery made a magnificent picture – just like a Christmas card. On the drive and on the minor country road, the snow became compacted into ice, leaving deep, six to eight inch tyre ruts on the unsalted areas, which were a hazard. Getting off the bus from work one evening, I lost my footing, slipped and fell heavily between the icy ruts, and lay stranded for some time struggling to get to my feet and feeling as helpless as an upturned beetle. I laughed at myself and my predicament, imagining how funny I must look, flailing with my arms and legs to try to get a foothold on something to lift myself up, but I was constantly frustrated because of my bump. My laughter stopped abruptly, when the beams from approaching headlights filled the dark sky; I concentrated all my efforts and one final flail brought me to my feet and I walked gingerly home, bursting into tears in John's arms as he met me at the door.

When our neighbours offered us a large bedroom in their warm house for a much reduced rent, I suggested that we take it, and I continued to work in Marlborough until April. On the 6th of May I went into labour and John was able to get me to RAF Wraughton hospital, and note – be back in time to go to work! With all the wards pretty full at the time, I lay isolated on a theatre trolley in the passageway of the hospital for hours, in pain and feeling rather sorry for myself. I would have loved to have him stay with me, but expectant fathers were not permitted to stay. Our son, John Elliott, was born in the early hours of the following morning, weighing nine pounds nine ounces.

After a few days in hospital, oh, how I longed to get home with my new baby, but the strict hospital regime, the statutory requirement of a ten day stay, plus rigid visiting hours made all the happy feelings that I may have had, slowly fade away. How times have changed! When I did go home, John managed a short time off from the busy work schedule at Transport Command, and that was only because of the kindness of his Wing Commander, himself a family man.

I suffered dreadful 'baby blues' and would burst into floods of tears for no reason at all – a problem misunderstood at the time – so I really didn't know why I was so down. All I was aware of was that I had this wonderful tiny tot, and I should have been happy and joyful; in fact, I became thoroughly tired and tearful. For weeks, I persevered with breast-feeding. Whatever I did, I could not pacify him, until the Health Visitor finally told me that I was, in fact, starving my hungry, crying child, and that breast-feeding wasn't enough for him and I would have to begin him on solids immediately. The thought of feeding a baby on bulk terrified me at first, but it did the trick.

Our neighbours had been so kind over those few months that we stayed with them, and their help during those dark cold, days were very much appreciated.

Almost until the end of June, the council lorries and workers were out and about, chipping away at the hard, compacted snow on the local roads which had carpeted the whole Wiltshire countryside.

Fortunately the arrival of John Elliott brought mega bonuses – Wow! We were allocated ten 'points' which enabled us to go on a shortlist for a service married quarter. When we finally did get to move, our son was six months old. It was a marvellous feeling; I was able to get down to all the wifely, motherly duties, and I had a husband who came home to lunch. Within days, there were friendly callers to coffee, and I was made to feel welcome. The blues miraculously disappeared and I began to enjoy living on a busy airforce station. Some of the young male and female officers would pitch up on our doorstep on the odd evening, carrying a few beers, happy for a break from mess life, and stay a couple of hours, sitting eating, drinking and talking in front of our raging fire. We often had a house full. One evening, before John came home from work, there was a knock on the door from one of them to say that our chimney was on fire. I rang the station fire service but, in fact, was able to put the fire out before the fire engine arrived; which was somewhat embarrassing, because John was also Station Fire Officer at the time.

As the campaign for Black Civil Rights surged ahead universally, we were witnessing a time of change and cultural unrest. On 22nd November, I was busy with the tea in the kitchen when John arrived home from work to tell me that President Kennedy had been shot. At the time that was all anybody knew. We sat and watched television while the full drama of the tragedy unfolded for the world to see. We were stunned and downhearted, and for days it was the topic of conversation everywhere. Then days later, whilst I held John Elliott on my knee, we witnessed together the shooting of Lee Harvey Oswald by Jack Ruby on the television.

John had to leave us to attend a couple of gunnery courses, one at Manobier near Tenby in Wales and another nearer home at Winterbourne Gunner near Salisbury. He was told that if he passed he would be posted to Singapore to join a new squadron going from Cyprus to Singapore, but the posting depended on him passing. He was never a technical man, but when he was set a task, he always applied himself one hundred and ten percent. He focussed totally on the job he had to do, working every weekend and studying every evening – it may have caused some severe fraying of the nerves, but he passed.

Chapter Eight

John flew out to RAF Changi in Singapore, to join 26 LAA Squadron of the Royal Air Force Regiment in the March of 1964. The squadron had arrived from RAF Nicosia in Cyprus some six months earlier, where they had been deployed to protect British lives and property, following the interracial Greek and Turkish disturbances which had broken out in Nicosia. The squadron personnel had all settled into their new jobs and accommodation before John joined them as the new man, in the position of Logistics Officer.

Meanwhile, I stayed in the married quarter at RAF Upavon with our son, John Elliott, and waited until accommodation and a flight out of England could be found for us. The squadron were very helpful in finding a place for us, and I flew from Stansted three months later with John Elliott, a day before his first birthday, on what was to be the last of the British United Airways flights to the Far East, via Istanbul and Bombay. It was a truly dreadful flight.

Unhappily, the flight attendants aboard the aircraft did little to make the thirty-odd hours journey a pleasant or comfortable one. Intent on getting their forward passengers drunk, the cabin staff scurried around them like ferrets. For the wives and families with youngsters, there was no such largesse, just irritation and utter frustration. We were all but forgotten, and I waited for an hour for a drink of anything. On the last leg of the journey from Bombay, I was terrified. In all the time I had flown, I had never experienced such turbulence and buffeting in an aircraft, as lights flickered on and off, and I truly began to wonder whether I would ever see land again. Perhaps I should have called for a spot of the stronger stuff being handed out so freely to the gents in front. John Elliott was irritable and inconsolable, because the jar of baby food that I had handed to the staff sometime earlier, failed to materialise. He was so exhausted that, when it finally came, he was too tired to eat, and fell asleep. As the journey progressed and buffeting continued, the noxious smell of regurgitated alcohol from people who had had a 'skin full', filled everyone's nostrils. I think every sick bag on board was filled.

On arrival at Paya Lebar airport, I was so happy to see John. He took his little son into his arms, and held us both close. John Elliott, sticky and travel weary, was asleep as we disembarked. He opened his eyes momentarily and glanced up at his dad, but was too tired to even acknowledge him, and closed them again. We drove home where we put him in his cot, in the air-conditioned room, still asleep and wearing the same clothes that he had travelled in; he slept until the following morning.

John had rented a lovely flat for us from a couple of Chinese doctors, who were working in England. It was on the second floor of a large tenement block, in Katong, a busy, populated area on the outskirts of the city. The back of the flat overlooked a swimming pool, with the front view from the balcony, looking out to the sea.

The place was beautiful, with light, cool, marble floors, and delicate rattan furniture with brilliant, vividly coloured seat cushions. Sliding colonial doors led on to the floral-decked balcony, looking out to the sea. It was indeed romantic, and in the cool of the evening, nothing could be heard, but the gentle sound of water as it lapped and stroked the wide sloping causeway, only yards from us.

Each afternoon, the local fishermen would congregate with their small boats on the waterfront, and by the early evening, they had ventured miles out into deep water to fish. Through the mysterious darkness of the calm evenings, the view across the water was breathtaking, with hundreds of glowing lanterns shimmering beneath the clear black sky. In the early morning, the waterfront came alive when the fishermen returned with their catches, ready to sell to the eagerly-waiting market traders, who surged forward, gathering around each catch, bartering and chattering. Their wriggling, jumping catches, carried in round flat baskets, invited everyone to look and buy.

On the squadron, I was greeted warmly by the officers and their wives, though I was young, new and green to the squadron ways. I had a lot to learn. Straight away, one was aware of a strong bond and unit loyalty on the squadron, engendered by the Squadron Commander, Gene Ledlie, and the Deputy Squadron Commander, Andy (Dempster) Anderson. Michelle, the Squadron Commander's wife, was the consummate hostess, with a gift of being able to entertain in style. She put on the most wonderful evening parties for us, and some of them were known to go on until dawn. The wives were encouraged to help to look after other squadron members' wives, and it was a solid, cohesive, happy unit, which had stuck together through the difficult times, as well as the good times.

Changi, on the north-eastern part of Singapore Island, had been transformed from mangrove swamps and virgin forests in the late twenties. Some of the trees at that time, reached over a hundred feet. One tree in particular, known as the Changi tree, stood over one hundred and fifty feet, until the sappers blew it up to confuse the invading Japanese during the Second World War.

The Changi that greeted us (once the main base for the transport aircraft in the Far East and the terminal point for the Transport Command routes from the United Kingdom), was growing fast, and by the time the Regiment arrived on the station, there were already flying squadrons of Hastings, Argosies, Meteors and the Shackletons from No 205 Squadron, which oversaw search and rescue and other maritime operations around the island.

The station was bursting with so many men and families that accommodation was difficult to find, despite the government housing at Toe Heights and Lloyd Leas. Most had to live in 'hirings' far and near, and few were able to enjoy the luxury of living on the camp at Changi.

Singapore, a beautiful island, and growing in prosperity, measured fifteen miles by nine, before reclamation began in the mid-60s. The city bustled with its multicultural population: Chinese, Malay and Indians. Its colonial heart, the Supreme Court, overlooked the Padang, where many sports, like cricket, rugby and soccer were played and where, some years earlier, the Japanese had paraded their captive British, Australian and other Allied prisoners, to inform them that Singapore would henceforth be known as Syonaan-to (Light of the South), only to surrender three years later to the British, when a Union Jack flag (hidden at Changi prison by inmates) flew once more over the colonnaded City Hall. Its large Hotels, Raffles and Goodwood, were favourite places for visitors, and the squadron enjoyed a few evenings there too.

Living in Katong meant a very early start for John to get to work in the morning. The hours of work began before seven in the morning and finished mid afternoon and were flexible – but work times were altered months later when the squadron was deployed due to the confrontation with Indonesia. Meanwhile, we took full advantage of the afternoons. We joined the Singapore Swimming Club, and often went to the beach.

There was a good bus route from Katong into the centre of the city, and to the air-conditioned stores, like CK Tang, Fitzpatricks and Cold Storage, selling exotic furniture and china. These superstores drew people like magnets, and I occasionally bumped into Moira (Andy's wife) and Michelle having coffee in one of them.

When my eighteen-month old inquisitive son, began to slide chairs over to the balcony railings, and try to climb over (shades of my sister Joan in Alexandria), I realised that he was no longer safe in the flat and sought to move elsewhere. It wasn't as easy as I had thought it would be. I found out that the only way to get to know about accommodation for rent was through the local tradesmen. There was always a relative who was happy to move out of their home in exchange for rent money from a service family.

We found a place at Tanah Merah not far from the Casaurinas Hotel, and only a couple of miles from the station at Changi. This time the flat was a two-storey, wooden beach house, with high, panelled fencing around the balcony, enough to keep little children in and intruders out. It belonged to a shipping magnate's wife. Built on the rocks, and jutting out to sea, it was modestly furnished, and the outside was painted green, so it merged with the background of tall trees and vegetation. Overlooking a white coral sandy beach, it was private and could only be reached from the outside by boat although we had private access via some steps. The rocky outcrop to one side hid the relics of an enormous, fortified, wartime, gun emplacement, covered by thick flowering bindweed.

Downstairs in the flat below us, lived a young, tall, black Tamil. He was kept on by the owner, as retainer and general maintenance man for both flats. He delighted in relating stories of bandits and smugglers. I'm sure some of the stories were true, but I think he achieved a certain sinister delight in their embellishment. The air was cool and calm in the day, but at night it was eerie with mysterious howls and noises, and I did often wonder whether some of the noises were coming from the downstairs flat!

Our nearest neighbours on the coast were David Marshall and his lovely family. Once a leading criminal lawyer, he became Chief Minister, and was pro-active in the talks regarding the colony's independence from Britain in the mid-50s. They were friendly and the first people to invite us to their home on the beach, where we ate waffles and drank juice. He never talked politics and was a great family man. Our other neighbours were Air Force, but they kept themselves to themselves and we didn't ever see them come or go. They had a white dog, which fascinated John Elliott, and I was horrified one day when I heard a shot from a rifle, and saw the animal lying dead in their garden with its shoulder ripped wide open; the sort of injury which could only have been from a dum-dum bullet. I had to drag my fascinated son away from the window. I never saw who killed the animal and didn't enquire further, but the episode was upsetting.

Living nearer Changi meant less driving for John and, after work, he would drive to the Casaurinas Hotel on the beach, and sit studying for his promotion exams. When I walked down to meet him after John Elliott's sleep, I would find him, sitting on the bench, under the shade of the bougainvillaea, with his books open, a sandwich in one hand and a cool Tiger beer in the other. After our drinks of orange juice, we would leave him and take our towels and sit on the beach, where he would later join us for a swim. We were often the only people on the beach.

Our early morning wake-up call some mornings was the bone-shaking roar of the Buccaneer aircraft that took off from another airfield, flew directly over the beach house and out over the sea, its burners flashing fire. It gave me a great feeling of pride and comfort at their presence in our midst during the early days of confrontation.

There were minor drawbacks to living where we did. The mosquitoes had a field day with us all, gorging themselves on our life's blood at night, then taking off like heavily laden aircraft to seek refuge in the darkness of the wardrobes and closets. The smouldering, slow-burning mosquito coils, kept them at bay for a few hours of the night while we slept, but there was no respite, once the coils had burned out. However, my greatest loathing were the swamp rats: opportunists and thieves, they delighted in sifting through my vegetable racks, and when I saw one, brazenly sitting, munching through my ready prepared vegetables for my evening meal, I almost had apoplexy, and had to procure help from the fearless Tamil retainer to get rid of it.

My fear of rats, stemmed from a horrible experience that I had in the Big House in Africa as a child. I saw one, sitting on top of the electric junction box in the hall, happily preening itself. It sat unperturbed and unnoticed by Big John, as he came and went by the back door, until I drew his attention to it. Rushing off to the kitchen, he returned with a long handled broom. Meanwhile, the rodent had disappeared up the cables, and into a gap in the ceiling, so we waited, until moments later it emerged. Big John was ready and, with one swipe of his broom, the rat fell off its perch and made a dash for the bedroom. With incredible agility, it leapt on to the bed, then the window sill, scampered up the curtains and on to the pelmet, as if it had practised the manoeuvre before. Each time he prodded it, the rat jumped and scampered to the other end. Finally cornered and pinned to the wall, it struggled free and made one frantic leap on to his shoulder; exacting instant revenge, it bit him on the neck and hurriedly made its escape out of the room. All this feverish activity took place within about two minutes, leaving Big John moaning and holding his hand over his bleeding neck, and me, rooted to the spot in shock and disbelief. Over the following few days, odd bits of tasty bait were strategically placed around the tops of cupboards, but the rat remained elusive, until one afternoon, there was an almighty flash and bang like a muffled gun shot, which came from the ceiling near to the electric wires: the rat, which had sought safety there, was finally dispatched by the cables which it had been nibbling.

We put up with these minor irritations, but when the chalk-white beach became polluted by thick clumps of black oil swept in on the daily tide, making the beach unpleasant and the water in the area unfit for swimming, we again looked for alternative accommodation. Fortunately, this time we didn't have to look far.

Meanwhile, the squadron, which worked hard and played hard, under the gaze of their dynamic Squadron Commander, Gene Ledlie, were winning sports trophies and almost every shield going on the station. Gene, of course, had recruited amongst his gunners before he left Cyprus, the cream of the marksmen and other sportsmen. Everyone and anyone who had anything to do with the squadron, including the wives, were encouraged to support and take pride in the squadron's achievements. There was an immense feeling of family pride and unity. The Flight Commanders were tasked with at least one sport to take charge of, and when John was given the water polo, I happily went along to show my support.

Apart from the fun side, the squadron took a very professional stance on important issues. There was anti-aircraft firing at China Rock, a firing range on the south east coast of Malaysia, as well as jungle training through heat, humidity and swamp. Tales of leeches, snakes and biting insects were not exaggerated. When the men returned to base, the stench of mud-soaked green uniforms and jungles boots was indescribable. On one occasion, I remember laughing at John as he walked up the stairs to the flat. Looking utterly exhausted, he expected to walk through to the balcony, sit down and have a drink before having a shower – well that was what he thought! I refused to hand him his eagerly-awaited cold 'Tusker' from the fridge until he had showered, in his boots and uniform, and rinsed off the stinking mud sufficiently to send them to be laundered. There was such a look of indignation on his face, and the events that followed meant that we both had to take a shower.

John was always a stickler for punctuality. If he had to be anywhere, he made sure he was ready and at his appointment well before time. However, on one occasion, in September 1964, the squadron deployed to China Rock. They had been given the opportunity to hold a live firing camp at the location and a battery of the Royal Artillery relieved the squadron from its deployment around Changi. The squadron personnel had about two days to check over the guns and mechanical transport, and amass all the necessary logistics to support a ten day practice camp. The whole unit was to move from the jetty at Fairy Point and sail to the beach on the mainland, some three hours travelling time, to the location at China Rock. The day before the move, John returned home very late and tired, as it had been his responsibility as Unit MT Officer to ensure that all vehicles were fully serviceable, refuelled and loaded prior to the move early the following morning. The two flights of personnel, guns and towing vehicles were to travel by the Royal Corps of Transport landing craft, while the squadron headquarters personnel, including John, were to travel one hour later by courtesy of a fast launch of the resident RAF Marine Craft Unit.

Anyway, that night John set his trusty alarm for 0430 hours and we both retired to bed at about midnight. We slept so soundly in fact that we did not hear the alarm go off and it was nearer 0600 hours when John leapt out of bed yelling that he had missed the rendezvous and that there would be terrible repercussions. He was in a dreadful state as he rushed to get dressed, refusing the offer of a cup of tea, and in sheer panic he drove to Changi at high speed and in record time. On arrival at the jetty, he was just in time to see the squadron sailing away, well beyond hailing distance.

The chaps at the Marine unit were highly amused, but they failed to tell him that his Squadron Commander, Gene Ledlie, was far from being amused. John hastily explained his predicament to the Flight Lieutenant in charge of the Marine Craft, but he offered no help, as the squadron had already taken their spare boat and the duty boat could only leave the jetty in the event of an emergency. He pleaded with him that – this was an emergency; but the Flight lieutenant wasn't convinced.

He did, however, telephone his colleague at the RCT Port Company who had provided the landing craft, and after much negotiation and bribery concerning crates of Tiger Beer, they came up trumps and promised a fast trip for my errant, but very grateful, husband to rejoin his unit – but NOT for at least another hour. This news did little to placate him until the smiling OC Marine Unit explained that due to speed and tides the squadron personnel would not be able to disembark until late in the afternoon. In fact, they would be able to deliver him at China Rock ahead of the main party.

True to their word, he departed from Changi some three hours behind the squadron, passed them en route and was on the beach to welcome his Squadron Commander and the squadron headquarters personnel when they disembarked. Luck of the devil! However smug he may have felt, he still had a rollicking from his Squadron Commander.

That year, with the heightened threat of Indonesian confrontation, the squadron was on full alert and deployed its light anti-aircraft Bofors guns to various points around the airfield and beach heads to support the land and sea operations in defence of the island. This was a twenty four hour, seven day a week operation which was sustained for about a year.

When we were offered a 'far hiring' in Siglap, half way between Katong and Changi, I was delighted and content to move. Situated in the centre of an avenue of modern dwellings, and opposite the local Chinese school, we were nearer the city and friends. We employed a 'live in' Amah during the week, who cooked and looked after us, returning to her own home and family at weekends.

We lived a short way from Andy and Moira, and Siglap offered us a number of grocery stores, shops and other facilities, within a short walking distance. One evening a week a large, open-air market was held along the length of the avenue, selling clothes, records, jewellery, gems and other goods. Beatlemania had reached the Far East and, as the market traders plied their wares, Beatles' songs blared out over the market hubbub. We were only a short distance from the rest of the squadron officers and their wives, and amongst many of the local Chinese community. Our immediate neighbour was a senior police officer in the Singapore Constabulary, Joe Teng, and his wife and son. John Elliott played amongst children his own age in the comfort and security of our high-fenced garden, and in the afternoons, when he wasn't sleeping, he was happy to play and keep cool in his paddling pool in the garden, under the shade of the trees. While our husbands were on duty, we were all in the same boat, and close enough to each other if any problems arose.

We hired a television, which was invaluable during the times of curfew. A number of killings took place and skirmishes broke out between the local Malays and Chinese in the local Kampongs, but we felt reasonably secure, with a 'call point' in case of any emergency.

John, with all his patience, taught me to drive our Morris Minor, bringing me greater freedom and peace of mind. As a celebration on passing my test, he decided to take me to see 'My Fair Lady' in the cinema in town. It was a couple of days before Christmas and, dressed for dinner, I drove into town on the understanding that he would drive home. We stopped at a hotel for dinner and at the bar we were joined by three Danish gentlemen. We talked at great length, and I hinted to John that we would miss the film if we didn't leave right away. The three men had other ideas and insisted that we join them on board their ship, moored at the docks. I was not keen but at that stage I knew I was outnumbered. There was no way that John was fit to drive – nor were they – and the evening was drawing in. So it ended up with me, driving four, noisy, slightly inebriated men, to the docks. I tried to insist that we stay for only a short while, and I intended to drive us straight home. With some trepidation, we found ourselves walking up the gangplank, into the ship and along to the ward-room of the Henriette Maersk, with the ships Captain and engineers. When they brought out the schnapps, insisting we join them in a toast, I feared the worst. I made my excuse – I was expecting a baby and I didn't drink. John, on the other hand, was not one to turn down a chance for one – two – or even three, and in ten minutes, they were all well away – singing and swearing eternal friendship to one another. I insisted, politely, that we leave; I thanked them, guided John down the gang plank, and led him to the car. I was totally disorientated, not from drink, but sheer terror. I hadn't a clue where I was, and I had never driven in the dark before. I must have driven around the same area about four times, until I reached a road that I recognised. John awoke the next morning to a chilly reception, and when he mentioned that he had invited the three friendly gents for Christmas Day lunch, I threw a wobbler on the spot. I insisted he ring the ship and tell them that I was about to give birth. They were very understanding, said they hoped I would be all right, and wished us both a Merry Christmas and good luck.

With more driving experience, I travelled further afield. We delighted in going out to Bedok Corner, on the coast. It was a favourite place to eat for many servicemen, families and local people, who congregated in the open air to enjoy the delicacies of oriental cuisine.

A last move to a 'near hiring' on the Upper Changi Road, meant we were much nearer to the station. We were also only a short distance from Changi jail, where the Japanese had interned hundreds of prisoners during the war (one of its prisoners was my boss from the showroom in Macclesfield). The garden of the bungalow at Upper Changi had been sadly neglected, making it an ideal haunt for snakes, so our priority was to sort it out. Within a week, we employed at our own expense two local labourers with picks and spades, to level and tier the slope into three level steps. John's driver purloined a number of granite boulders, which he loaded into the back of the Land Rover and brought to the house for me – I never asked where they came from, and I was able to put the finishing touches to the landscaping by planting grass and flowers. By the time we were due to leave for the UK, the garden looked beautiful. (When we returned to Singapore in the early 1990s for a holiday, I was happy to see that our bungalow was one of the few buildings along the road still left standing, with the garden unchanged.)

The saying amongst the personnel in the Far East was

that, either one returned to England with a camphor wood chest or a baby. Well, Anne, Tina (both Squadron officers' wives) and myself, managed both!

Prior to our move, we had bidden, Andy, Moira, and their two daughters farewell from the squadron, on their return to England and a new posting. We took Andy and Moira out for a farewell cinema show and dinner – the film was awful! However, we consoled ourselves with an excellent meal and wine at the newly opened Troika Rooms Restaurant in the city, and the following day we drove to Paya Lebar airport to see them off.

After a long time of standing and dancing at Temple Hill mess one evening – and one gin and tonic (my first introduction to the hard stuff), Peter, decided he couldn't take any more, and was born at Changi Hospital on the l3th of September 1965, a couple of days before he was actually due. John Elliott was not exactly overjoyed with the arrival of his new brother, and he had a few tantrums, and calls of, "I want you to send him back!". Quite expecting to have an instant friend and companion he could relate to, he found instead only a small tot that cried and took up 'his' quality time. When he finally resigned himself to the fact that his brother was staying with us, the tantrums disappeared, and he warmed to him, piling all the toys he could find into Peter's cot.

From England, we received news that my grandmother had died from cancer. It was upsetting being so far away at the time, and I regretted my very infrequent letters to her. All the wonderful childhood adventures of our first home with my grandparents in Small-Heath, would be a closed chapter in my life, but the memories will remain.

John and Anne Morgan-Jones's departure from the squadron, followed a couple of months after Andy's. Anne had her hands full with four youngsters now. Their small daughter, Jane, with her broad smile, was a pretty baby who had spent many hours with us while her parents had a break in Malaya with their boys, and was always the daughter that I never had. John and Anne were good friends, and we treated them to an evening at the Goodwood Hotel before their departure from Changi.

By the time that Gene had handed over to his successor, all the original squadron members had gone to begin new tours at home in England, and the increasing commitments at work caused the tight, cohesive regiment family unit to all but collapse.

I embarked on a hairdressing course at a salon just around the corner from the house, which took up a lot of my time, and the Amah was wonderful, cooking and looking after the two boys in my absence. We bought a washing machine, which made life much easier for all of us, and my neighbours took full advantage of it as well.

With the squadron fully deployed and all the Flight Commanders and airmen spending endless hours on duty at the gun emplacements, the wives and families saw little of their menfolk, arousing some discontent. The Command Post Operations Room, began a round-the-clock shift system of work, and the heightened state of alert, brought more restrictions for everyone.

On Christmas Eve, while John was on duty in the Command Post, I thought that I would boost the evening shift's morale, and decided to sneak a crate of beer in to them, much to John's consternation. As the guard on duty pointed his rifle at me, I persuaded him that I was not a foe, but a bearer of Christmas gifts. They didn't refuse the beers! I didn't stay around, and had only been gone a short time, leaving John Elliott asleep in my room, and the Amah baby-sitting from her room. I was greeted on my return by a worried Amah and a sobbing, bleeding John Elliott, who had climbed on to the bed-head to reach the fan switch, and fallen on to his face on to the concrete floor, dislodging his front teeth. I was beside myself with remorse and worry, as I bundled him into the car to go to hospital to be treated. Poor little soul, he eventually had to have his front teeth removed.

John's tour was finally up after two years, and we received his posting notice for England. I was quite ready to leave by then. We had had a pleasant time, but I looked forward to some normalcy in our lives once more.

Both of our families had been brilliant with letters and news from home. My sister, Joan, and her husband had a young son, Richard, and my youngest brother, Robert, was being thoroughly spoiled by his older siblings. Martin had joined the Royal Corps of Signals, Mary was a Queen Alexandra naval nurse in Portsmouth, and Peter and John were at school.

Back in England, the fashions were going haywire, with hem-lines getting shorter, and hair styles more bizarre: as my mother put it – trashy! However, there was a growing self-confidence amongst the younger generation and an air of defiance, with the emergence of 'flower power', radical songs and sexual freedom.

England won the football World Cup in July 1966 and

the whole country rejoiced when Geoff Hurst scored in the closing seconds with those immortal words by Sports Commentator, Kenneth Wolstenholme, "They think it's all over... It is now!"

The United States, who had seen the emergence of the Civil Rights Movement, and were very heavily involved in Vietnam, were steadily becoming engulfed in civil unrest at home, as a result of both.

We were unable to join John as a family on the station at Watton in Norfolk, as there were no married quarters available, so I stayed in Newcastle with his parents for a few weeks. Being the Regiment and Fire officer on a large flying station, John was required to live on base; he was kept on his toes and busy with ground defence training and so on, and was unable to get away to see us much. Eventually, a place was allocated to us: a substandard, prefabricated, two bed-roomed house on base. Having no choice and little option, John insisted that we take it, fearing that if we didn't I could find myself spending months in Newcastle with our two youngsters. That wasn't an option I was prepared to take, as John's father, who had been treated for TB a couple of years earlier, was not a well man. He needed his afternoon rests, and trying to keep two small boys quiet for long periods of time became increasingly frustrating and difficult, especially on wet days, when we couldn't leave the confines of the house. There had to be complete silence for the hourly weather bulletins – John's father was obsessed with them. I hated the intensity with which the weather forecasts had to be watched and listened to. John's mother was very tolerant, but I think it was a lot for her to put up with during those weeks with us around.

The boys and I caught the train to Norwich as soon as we could. The substandard prefab wasn't too bad after some minor improvements and a lick of paint. I bought some carpets to cover the lino floors, made new curtains, and bought a few items of furniture; and the place was warm and cosy once our crates arrived from Singapore and we filled the rooms and got the coal fire going.

Each morning, with Peter in his pram, we walked John Elliott to nursery school on camp. I bussed or walked everywhere before we bought our first new car, a red Volkswagen Beetle, which we loved. Then we did a fair bit of motoring around the Norfolk coastline, its pretty beaches, and the Broads, and we marvelled at the diversity of its wonderful bird life. We loved the area so much, that we even talked of one day settling down in Norfolk.

Later on in the year, the television relayed Cliff Michelmore at a scene of devastation as tragedy struck the infant and junior school in the small mining village of Aberfan. There cannot have been a dry eye in the country, and I felt emotionally drained by the time the small children's funerals had taken place. I remember going into my sleeping boys' room that night and waking them as I held them in turn in my arms. The disaster was to wipe out a whole generation of the village. For weeks we mourned quietly for the families, and the small town which few would have heard of, but which would now be mapped in our minds for all time.

John received his promotion to Flight Lieutenant, and was tasked with organising and preparing the station's personnel in readiness for its official Triple Standard Parade. He thoroughly enjoyed his work on the station and put his heart and soul in to it – so much so, that one night, he sat bolt upright in bed in his sleep and uttered the words, "God Save the Queen – God Save the Queen – God Save the Queen," and fell back on to his pillow fast asleep: the Queen would have been proud! In the morning, he didn't believe me, when I told him what he had said in his sleep. The parade was magnificent and I was indeed proud of him on the day.

He went up to the Regiment depot at Catterick to attend, and help with, the Royal Air Force's golden jubilee celebrations, where he was able to meet friends and catch up on Regiment news. Station life at Watton, was hectic and great fun. I had the opportunity of putting my hairdressing to some use, until my legs began to complain, because I was expecting our third child.

We finally moved into a standard quarter, in Tedder Close, near to our dear friends, Rod Donnelly, the Station Medical Officer, and his wife, Judy, who worked as a nursing sister in the Norwich hospital. Away from work, the four of us shared some memorable wild times together at the mess. Tom Jones was all the rage. For umpteen weeks, everybody on base was glued to the box to watch the 'Forsyte Saga' and, if anyone missed an episode, there was always someone who could keep you informed as to what had happened.

In 1968, the shooting of Martin Luther King, Jr., caused universal outrage and was followed by Robert Kennedy's assassination three months later. New, revolutionary ideas called for radical changes, and we knew it as the pot, pop, and protest culture, which would eventually see the voting rights given to eighteen year olds.

In Africa, a number of Asians were leaving Kenya, fearing mass deportation and taking what they could. Many entered Britain, having left their thriving businesses, to face an uncertain future. The employment exchange were happy to call upon my father's talents, to help get many of the families settled into employment, because he spoke fluent Swahili, which was vital as many of the Asians knew no English at all.

Now at this stage, you may wonder – did, she do nothing but watch television? Well, I did! Times were changing. A couple of the officers' wives went out to work – a new phenomenon, but a sign of the times. I did a great deal of baby-sitting for friends while I was pregnant, but I eased up when my legs became too painful. There were two other officers' wives nearby, who were to become mums but sadly not everything went according to plan for them – having a scan wasn't the norm in those days. I spent an anxious few weeks, before my baby was due, wondering if everything would go smoothly and on 15th March 1968, our third son, Richard, was born at Ely Hospital in Cambridgeshire, fit and well, and beautiful – I counted each finger and toe. We were so relieved. We had him christened four months later, with Squadron Leader Eric Denson (a Flight Commander on Canberras) and his wife Shirley, and our friends, the Donnellys, as his four godparents. I had a fit of the giggles as Judy gave up her godson into the arms of the Padre. Richard looked up, smiled and gurgled away, causing us all great amusement – he didn't know what was to follow!

At about this time, the station had to come to terms with three very sad and sensitive incidents, amongst them, a fatal air crash and an horrific suicide in the officers' quarters.

Sadly, Eric was to take his own life in 1976, after years of suffering the effects of radiation sickness. In 1958, he had taken off from his base in Lincolnshire in his Canberra aircraft, on a secret mission to Christmas Island. His task was to collect samples of cloud to test for 'fallout' dust particles. After that terrible day, life for him and Shirley would never be the same again. On his return from his mission, he entered the door of his married quarters, unable to divulge what had taken place and burst into tears, with the words, "Into the jaws of death, into the mouth of hell!". What on earth was he talking about? Shirley had no idea. In fact, he had received the equivalent of 6,500 X-ray doses on that day, as he flew through the clouds of radioactive fallout! Unhappily, Shirley was to carry on married life with her husband weaving in and out of terrible, deep depression, unable to tell a soul, and the doctors could find no explanation for his rashes and mood swings. She was unable to share her worries or fears with any of us at the time, although Judy and I tried to help, but we were unaware of the reason for his illness. It was not until the end of 1999, that the real reasons for his illness were finally brought to light. Meanwhile, over those lonely years, Shirley was left to bring up four daughters on her own. We had all been close friends and shared many happy times together. We all still keep in touch.

When John's tour at Watton came to a close, he went to rejoin 26 Squadron, who were based at Bicester in Oxfordshire, as Deputy Squadron Commander under their new Squadron Commander, Marcus (Mickey) Witherow, a man whom John held in very high regard. He could hardly contain his delight as he rushed off to join them, while I stayed behind to pack and clean, ready for the handover of the keys to the quarter.

There were other RAF units and personnel at Bicester before the two Regiment Squadrons Nos 1 and 26, which made up 5 Wing, arrived. Most of the regiment personnel knew one another from other squadrons, most having served together in other parts of the globe and, once again, there was a good rapport between the squadrons and families.

Mickey, who wasn't yet married, asked me if I would help with the welfare of the families, and squadron functions, which I was more than happy to do, and often meant going out with my young baby, sleeping happily in the back seat of the beetle, as I travelled around.

The day came for Mickey to be married to his fiancée, Mary, a Princess Mary nursing sister. It was also my Richard's first birthday, so he stayed at home with my home-help, who had organised a party for the three boys for that afternoon. There was a flurry of excitement in the morning as we all prepared ourselves for the wedding. John and the wedding guard of honour went ahead, and the rest of the officers and wives from both squadrons travelled on a bus to the church and reception. It was a wonderful, sunny, warm day. The bride and groom looked very happy and everything went well. The return journey on the bus was hilarious, with jokes and singing, and many folk feeling a little 'tipsy'. It was a great day out for us all, which we will never forget.

When troubles brewed on the Island of Anguilla in the Caribbean, John flew out with some of the regiment in an uncomfortable thirty-hour flight in a Hercules to Antigua, to relieve the Parachute Regiment. The whole move was done with great secrecy and no one was able to talk about what was going on. John was wonderful with letters, and wrote tales of giant crabs which invaded the tents at night. He was entertained each night by strange animal noises, whistles and peals of laughter coming from the tents next to him, where the young officers would make up stories about the little, pink, wooly-dew-drop characters and friend, Soup-Dragon, from the television series *The Clangers*. He talked of the hot sunny days and the beautiful beaches. The biggest problem most of them faced was sunburn. When the island was hit by a hurricane-force storm that caused a great deal of damage, the airmen were tasked to help with clearing-up operations and praised for all their rescue work.

Meanwhile, at home, life carried on in John's absence, with three small boys keeping me very busy indeed. I cycled Peter to his play group on camp each morning, and John Elliott went off to the local primary school and was introduced to the new form of teaching. Gone was the formal serried ranks behind desks all looking ahead, hanging on every word from the teacher. As I looked through the window, there were just small groups of children – many wandering around the classroom aimlessly while a teacher sat with another group. I was very worried that he wouldn't learn anything, especially if I was anything to go by, and I set to work to try to teach him at home, firstly by making a blackboard for the kitchen, where he could doodle, write and draw. (As it turned out, my worries were groundless. He is now in commercial banking in the city of London, has a sound financial brain, and a good knowledge of business law under his belt.)

I had to keep a watchful eye on my youngest, Richard, who tried to run off at each opportunity to look for Peter at play group, and there was more than one occasion when I caught him looking through the play group railings. Another time, Mary Witherow brought him back home to me, when I wasn't even aware that he had left the house. He just couldn't understand why his brothers were not at home with him during the day. We had our routine, and at the weekends, the three boys played safely in the back garden, or with friends on their bicycles, on the road in the front of the house.

They went through the usual childhood diseases, chickenpox and measles and, as I had little faith in our local doctor in the town, I relied entirely on Mary's nursing knowledge and ability to help me through the difficult patch. She was very kind and a great help to me during that period when John Elliott especially was very poorly.

The boys missed playing football with their daddy in the early stages of his departures but, like all children, as long as their meals are on the table and they have a routine, they soon forgot that daddy was away.

I think that secretly, John was delighted to have a long break away from three small children. When he agreed to do another ten week stint in the Caribbean, I was so angry and upset that I walked out on him, leaving him with Richard on his knee and the boys playing in the garden. For a couple of hours I sat huddled on a box in the coal shed, wearing my winter coat against the cold. I had nowhere else to hide, and sat and shivered, feeling very sorry for myself. I could hear John call out to me, but the coal shed was the last place he would have looked for me. I derived some pleasure and gratification when I returned, to see him looking so downcast and worried and wondering if I had indeed left him for good. It was our first major falling out, and we often laughed about it afterwards. It made no difference, however. Off he went to complete his ten weeks in the sun, with me waving a tearful good-bye. However, his efforts had their rewards and he was awarded a special Laudatory Report for his work in the Caribbean.

Our red Volkswagen Beetle was almost written off when, coming home from Oxford one day, someone ran into the back of me at a traffic lights. Seat belts were not compulsory in those days, but the realisation that we could all have been badly injured stayed with me for some time; for a while I didn't want to drive out at all. We were shunted forward, with my mother-in-law clutching Richard on her knee in the back seat. The perpetrator found his front bonnet and engine mangled and belching smoke. He emerged from his car, looking shaken, and apologising profusely for his carelessness. Apart from severe whiplash to us, nobody was hurt, thank goodness, but the car was badly damaged.

We enjoyed our tour at Bicester. The boys loved their trips out with friends around and about the Oxford area. We went to Banbury for tea many times, and to North Hinksey Park to punt down the river.

My father received an invitation to return to Tanzania, for the opening of the new Kilimanjaro airport at Moshi, and was happy to accept, relishing the prospect of seeing old friends. Accorded VIP treatment, he had a Land Rover and driver to meet him. After the official ceremony, he was taken to visit the prison and grounds. He took some films of the occasion, but he felt that the driver had been instructed to show him only what they wanted him to see, as he was rushed around from place to place, giving him only a scant view of the area. He noted with dismay, that the giant tree which had towered over the Big House, had been cut down.

John was sent to RAF Fairford on a sensitive mission to help organise and train the funeral guard for the officers and airmen who died in a Vulcan crash. It was a sad day for the wives and families, and he looked physically drained by the emotion of the event on his return.

The squadron heard that they were to move to Gutersloh in Germany, and Mickey had hoped to be with them on their move. However, he was posted to RAF Catterick.

My adventurous boys were out playing one afternoon, with a number of other children from the quarters, in the front of the house. The next thing was a knock at the door by a couple of the older children, and John Elliott was standing in front of me, holding his arm. Right away, from the angle of it, I knew that it was broken. Leaving my other two behind with a neighbour, I rushed off to the John Radcliffe hospital in Oxford. Poor little soul, he sat patiently, whimpering in dreadful pain as we waited our turn in the busy casualty waiting room for ages before he was seen and x-rayed. He was admitted that evening and went down to theatre to have his elbow pinned the following day. The surgeon at the hospital was marvellous. The surgeon hoped that John would get perhaps ninety percent of mobility back, but he couldn't guarantee anything. I was happy with that at least, but hoped for the best. After the plaster was removed, he underwent intense physiotherapy which was painful for him, and it hurt me to see him crying. I had strict instructions to get him to use his arm and do as much for himself as possible, but within a week of his return my young son had turned into a demanding little tyrant. If I heard the words, "I can't do," once, I heard them a hundred times. I tried to encourage and help, but my best wasn't enough. Having been thoroughly spoiled and pampered by his caring nurses, he demanded the same all-caring treatment at home, until one day, he informed me that he didn't want to live with us any more, and preferred to go back to the hospital. Finally, I suggested that in that case, he should pack his little suitcase. Off he trotted, with a small rolled up bundle of clothes in his plimsoll bag. "Well, I'm off," he said, looking across at me at the kitchen sink, awaiting my reply. "Can you hear me? I'm going now."

"Go carefully," I replied.

"I mean it, I'm going."

"Yes, all right then – bye."

Clutching the door handle, he continued, "Did you hear me? I'm going." Then out of the door he went. I didn't turn to look. I left him for about ten minutes, then got the car out and trailed him down the path which led into town. He hadn't gone far, and I overtook him. Glancing in the mirror, I saw a frantic waving of hands and heard calls of "I'm here." I continued to the end of the road out of sight and came back to pick him up. He climbed into the back seat without a word, and we went home for plenty of cuddles; I never had an ounce of trouble after that.

In life, the moments you remember with clarity are more often the worst or the best of experiences. I must draw a veil over the squadron aspects of our eighteen months in Germany. Suffice to say, that John and his new boss had a mutual dislike of one another.

The squadron left from Brize Norton to Gutersloh, and I followed later with the boys. I shall not forget the kindness, shown to me by David and Betty Bolton before my departure. David had taken command of No 1 Squadron from Mike Welply. Despite their busy schedule (with civil disturbances in Northern Ireland the squadron was deployed in Ulster) and the families on the station to take care of, Betty made time to take us and our baggage to the railway station while David handed over the quarter for me.

Gutersloh, once a flying station for the Luftwaffe, was now a vibrant station with three British Lightning Squadrons, and two helicopter squadrons, as well as our regiment and others. With the airfield only a few miles from the East German border, two Lightning aircraft stood on 'battle flight' readiness in the hangars.

Our quarter was only a stone's throw from the mess and station amenities. And because it was a short distance for John to walk to work, I kept the car, VW Beetle MKII, for my use with the boys. Alan Johnson, the Station Medical Officer, and his wife, Denise, were our good friends, and we shared some great times together. The boys loved to walk to the open airfield and wave to the pilots, and the pilots always waved back. They could watch the Lightnings taxi to the end of the airfield, take off and circle around doing their circuits and bumps. The pilots were a great bunch of men; we knew them all and could see who was in the aircraft taxiing down the runway at any one time. My boys were overjoyed when they were shown around the Lightnings and allowed to sit in the cockpit of the aircraft. Many of the pilots went on to become civilian airline pilots; others were promoted and eventually had their own stations to command. I am happy to say that most remain my good friends.

Because I had the use of the car Denise, her son Robert, and my boys, got around the country a fair amount, sightseeing in the Black Forest and walking along the length of the mighty Mohne Dam, where we picnicked down by the water's edge. We managed a weekend in a bed and breakfast at Rhudesheim, and sat on the banks of the river Rhine, with the calm water lapping on the pebbled banks, and we watched the long barges, some tied to each other in twos and threes as they plied their wares up and down the mighty river between the industrial cities. With many small cafes, along the Rhine, we drank and ate alfresco.

When John took his first leave, we embarked on a one-off camping holiday for a fortnight in Austria and Italy. Neither of us being campers, we booked through a camping holiday firm. Leaving Gutersloh behind, we drove to Munich, where the road passed right by the stadium which was in its final stages of completion for the Olympic Games in September 1972. Sadly those Olympic games would be remembered for the deaths of eleven Israeli athletes. We drove south and stopped for a night in Ulm, then left for the Plansee in Austria the following day. We arrived late in the afternoon at the campsite to find the whole area ankle-deep in mud. The place had had a fortnight of continuous heavy rain, said our fellow campers, and they were glad to be getting the hell out of there! Those who were leaving had to have their vehicles towed away from the field by tractors, which churned up the heavy ground even more, leaving deep mud tracks everywhere. We were warmly welcomed by a couple of English university students, and we were not going to be put off by the mud, so we made ourselves comfortable in our tent.

The cooking facilities were primitive but clean, and once I got the hang of things, we sat down to sausages, bacon and egg. The boys were quite excited by it all and happy to play in their side of the tent; John and I opened a bottle of wine, and unpacked the rest of our suitcases. I was put off slightly by the hordes of earwigs which had taken refuge along the dry folds of the tent curtains.

In the morning, we were awakened by the jingling bells of the cattle herd in the field, right beside us. It was cold with a heavy dew as John walked to the farmhouse to collect the warm, fresh milk. Peter was fascinated with the cows, and couldn't wait to run up and stroke them. They were gentle and didn't mind him one bit, but grazed unperturbed, and each morning this became a ritual for Peter; he would be up and out into the fields with the cows before breakfast.

The sun shone for the whole week that we were there. The warmth of the day filled us with happiness, and we swam in the ice-cool, clear lake within the shadow of the lush green hills high above us. The boys were happy to play with friends near to where some canoes were tied up at the edge of the lake, and we kept an eye on them from the tent. Within moments, I was astonished to see my three-year old afloat aboard a canoe on his own and being carried out into the lake by the current, with two very guilty looking brothers standing shouting to him from the edge of the water. By chance, a quick-thinking German gentleman, suitably attired, swam out into the lake to rescue our stranded son. Who let the canoe loose, is still being debated to this day!

The second week of our holiday took us through the Dolomites but, when I ran into a large boulder en route to Ravenna, damaging the car sump, we were forced to find local accommodation in Bolzano for a couple of days, while the car was being repaired. The weather was kind to us all the way, and our boys were marvellous little travellers, and slept during the long hours in the car.

The camp tents, at Ravenna were dispersed amongst

tall eucalyptus trees and sand dunes near the sea. It was the height of the tourist season, and we were appalled at the sight of hundreds of bathers, swimming with their tiny tots in some of the dirtiest water I had ever seen. I only noticed the raw sewage floating around the foaming waves after we had entered the water. I quickly removed my protesting boys, who wanted to stay and swim. On our second night we were almost blown away by a violent sand storm, which threatened to take us along with it, as we rushed around battening down everything we could. The tent never recovered its shape. Some people lost their shelter while they slept, leaving clothes and debris scattered about the camp site, and sand everywhere. I felt that we had no sooner arrived at the camp site than we were packing to return home. As we drove off, I had that awful sinking feeling that all the holiday had done was to postpone a showdown between John and his boss.

John's mother flew out from England to stay with us for a week, leaving behind his father who could no longer withstand long journeys and never really recovered his strength after his bout of tuberculosis some years earlier. He continued to work for the Forces Help Society in Newcastle, but he became increasingly breathless and even the short walk from the bus, up Grey Street to his office, was an effort. He had survived a gas attack in the trenches during the First World War, and I always remember him as a frail man with a persistent cough, yet he remained a man of quick wit and lively brain. He took a keen interest in John's career and meticulously mapped out where he had travelled. All the photographs and letters which he had received from John when he was overseas, were carefully put into albums and brought out on occasions for us all to look at and talk over.

At home in Macclesfield, my father had had a close brush with death while carrying out some maintenance work beneath his car. The car jack snapped, trapping him under the vehicle. With no one around to help, it took my mother's super-human effort to lift the vehicle off him enough to free his legs, so he could scramble out. He emerged with badly cut legs and other superficial wounds and was well aware that if my mother had not been in the house and heard him call, the consequences would have been very different. My mother despaired of him when, months later, he took off the end of his index finger on the circular saw while cutting wood in the shed.

John returned to duty after our holiday in Austria and Italy, hoping that the break would mend the growing rift between his Squadron Commander and himself, but nothing had really changed. In fact, I could say that the tension became worse. John looked so downcast and miserable and I looked on, powerless to help, as the whole scenario began to have an effect on our lives.

I had a husband with impeccable morals, and whose loyalty to his regiment knew no bounds. He had a great respect for any officer who knew his work, but could be dismissive of those who only 'played the game'. Known as 'Fighting John' to many, he believed in encouragement, firmness and fairness to all those below him, and respect and loyalty to those above him, and was deeply wounded and offended when he was more or less accused by his boss of disloyalty! "Disloyalty to whom?" he asked. "The man or the unit?" His loyalty to the regiment was unquestioning, and he strove hard to learn his trade – after all, he had been taught by the best! He was an honest man. Honesty in the sense of not being afraid to say what he thought, even if sometimes it didn't suit everyone. At Gutersloh, he despaired and grew frustrated with a boss who was more intent on making a name for himself on the golf course, and whose judgement sometimes he felt was questionable. Other members of the unit, despite their grievances, were not able to speak out, because in the end it was all about people's careers. John was not afraid to speak out, but it did him little good; it wouldn't be the station that would write his confidential report! Suffice to say, there was no redress, and he did not get his promotion.

However, there were compensations. We had had some magical moments with loyal friends, which was an enormous help through the difficult times. I was overcome when they threw a great surprise party for us a week before we left, and I'm glad that I can count on them as my friends to this day. I felt sad that we were saying good-bye to them, but I didn't look back as we boarded the aircraft to leave, and I wasn't surprised when his boss didn't come to say good-bye.

Chapter Nine

In the spring of 1972, John began a new tour at the School of Recruit Training, at RAF Swinderby, half way between Newark and Lincoln. A tidy, neatly landscaped station, it was divided by the main Lincoln to Newark road, which ran through the centre, between the quarters on one side and the hangars and headquarters on the other. There was always an air of peace and calm about the place, and we loved it there. It was to be the happiest station we were ever on, for both of us; not least because it gave us a chance to wind down from a busy flying station and to put our lives in order, free from the stress of the past, and once again, we made love as we used to.

Having moved around so much and lived in a variety of accommodation, we decided to make our quarter look like a real home. Returning all the Air Force furniture, we bought our own beds and sitting room furniture and, for the first time, I wasn't going to worry about knocking a nail into the wall to put up my pictures. I put up shelves, and my own curtains, and it felt like a real home. Our kitchen window overlooked a vast expanse of open field and the side entrance door of the mess, which was useful: I could time the kettle to boil, as John walked through the mess door, crossed the field and came into the garden through the gap in the hedge.

John spent hours teaching the boys football and playing cricket with them on the field, and they rode around the 'patch' on their bicycles with the other children, in freedom and safety. With a rounded mixture of officers, station life was fulfilling, unhurried, and happy. We entertained or played tennis in the evenings; he taught me how to play squash, although he didn't care to play much himself.

We endeavoured to make time to visit both sets of parents equally on the odd weekend. My brother Martin and sister Mary were now married and starting families of their own, and Peter, who was in the Cheshire Police, was engaged to marry his sweetheart, Rowena, a policewoman. Wherever we were, the family kept in touch.

I had always admired John's ability to teach, and I suggested to him that I embark on a few GCE 'O' level courses at night school and that I would be happy if, with his encyclopaedic brain, he could help me at home with some of the study. Again, I toiled at a desk with him keeping me topped up with cups of tea and the odd bar of chocolate. Studying did not come easy to me, and I felt I had something to prove to myself now that I was much older; it was something that I had always wanted to do and never had the opportunity. John was a great motivator and never, ever patronised, and with his support and unerring patience, I passed.

I ran the station Thrift Shop and, under the supervision of the Station Commander's wife, Betty Groocock, a number of us also embarked on a charity 'quilting bee' project on camp. The station had a huge, fun crowd of people on the married 'patch', and we all gelled wonderfully together. On Christmas and Boxing Days, we opened one of the large station hangars, which was equipped for football and badminton, and got together some of the parents and children for a day's family fun. It was hilarious, finishing up at the mess and our house.

The Regiment Officer on any station holds a unique position, and his skills are highly valued. John got on very well with both of his Station Commanders and his ability as their Regiment Officer was highly respected in return. He spent some time on public duties in London, which gave him great pleasure. This was a tradition which began in 1968, when Andy Anderson took charge of the Queen's Colour Squadron and paraded the first Queen's Guard, at Buckingham Palace, The Bank of England and the Tower of London. Being allowed guests was an added privilege for John, and the invited could watch the parade from inside the ground and attend a very pleasant lunch at St. James's Palace.

In the summer of 1973 I had been over to Cheshire to see my parents with John and the boys on quite a few occasions, and we went sailing on my father's boat at Rudyard Lake and played cricket. Equally, my parents drove to see us at Swinderby. It was about this time that my mother began to show signs of being unwell, but she was never a complainer, having been a fit person all her life. However, she began a series of tests for what the doctors thought was rheumatoid arthritis. I was worried of course. For weeks she came and went to the clinic, until finally being admitted to the Manchester Royal Infirmary for further blood tests. When we heard a fortnight before Christmas that she had leukaemia, we were devastated.

At the hospital she underwent blood transfusions and further tests until her arms were black and blue, and the nurses ran out of veins to inject. My father was motoring in and out of Manchester visiting her each evening, and he looked worn out with worry. It was a terrible time of trial for him. My brother John and youngest brother Robert, who was only eleven years old at the time, found their lives were put on hold during the evenings too. I tried to get to see her as often as I could. She looked pale and tired, and on occasions became irritable. I realised later that her dilated pupils were due to the morphine that was being administered. She was so happy to have a simple thing done – like her hair brushed, as she hadn't the strength to lift her arms to do it herself. We worried and prayed for her at that time. It was during the miners' strike, and the hospital staff were constantly on the alert in case of sudden disruption to the sensitive electronic equipment. Twice, she had to be rushed to theatre to be given emergency resuscitation and oxygen. Although we knew the prognosis was poor, and there was little chance that she would live beyond a few months, we tried not to lose hope. There was added frustration when my brother, Peter, on a visit to see her, had his car stolen outside the hospital and had to taxi back home.

We were unprepared for the news that came a few days after Christmas. We hadn't a telephone at home, so when we received an urgent message from the station guardroom one evening, to ring home right away, we knew it was bad news. My father, with a quiet, sombre voice, just said, "Your mother died at nine this evening." I was beside myself with grief – I knew it was coming and I thought I was prepared, but in my heart I wasn't. She was a wonderful lady who had come into our lives at the time of our greatest need. She had been a good mother, and asked few favours from life; a caring, honest and thoroughly maternal person who always smelled of fresh Johnson's baby powder.

Our dear friends, Milly and Derek Ikin, were a source of strength to me at the time, as were Maurice and Claudia Benee, who took care of our youngsters while we went to attend the funeral and stay on to give some support. All our family were there. We were close, joined together again in grief, and once more my father was facing the future on his own, bringing up Robert. Borne down with grief, and perhaps bearing some feelings of guilt about the past, my father began to look a broken man. I know that in his heart, though, he had truly loved her.

1974 saw us on the move again. This time to quarters at RAF Middleton-St.-George, in County Durham (now Teesside Airport), where John was to begin a tour on Ground Defence Training with the Royal Air Force Regiment at Catterick, the home of the Regiment.

John Elliott began senior school at Hurworth, which meant a long bus ride each morning for him, and Peter and Richard attended junior school in town. John left on the station bus each day with others, to drive the twenty-two miles to camp, leaving early and returning late in the evenings. We liked the area, had nice neighbours and I was content to help with the nursery school while we were living there. However, after eighteen months, I became frustrated at the length of travelling time it took to get to see my friends and I missed much of the social life on base.

With the boys having had so much disruption in their education, we contemplated boarding school for them, with a possible move nearer to RAF Catterick for us, and we made enquiries via friends about Ashville College, a public school in Harrogate. We paid a visit to the school and liked the Headmaster. If John was to attend, he would need to pass both the school entrance exam and an interview. He worked very hard at his studies, even working some weekends with John, and we were proud of him on the day of the interview, when he passed with flying colours. His uniform list was incredible, and again, there were those labels!

We looked around Catterick Village for a house, and bought our first home together: a Georgian, three-bedroomed house. Ideally situated on the A1, with access to the North and South, we were near to friends, and Peter and Richard were able to walk across the road to their new school. Harrogate was less than an hour away, so we were near to John Elliott, and we were half way between John's parents and my father.

Catterick was a happy station for us. Group Captain Kingsley Oliver was the Station Commander at the time, and he and his wife, Isobel (a leggy, Lauren Bacall look-alike), had sons the same age as ours. We had known them both from our old Changi days, and we became good friends. John was happy. He was working amongst people he knew and liked and had served with many of his colleagues before on other squadrons. There was a sense of camaraderie on base and, again, we were able to take part in station life, which made it doubly enjoyable.

At home in the quiet, pretty village, I tackled the

gardening, and wallpapered, decorated and painted until the place was more or less how we wanted it to be. We got to know some of our neighbours and generally liked the place. Not far from the race course, open fields and the river Swale, the boys enjoyed freedom and liberty to a greater extent than before, but I was strict with them (perhaps overly so at times), but they were now in their teens and I had their safety and welfare in mind. Our neighbours, Shaun and Lesley Clarke, were expecting their first child. Shaun was a member of the mountain rescue team; he was also a mean player on the banjo! Before long we were introduced by them to the fascinating beauty of the Dales. From Richmond to Leyburn, and Reeth to Wensleydale, we spent hours on long walks, with the boys, who loved picnicking on the soft, grass verges beside the narrow, winding stream at Grinton. Peter played for hours, practising his engineering skills, by damming up the river with stones, and watching the water flow over them. We watched the sun's rays cascade amongst the purple-heathered hills, walked across narrow fords and amongst black-faced Dales sheep. We also got to know the small, local pubs, who welcomed their walkers; they all knew Shaun, of course, so there was always a warm welcome for us, with a roaring fire in the grate, and a glass of the local brew.

Sadly, but not entirely unexpectedly, John's father, who had been unwell for some time, died in Newcastle. John's mother was very family-orientated, and John went north to help her during this very difficult period. Happily for us, she was an independent, mobile lady, who loved playing Bridge and meeting up with friends once a week at Fenwicks for coffee; but we tried to keep in touch as often as possible by going north to take her around the beautiful Northumbrian coastline and out to lunch.

At about this time, news reached us that our friend Maurice Benee was killed in his helicopter while on exercise in Norway. His tiny daughter, Tamsin, was only a few weeks old when the family came to stay with us at Catterick, and only a few months old when her father died. We did not hear from Claudia, his lovely wife, again and we lost touch altogether, although I have a happy footnote to add to this sad event. Many years later, I was watching a programme early one evening about the training of Air Force cadets from Cranwell. A young female Officer was being interviewed, by the name of Tamsin Benee. Could this be the baby I once held in my arms? I had a few photos which I had taken at Catterick at the time of their stay with us. I gathered a few together; one was a photo of her as a baby, and a couple were of her parents, and I sent them with a letter to Cranwell. I received a lovely reply. Tamsin was indeed Maurice's daughter and, like her father, she was training to be a helicopter pilot. She was overjoyed with the photos – the only ones, she said, that she possessed of her father in the early days and I was delighted, of course, when I later received a phone call from Claudia after so many years.

Shortly after we saw Peter away to Ashville College, I decided to run a small 'play group' from my home, for about six youngsters of pre-school age. I put my DIY to use and built storage cupboards to take the stock of toys that I had to buy, plus books, paints, puzzles and loads of Lego. The children were a grand little lot, with lively personalities. All of them could count, knew their colours, and could do simple jig-saws before going to primary school, and I was quite proud of that. I finally gave it all up after almost two years, to fulfil my lifetime ambition – to nurse.

It had been quite a few years since I had gone for an interview and when I put on my grey suit I knew that I looked good. As I walked through the hospital doors, I almost chickened out, but John had had such confidence in me, that I felt I couldn't let HIM down. The interview must have gone well as, a fortnight later, a letter of acceptance dropped through the letterbox. Then all the nerves began and I thought of all the studying, the nagging self-doubt in my own ability and such. In all this time, John was a tonic for me. "Of course you can do it," he would say; with all my self-doubt, he never once lost confidence in me. During this time, John got a short posting to RAF St. Athan in Wales.

When I began training at the Friarage Hospital in Northallerton, it was all that I hoped it would be. We bought a small Mini for me to get to work and John had a Toledo. It was a long drive to and from the hospital. There were high times, lows, some sad times, and rewarding times. I met some lovely people in the course of my training. I especially loved the orthopaedic wards, and I found the workings of the skeleton reasonably easy to understand: the working bones and muscles, levers, hinge joints, gliding, pivot, ball and socket. I was in my element; with the origin being fixed and the insertion being freely movable... flexion and extension... how could I go wrong? I had a clever bunch of colleagues – there were nine of us altogether on our intake; we had fun!

All through that time, I had a great deal to thank my husband for, because for eighteen of those months, I only saw him one weekend in the month when he came home from RAF St. Athan. He was very supportive throughout, especially when I came home feeling rather weary, having had a long hard day on my feet, to more study, and – oh, boy, did I put some hours in! When I finally completed my studies, he knew more about a myocardial infarction and how the body worked, than many of the nurses.

I was still nursing when I received the good news of a posting for John to RAF Leeming in Yorkshire; we were both elated. The station was only an eleven-mile drive south, which meant that we could stay put in our home in Catterick Village. Having always loved working on a flying station, and Leeming was then growing, the posting proved to be an excellent move for him in more ways than one. Appreciated for his enthusiasm and dedication, he was well thought of by his Station Commander, Group Captain John Curry, and everyone else. Aside from his normal duties as the Station Regiment Officer, there were two royal visits, and the freedom parade and remembrance parades in Northallerton to arrange. When Prince Andrew began his flying training on the station, John was asked to stay on for a further few months, which he was happy to do.

At some stage in 1982, he spent a time at the Ministry

of Defence as one of the many advisors during the Falklands war, when 63 Rapier Squadron, commanded by one of our friends, Squadron Leader Ian Loughborough, left Germany on the QE2 bound for the war zone. The Falklands became the first "media" war. It was not a major world conflict, but a war fought in the frosts of winter; a war of shadows and darkness; and where those who fought along side each other, discovered something new about themselves.

Certainly it was a war which brought heartache and pain to many who could only watch and wait as the conflict unfolded before their eyes. We were concerned as we knew many of the service people involved, and prayed for those families whose loved ones did not come home. Finally, we all breathed a sigh of great relief when the conflict ended in June.

Months later John flew out to Fort Bragg in the United States to do the Psyop War course, working until the early hours of each morning. He kept himself fit by running through the pine forests of the camp every day during his lunch hour. He graduated top of the course, amongst all the American and Allied Officers present – all twenty two of them – and I felt proud of his achievement. The United States Army showed their appreciation, and made much ceremony of it, awarding him a desk-top set and an honorary medal from the Eighty-second Airborne Division, which he was most proud of. He enjoyed his time in the States, made friends and, being an avid reader of military history, took the opportunity of visiting military museums and places of interest.

Our final posting, to Biggin Hill in Kent, was a contrast from the hills and dales of the north. John took up the post at the Officer and Aircrew Selection Centre, but before he left Leeming, he was awarded his promotion: we were both over the moon.

I stayed in North Yorkshire to graduate, finish my nursing, and sell the house in the village, which had been our home for eight years. John Elliott's dedication to his studies, and sport, at college produced good grades, and he left home to begin working at Lloyds Bank in Darlington. Peter, who was waiting to go to Nottingham University to read Chemical Engineering, worked for a few months in Bromley with a couple of holiday tour firms, and Richard, was in his last year at Ashville. When I eventually joined John at Biggin Hill, he was well settled into station life and work. We moved into quarters on camp once again and we turned the smallest bedroom into a study; he would sit for hours writing out his reports on the young cadets that had been interviewed that day, while I kept the coffee going.

We loved the area and, living on the station at Biggin Hill, you could almost feel the history of the place. Pictures of pilots, long gone, hung on the walls in the officers' mess. A Spitfire stood as a reminder of the station's historic past in front of the beautiful St. George's Chapel, with its stained-glass windows, dedicated to the war heroes. A closer look at one of the windows reveals a minute mosquito insect, which had been cleverly incorporated into one of the coloured panes.

London was only a short train journey away, and we

were able to enjoy shows, museums, and all the places of interest. I saw more of my father, my brother Peter, now a marksman with the Metropolitan police, and Mary, who was nursing at the Naval hospital at Haslar in Gosport. I was also able to meet up with my friend Jenny Loughborough once a month. She would travel into the city from one end of London, and I from the other. We would eat our lunch at Lewis's, do a spot of shopping, stop for tea at Selfridges, then go our separate ways home.

Richard joined us on camp after his term at Ashville and found himself a small part-time job. My sister's sons, Richard and Stuart, would come to stay and the whole lot of them, in their exuberant youth, began to explore the highlights of London. Richard started six months training with the Air Force at Hereford. Up to now, nothing in my life had been so demanding yet so enjoyable as having my boys and watching them grow up and turn into fine young men. I was proud of their achievements, although I didn't always take the time to tell them so. And yes, I missed them when one by one they left home to make their own way in the world, but I was proud of the fact that they were very capable and thoroughly nice young gentlemen.

For the first time since being married, John and I felt free to take a holiday abroad and headed for the beauty and warmth of Tavira in the Algarve.

With only a couple of years to go before retirement from the Air Force, and the possibility of OASC, moving elsewhere, John felt that the time had come to look for a new career that would take him to sixty, and that this should be done sooner, rather than later. He answered an advert for a vacancy as a tutor at the Civil Defence College at Hawkhills in Easingwold, North Yorkshire, and was granted an interview. Leaving by train very early on the Friday morning for York, wearing his dark, pinstriped suit, he looked confident and good. It was a very hot day. Before he left, I suggested that he wear braces instead of a belt for his trousers – this, I said, would give the suit a better line and therefore a neater appearance. On his return in the evening, he said that he felt that his interview had gone well. However, he didn't thank me for suggesting that he wear braces under his jacket, for when invited to take his jacket off, he felt he couldn't, so he sat and sweltered all through the interview, while perspiration ran down his back. There had been a great number of candidates for the post, some were senior military personnel and as a result he doubted he would hear anything further. He returned from Yorkshire, feeling that he hadn't lost anything by attending the interview, and he put the day's proceedings to the back of his mind. About three months later, he phoned me from work to say, that he had been offered the post at Hawkhills, and that they wanted him to take up the post as soon as possible. The news threw us into a minor panic: we suddenly had an awful lot to do, not least to find somewhere to live again.

My father had moved to Warsash near Southampton a year earlier to be nearer my sister and the comfort and warmth of the south coast – which would be kind to his bones, he said! He so loved being by the sea.

John and I had become accustomed to being in the

south and quite liked the area, so we put a deposit down on a brand new three bed-roomed house near Warsash, mainly as a bolt-hole for the boys to come home to. We were assured that there were quarters available at the college to rent, so John and I drove up to take a look. What greeted us was a nightmare. We were shown around a couple of houses, both of which were in a dreadful state, and there was no way I was going to begin cleaning before I could move in. Suddenly, we were catapulted into activity. Our well-laid plans were thrown into turmoil; so much so, that we had to alter our plans to buy in the south, try to recoup some of our deposit, and endeavour to look for a house in Easingwold itself. Whatever we were going to do, we had to think carefully, and fast.

Meanwhile, John and I attended his last ever guest night in the service and we were happy that our dear friends, Air Commodore and Mrs. Anderson, despite their busy schedule, were able to come as his guests – an excellent and fitting finish to John's RAF days – Andy and John went back a long way. It was a wonderful evening: we had a lobster dinner, which was a great surprise.

There were two retirees being dined out that evening. The first officer, who gave his thank you speech, read through a dozen pages of script on his service career and had the listeners falling asleep by the time he got to the end – no one would have minded much if it had been amusing, but it wasn't. John thankfully, spoke on his feet and kept his words to a minimum.

At the first opportunity available to us, we rushed

north for a weekend to look for property, but we really hadn't got a clue where to begin, and walked around York and Easingwold, collecting as many brochures as possible. Fortunately, I met a colleague from my nursing days, and she kindly sent brochures of house properties in the area to us, which was a great help. After another visit to the town and a look at three houses, we finally settled on one that we liked. Within two hours, we had driven to Darlington, settled a mortgage, returned to the house and arranged a date to move in. John set about finalising his premature retirement from the service – he still had two years to serve, and hoped that there would be no last-minute hitch.

When John began work at Hawkhills, I remained in our quarter to arrange for the removal men to collect our contents, and I then drove north to be ready to see the crates into our new home, then back again to the quarter to clean and tidy – I was more than well-versed on hand-over; the Families' Officer would arrive with the file of the contents of the quarter: plates – six, glasses – six, and so on, broom – one, plugs – eight, as you scrambled around checking the lights and electrical equipment. Now I suppose everything comes with plugs attached! Thank heavens there would be no more of that! Every scrap of the cooker in pristine condition – as new; washing or polishing the kitchen floor backing out of the door. Anyone who has ever lived in a service married quarter will know the routine. Checking the dustbin and stuff in the garage – the list could be endless and there was always a great feeling of relief when 'march out' went well.

In the early eighties, the IRA stepped up their bombing campaign on the British mainland and I shared some worries with my sister-in-law, Rowena, in London. The miners began their long strike, which turned families against each other, and in April we watched the Libyan siege on television, knowing at the time that my brother was one of the marksmen on the roof, and were deeply saddened at the shooting of Policewoman, Yvonne Fletcher.

We went up to Hereford to attend Richard's passing out parade and stayed with friends. The day began with sunshine. John and I, quite emotional with pride, watched our youngest son and his young contemporaries, looking tall and smart in their blue uniforms, white belts and gloves, march on to the parade square. The weather forecast threatened rain, and contingencies had been made for a hangar parade, just in case. However, the parade revue was well underway in the open air, before the heavens opened, with an almighty downpour. It was too late for any change, and everyone was soaked to the skin. When it was all over, the relatives and friends gathered afterwards for refreshments and to meet the training staff. After all the formalities, we drove back home with Richard. When a careless owner of a Volvo reversed back into us at a petrol station, we sustained a broken headlight and front wing damage. The damage was enough to cause us some grief as we joined the motorway with hundreds of other vehicles, in the dark, and in torrential rain.

Richard finally left home to take up his duties with Air Movements at RAF Lyneham in Wiltshire, Peter had begun his studies at university, and John continued to work his way up the ladder in banking. Suddenly the house seemed very empty indeed.

Easingwold, a place that I had not heard of before going to live there, was a growing market town, about nine miles away from Thirsk. It nestles amongst the tall undulating Hambleton hills and rolling countryside of the Vale of York. It has a wonderful mild, moderate weather system, with no extremes; winters are not the harsh winters we had at Catterick. John and I spent a few weekends exploring the area. The York we see today, is vastly different to the York I saw when we arrived in 1984. There had been a great deal of adverse criticism about the area meted out in the press from overseas visitors but perhaps the greatest publicity came after the Minster fire of that year. Now, it's the prettiest place to see, with many derelict areas renovated, new homes, and a revitalised city centre, and with so many places of interest, it has got to be the best place to live.

I registered with the nursing bank, where the work was varied and the hours flexible, and my work took me around the local countryside.

Chapter Ten

1986 had all the promise of good things to come and, free from constraints, we returned to Africa for a three week holiday through a tour company, to Kenya. Nairobi had changed quite a bit in twenty-odd years, but there were still places we could recognise. There were more hotels in the centre of the city, catering for tourists. Hawkers stood on every street corner, and the traffic was a nightmare. We visited a couple of game reserves, with their immaculate up-to-date game lodges, and stayed at the Kilimanjaro Safari Lodge – initially known as the Kilimanjaro Safari Camp. I understood that it was from there that Ernest Hemingway gazed, from what must have been a tent then, and was inspired to write *The Snows of Kilimanjaro*. My father had known Ernest Hemingway and remembered him more for his partying than his writing. Kenya's wildness, had been tamed by the many tourist carriers that rushed around to catch glimpses of the animals, churning up dust, leaving hundreds of dust devils swirling around. There was still a magic about the place, though. We followed our safari with a short break on the coast at Mombasa, visiting the ruins at the lost city of Gedi, and touring the ancient, indestructible Fort Jesus, with its museum of coastal antiquities, ceramics, and carved doors. John had the opportunity to hone his Swahili, which the Africans appreciated and loved, and when we arrived back in England, we vowed to begin saving right away, for another trip to Africa.

A week before our return I hadn't been very well and

put it down to a food bug. However, when the sickness persisted, I knew it was more serious. Blood tests proved that I had hepatitis. Eventually turning a sickly yellow, I lost a stone in weight and itched and scratched myself almost raw for twenty-nine miserable days. John again was patience itself and was there for me. On the thirtieth day, like some miracle, my colour returned, and I felt trim and looked good. The problem after that was that I didn't want to lose any more weight and began eating my heart out to put weight back on – how foolish can one be!

That year, and only months after joining the Air Force, Richard surprised us with news that he and his girlfriend were expecting a baby. The news hit us like a hammer blow at the time as both of them were still very young. However, I tried to have positive thoughts about their situation – what had happened, had happened, and we had to do what we could. Strangely enough, I fretted more about how I was going to explain the situation to John's mother – to my knowledge, nothing like this had ever happened in the family before. I need not have worried; she was marvellous, gave no opinions, and was extremely supportive. Having got that off my chest, I went down to stay with my father for a few days, and told him. I can't say that he took the news so lightly – the word irresponsible comes to mind!

At the beginning of the December, we received a very cheerful telephone call from Joan's eldest son, Richard, who was overjoyed with the news that he had been chosen with nine other young service cadets to go to Kenya to help the Royal Engineers with a building programme for a local school at Isiolo, and to help with digging and fencing for the Rhino Conservation Trust. He could hardly contain his enthusiasm, as he talked of his excitement, and of wanting to experience some of what his grandfather and his mum had experienced. We were delighted for him. He was always enthusiastic in anything he did, and he was a personable, handsome, fit young man, who loved to try his hand at everything and loved life.

We saw Christmas in, and prepared ourselves for a year that would alter some of our plans. Richard rang from hospital on the afternoon on 24th January, to say that Minnie had had a son. I was delighted that he was so happy. A few days later, I went down by train to stay with Mary, and arranged for Minnie and Richard to come down to meet me at her house in Stubbington, as I had no car. They were only an hour away and I looked forward to meeting Minnie and my new grandson, Nathan, properly. We had tea, and talked at length about what their plans were for the future. Mary's Siamese cat, Gizmo, caused us much amusement because each time Nathan cried, he craned his neck to look in to the carry-cot, quite bemused at the baby's cat-like cries. After tea they left to go back to Lyneham, and I was left wondering what life was going to be like for the two of them with a tiny baby to look after. Neither talked of getting married, and I didn't know how the service viewed couples living together in quarters, or if it was even possible. When they left, I felt helpless, but Minnie was not my daughter and I had no rights over the baby. That evening, 5th February, Mary had arranged for us to have a supper party for my father's birthday. We sat around talking, joking and feeling light-hearted and happy, and I tried to put any problems that I had out of my mind. Just as we were about to sit down to dinner, we received the most devastating news possible. It was from the Reverend Davey, in Liskeard. He said that he was at home with Joan, who had just received news from the army that her son, Richard, had died at Archers Post in Kenya, on the 4th – the day before. He was only twenty-one years old, and had only three days to go before he was due home. To add to the sadness, he had died on his younger brother, Stuart's, birthday. The whole room was hushed. My father, uttering the words, "Oh my God," left the room and went home, and I felt ill to the pit of my stomach. Although Mary insisted that we eat our meal, none of us felt like eating. We felt helpless, and I just knew I wanted to be with Joan at that moment. I hired a car the following day, drove the four hours down to Cornwall, and was greeted at the door by one of Joan's friends. The sight of my sister, sitting rocking herself in the chair with red, swollen eyes, and tears running down her cheeks was more than I could bear. How could God let this happen I thought! I put my arms around her, and we cried together. By the time I arrived, people had beaten a path to her door. Surrounded by beautiful flowers and cards, from caring friends, I felt inadequate in such a situation, and just let her talk, hoping that she would gain some comfort by my being there. Stuart, who was away serving with Royal Electrical and Mechanical Engineers (REME), had been told of his brother's death, and was on his way home from the army, and Victoria, who was suffering from the loss of her eldest brother, went to school that morning to be with her friends. The press had called a number of times, and local television news announced his death.

Meanwhile, Joan and Brian awaited further news from the army as to when he would be flown home after the post mortem. I rang John at Easingwold to tell him of the tragic news, because he had expected me back home the following day. I then rang my Richard at Air Movements RAF Lyneham to tell him, and to say that there was every likelihood that his cousin's body would be flown in to the station. It was a painful couple of weeks for Joan and her family as they awaited further news from the army, and the outcome of the post mortem, which was to be carried out in Nairobi. Ironically, a few days later we received postcards from Kenya, which Richard had written the day before he died, saying what a wonderful time he was having out there.

I returned home to Easingwold to John, who had kept the fact quiet that he had been confined to his bed for a few days with back pain. He was given tablets to ease the pain, and had relied on two old walking sticks, which he kept by his bedside, to get to the bathroom. He had managed to get down the stairs to answer the door, by sliding on his bottom. He was in dreadful pain, despite the pain-killers he had been given by the doctor. Our good neighbour had cooked a meal for him, and he hadn't been short of visitors from work.

In Nairobi, the post mortem on Richard established that he had died of anthrax. He was cremated out there, and the casket returned home to England with the army. It was a sad day for all of us, as we gathered together, with Major General Mathews, his Commanding Officer, Major Bennet, Officers and Soldiers of 300 Troop and other service colleagues in attendance. A green beret was placed upon the casket, and Reverend Davey was quite emotional as he spoke kindly of him, and praised his work for charity. The casket went to rest in the church cemetery in Liskeard.

I spent a great deal of time travelling down to the south of England that year. My Richard and Minnie married six months later, moved into a high rise block of army flats in Woolwich, and settled down to life with their baby. We saw them often, as Minnie loved the Yorkshire countryside. For John and I, it was a great joy to have a small body around again; we watched him learn to roll over, then sit up, then crawl and, finally, stand. He was loved, cuddled and swooned over, and became the apple of his grandparents' eye, and he brought us great happiness. However, all good things had to come to an end, and after eighteen months they left Woolwich for a tour in Sardinia, which they were very happy about.

Minnie wrote regularly, and we received tapes of Nathan beginning to talk. I missed them so terribly, but was filled with joy, when John came home one day to say that he had booked a holiday for us in Sardinia, at a hotel chalet near the coast at Marie Pinetta; about half an hour's drive from Cagliari. We flew out to stay for a fortnight, occasionally seeing them at their flat in town, and every other day they drove out to the coast to see us. Nathan loved the beach, and the hours I spent with him in the swimming pool. In that fortnight, he began to paddle around with his arm bands on, and by the time we left, he had learned to swim; I captured hours of his progress on film. With little respite from the extremely hot weather which reached the nineties each afternoon, he slept on our bed with a small fan whirring across him to keep him cool. Richard's small silver Mini wasn't able to take the four of us on long trips, so he hired a dormobile to take us around the pretty parts of the island and beaches. We enjoyed our break with them, but I was aware of something in the air which I couldn't put my finger on – an intuitive feeling that all was not well. I left Sardinia with a heavy heart, knowing that I would not see Nathan again for another two years.

How wrong I was. A few months later, while we were taking a short break, motoring around the south coast to see my sister and stopping off at Lyme to see Andy and Sandra, Richard had been trying to contact us on an urgent matter. On our return to the house, there were frantic telephone calls asking, where had we been? The phone calls were to alter all our plans for the next ten years at least. A break up of any marriage with children brings its own unique problems. We were to experience some of the heartache of what many families go through. Trying not to take sides brings scorn and mistrust, but I decided that whatever had happened I would stand by my beliefs, blame no one and try my utmost to be fair and supportive. The most important person to me was my little grandson.

After a few months, a lot of soul searching, and many prayers, we were given care and control of Nathan, while Richard and Minnie had joint custody. When it came down to the real business of looking after him, John and I took sole responsibility for his welfare. Richard was able to continue in the services, and was responsible for financially supporting him. He loved his little boy, and knew that as long as he was with us, we could give him a loving, stable home. The Air Force were very sympathetic with his predicament and posted him to RAF Leeming. The Station commander at Leeming at the time was Rick Peacock Edwards a friend from the Gutersloh days. During the Gulf conflict, Richard was busy on the station, but at least we knew his little son had the opportunity to see him after work most days.

Two days before the end of the Gulf War, John's mother was admitted to hospital. She had always loved to embroider and read, but her failing sight had gradually denied her these pleasures. After consultation with a specialist, we were told that she could have an operation to remove a cataract, but before anything could be done she suddenly had a stroke, which left her unable to communicate and she died a week later. It was a sad time for John. He was about to retire, and we talked of taking his mother on holiday with us after her operation; instead, he was having to go up to Newcastle to sort out the house that he had been brought up in, with all its memories. Three months later, my father, who was on holiday in Cornwall recuperating from an operation, contracted shingles and died suddenly. The aneurysm, caused by the trauma of being run over by a tank years earlier, had finally ruptured. It was the end of a wonderful, caring generation and once again it was an awful low time for both of us.

We managed a short break to Lincoln after John's

retirement from the College, visiting places we knew. Knowing how he enjoyed playing the piano, I splashed out on one as a retirement present and watched the beam on his face when he saw it. I loved to hear him play.

Looking after a youngster wasn't exactly what he had planned for retirement, so it pays to be open-minded in life. We decided that we would enjoy our grandson, for whatever length of time he would be with us, and we got on with our lives, with minor adjustments to our situation, determined to make the most of it.

As Nathan was growing, he kept us busy and on our toes. All the shops and stores, thank heavens, were pushchair friendly – no such perk when mine were young; the only choice then was either to struggle with one child on my hip and one on reins, or leave them in their pushchairs outside the store! We became used to keeping the kitchen cupboards tied up with a long length of string through the handles, to keep inquisitive little fingers out, and the front and back doors had to be locked, when he could finally reach the handles and open the door – I caught him trying to make his escape one afternoon when I forgot! He was an intelligent and likeable child, with his wide, dark, almond-brown eyes and his pretty smile. He attended play group, and then nursery school in the town. Surrounded by young mums, I was introduced to the joys of the Early Learning Centre where Nathan would play for ages with the toys, and so trips to York with him were frequent.

When he began to show an interest in football, John was in his element and encouraged him to play at every opportunity, becoming even more enthusiastic perhaps, when Nathan showed that he possessed reasonably good eye and foot co-ordination. We watched him growing up with a great deal of pride, and were introduced to the 'new age' reading – Roald Dahl's *The Enormous Crocodile* was one of his particular favourites which we read over and over again to him at bed times. When finally we bought him a toddler's tape recorder, *The Incredible Mr. Fox* could take over on the odd evenings before bedtime, while we retired to the sitting room for a long, well-earned drink.

When he began reception class at primary school, I went along to help with the children's reading group. I was never too worried with spending time with Nathan as he was a good reader, and of course I had all the time in the world to read with him at home. Some of the youngsters struggled with their reading and my heart went out to them, as I can remember the difficulties that I had as a child – unable to read properly until about the age of eight.

I shared in a 'school run' with neighbours whose children went to primary school, and waited with equal anticipation with other 'mums' at the school gate for the end of lessons in the afternoon. When the doors were opened, hordes of excited youngster would rush out waving bits of paper or drawings in their hands. The neat youngsters, with their oak and leaf emblazoned crest on their blue or red jumpers, that had left for school in the morning, bore little resemblance to the ones that emerged a few hours later, carrying or swinging their assorted coloured satchels, jumpers being swung in the air, and coats half on, being dragged along the path, as others would dally at the door to swap stories with their friends. Nathan was often one of the last to emerge, kicking a football – not quite the neat child that I had dropped off at the school gates that very morning.

John concentrated on Nathan's particular football skills on the field, with the emphasis on 'ball control' when he got older, much as he had done with our boys. Nathan was almost as good with his left foot as his right one. Before long, a number of his friends began to join in, until there would be about eight of them at the field each weekend, all trying to outdo each other with their football skills.

Like new parents, because of school we found ourselves constrained to school timetables, but we delighted in Nathan's progress and, when his Headmaster chose him to play football for his school, John bubbled with pride as he stood on the side lines cheering him on, although John's shouts of support from the sidelines could be a trifle embarrassing at times and, on a number of occasions, I had to remind him that there were other players on the field too. Despite his praise of others, there was only one brilliant player on the field as far as he was concerned and, that was HIS grandson! In Nathan's early days, there was no football in the community, and so we were delighted when a youthful man, named Peter Nottage, with his infectious laughter and personality, came to Easingwold. A family man and father of two, he took the 'bit' between his teeth, and rallied parents and teachers alike to get something going for the youngsters in the town. The scheme became a great success and soon fifty or more youngsters would appear at the football field for Peter's Saturday morning football sessions – the numbers kept growing. Soon, there was the purchase of football colours, and the Junior League. Nathan went on to captain his school and Easingwold juniors and at one stage Peter suggested that he go to Leeds for junior trials. I felt he was too young, and John and I agreed that he should just continue to play his football at home and keep up with his tennis – all we really wanted for him was to be a good all-rounder at sports, which would give him all the communication skills needed for the big world outside. We would never need to worry about his competitive skills – they were as sharp as ever. We all loved the weekend away match days, come rain or shine, and I was happy to supply coffee for the folks on the sidelines and juice for the youngsters.

We were lucky to have a good neighbour who was a piano teacher and, when Nathan showed an aptitude for piano, he began lessons in earnest. When he ran into difficulties, his grandpa was ready to help – there were wonderful moments, when both of them would be at the piano playing and improvising. Playing the 'Blaydon Races', and jazzing it up as they went, would end with them falling about in laughter.

There were trips to see Newcastle United play and, of course, the black and white team shirts were worn. Kevin Keegan, who was adored by the fans in the north, was a wonderful PR man and each time Nathan wrote to him, there was always a reply from the man himself. Nathan was taken to play football a few times at Benton with 'Football In The Community', a programme run by

Newcastle United for the local children. Then came tennis and cricket, in which he also showed an interest and aptitude, and we were both happy to indulge and encourage him; he was a natural sportsman.

We had the usual childhood illnesses to worry about, and a couple of stays in hospital. One was to have his tonsils removed, after monthly bouts of sore throats and continual use of antibiotics, at which I despaired. Then he had to be admitted for appendicitis. Each time he entered hospital, I worried like any other anxious parent until his homecoming.

In 1994 John and I went off for a short break to the Far East, while Joan looked after Nathan; by now, she was also a grandmother.

We arrived at Changi, after a long but pleasant flight by Singapore Airlines jumbo jet. The memories flooded back of the times we were there many years earlier. The huge terminal building is where RAF Changi once was. Everywhere we went to in Singapore, was clean and the people were smiling and happy as they went about their business of preparing for their twenty-eighth national day parade to be held on the Padang.

Our hotel, Melia at Scotts, was plush, and we swam in the pool which was three stories up, in the shade of a palmed patio, drank our first ice cool Tiger beers, and had our evening meal at the Goodwood Hotel just down the road. The underground Mass Transit Railway (MTR) stations were clean and had a friendly atmosphere, and we used the MTR to get to Raffles where there were a couple of nice eating places, as well as the museum. With tall, glistening skyscrapers competing with the oriental pagoda-like structures and the neat colonial buildings, Singapore is truly a fashionable melting-pot for all races of Chinese and other ethnic groups who are happy to call themselves Singaporeans. Sadly we did not have enough time to visit all the places we would have liked.

After four days, we flew off to Hong Kong and stayed at the Tower Hotel in the centre of the Chinese community in Kowloon, not far from the golden mile in Nathan Road. That evening we met up with our good friends, Sam and Linda Hunt, who we knew from our Gutersloh days. Sam was then commanding Sek Kong and lived at Air House. From our hotel room, we watched the assortment of aircraft negotiate their descent in to Kai Tak airport between the dense high-rise buildings of the busy city.

The weather in Hong Kong was unbearably hot, and the place positively heaved with a sea of bodies, pushing and rushing about. Of all the places I had seen and travelled, I found it quite a culture shock, and a complete contrast from the beauty and calmness of Singapore and its people; in fact I found it almost claustrophobic and intimidating. We managed to see a good part of the island by the Star Ferry, or bus and MTR and spent a blistering-hot day visiting the summit of Victoria Peak, by the funicular peak tram. From the viewing deck at the top, there was an incredible view over the mountains of the New Territories and some of the islands of the South China Seas.

Linda rang us at our hotel one afternoon to warn us of a typhoon threat later that evening and invited us to stay at Air House with them overnight – we were to grab what we could, head for the underground, and she would meet us there. Later the wind blew up and shops were closed and boarded; signposts and billboards were flung about; papers and cans rattled and littered the streets. In fact it was not safe to walk around outside. Even the security staff at Air House were sent home. The next day, clearing up operations began in areas around the island. We caught the bus back into town to our hotel, in time to pack and leave for Kai Tak airport to fly home.

It was after our return from holiday, that I noticed that John looked pale and unwell; certainly the heat of the Far East had affected both of us, but him in particular. On the first evening in the hotel in Singapore he had perspired profusely and was dehydrated. He didn't complain, but I insisted he see a doctor on his return home. An ECG, revealed a mild problem and arrangements were made for him to be admitted to the Coronary Care Unit at the District Hospital for further investigation. After a couple of days he was discharged and I wasn't unduly worried. He looked well, and, after all, people live with irregular heart beats for years. Some months later, he was to experience two more serious scares which followed weeks of endless, interrupted nights, with him waking up breathless. I would sit with my arms around him, trying to comfort him. When you look well, it's difficult to get anyone to take your illness seriously, and he struggled on in the nights with bouts of breathlessness, until he was finally admitted to hospital and given emergency resuscitation, and kept on oxygen. Knowing that he was in the safe hands of the medical staff of the care unit at the hospital, I went home and for the first time in ages I slept through the night.

John had always been a physically fit man and even at sixty-three, he had the physique of a man half his age. He had enjoyed the outdoors, played sport, and being the person he was, he wasn't about to give in to any illness. In hindsight, however, misunderstandings, and a chain of events, would lead me to look further into my own failings, that maybe, I should have insisted that more be done for him earlier. Instead, he looked well, although his heart had struggled for weeks. I will always wonder if I could have done more!

I was frantic with worry the third time he was admitted to hospital and, as I lay in bed in the evenings, I dreaded the phone ringing. Our sons rushed to his bedside once more, after we were given the prognosis that he may live a few more months, maybe a year. We sat silently and I held his hand in mine. I'd heard these words before when I was nursing – but this time they were being said to me. I was stunned. I looked at the man I loved as he lay in his hospital bed, and for a moment, neither of us said a word.

Richard flew off to the Falklands for a four month stint of duty, and John and Peter went back to work, not knowing whether they were seeing their father for the last time. We were all emotionally charged and, at home, I wept and prayed alone, hoping that Nathan wouldn't see me.

John left hospital with enough pills to sink a battleship, vowing to take life a little easier, but he remained positive and optimistic about the future. I admired his personal courage, and he hadn't lost his sense of humour. He could always make me laugh and I loved him for that. Most of all he had the will to live.

We took more short weekend breaks with Nathan, visiting old friends, who we had always promised to see and never made the effort to. Although I worried continually about John, I was buoyed up by his positive attitude and, in the end, if he could be positive then I felt that I should make an effort too. Each time his cardiac clinic review day came, and he was to see Dr. Roger Boyle, he dressed in his suit and tie and looked the picture of health. He was a good-looking man and the nurses looked forward to seeing him. After the first year was reached, to the day, we both – psychologically – breathed a sigh of relief. I worried less when he left for town, or drove anywhere, and began to put the difficult times behind me, as if life would go on for ever.

We went off to Protaras in Cyprus on a short break to join Joan and her husband who had hired a friend's house for a fortnight. John felt fine, took it easy and kept out of the sun. He was always happy to sit and read under a shade on the beach, while we swam down near Fig Tree Bay on the south-east of the island. We hired a moped and bombed around the small picturesque area in a carefree manner.

The following year, we went off to Portugal, again to Tavira, a place where Nathan loved to go. It was our third visit to the area, with its exquisite monasteries and churches, and beautiful floral arcades. A real jewel of the Algarve, it's a place of tranquillity, where tunny and sardine fishing still provide the local fishermen with a living, and where, within a few minutes walk or drive, you can be near the clear waters of the warm Mediterranean. We loved the laid-back, gentle, carefree life of the place and its people, and we promised ourselves that we would make it our holiday destination once a year if we could, providing everyone kept well.

Richard left the Royal Air Force after his term was up and decided on a career in civvy street. He moved to Nottingham and with his personality and sound background of air force discipline, had no difficulty whatsoever in finding employment. He shared a home with Peter for a short while, and began working for a cargo firm at East Midlands Airport, working his way up the ladder to management.

We watched proudly, as our happy grandson grew, made friends and was becoming a thoroughly nice young man. When Richard bought his own property in the area, he wanted Nathan, eventually, to join him, which came as a bit of a shock to John. I was taken aback at the time, but we knew that the move would have to come one day. We decided, mutually, on his leaving us the following year, which would see him complete his primary school education. It was only right that father and son should be together and, what's more, it would give us the freedom in John's retirement to do what we wanted. Meanwhile, Nathan continued to be the apple of his grandfather's eye, and was supported in all activities at school and at football in the community.

We were delighted when our eldest son became engaged. He met his fiancée at a tennis club and, by a long arm of coincidence, her father, Jack, and my husband had both been born and brought up in Heaton in Newcastle, not a stone's throw from each other. Both men had attended the same grammar school in the 1940s. I cannot begin to count the many coincidences I have encountered in my life. It is strange to know that we rub shoulders with the most wonderful people and yet seldom are we able to spare the time to get to know many of them well. We are inextricably linked and in many ways our lives are intertwined. If we stopped to think for just a moment, we would observe that we are no more than a handshake away from people and friends that we have passed along the way. We were very happy for John and Claire and looked forward to their wedding the following year.

In the June of 1997, we took ourselves off by train to the lovely city of Edinburgh for four happy days. It was a place I had always wanted to see and never had the chance to. We booked ourselves into a bed and breakfast hotel near the city centre and had the time of our lives, visiting the castle and the historic sites and museums. We found our way around mostly on foot, and bussed over the Forth Road Bridge to Sea World. The weather was warm and kind to us and Nathan even managed to get his grandfather to climb the winding staircase of The Scott Monument.

We returned home revitalised and ready for Andy and Sandra to stay for a couple of days while they went house hunting. A week later, my sister, Mary, her husband, and Richard came up to stay, and joined John and I to celebrate our thirty-fifth anniversary with a meal out.

We had had a busy three weeks and, when all our

visitors had gone, I decided to take Nathan and go to Nottingham for a few days on the Sunday, giving John time to rest and relax at home on his own, fully intending to return on the Thursday, for his birthday the following day. He rang me on the Monday evening, and again on the Tuesday and seemed happy, and he spent a long time talking to Nathan about football – Tino Asprilla was on the transfer list and there was great discussion about that. Nathan always finishing off with the words, "Love you, Grandpa; bye."

On the Wednesday morning I took Nathan in to Nottingham to shop. We met up with Peter for lunch, and he brought us back by car to the house. I was often reticent about ringing John in the afternoons in case he was resting, so I waited until after four o'clock to ring him to arrange a time to be picked up from the station on Thursday. The afternoon came and went, and I still couldn't contact him. I could only think that he was in Newcastle for the day, which he occasionally took a mind to do, in which case, it meant that he would not return until seven in the evening. Peter and Richard drove us to a park for a walk by the lake, and for some reason, I couldn't get John off my mind. I tried not to let my imagination run away with me, but I didn't enjoy the walk and was glad to return to the house, where again I was on the phone. Seven-thirty came and went, then eight o'clock, and then eight-thirty. I must have rung a dozen times, each time thinking he would be home now. As the time went on, my imagination was running riot, and my nerves were crumbling. I could stand it no longer, and at eight-forty, I rang a dear neighbour and asked her to call at the house.

When the phone rang a few minutes later, I was quite expecting to hear John's voice. Instead, this gentle voice said, " Joyce – John is sitting in the garden, he doesn't look very well, I think I'll just get the Doctor." My heart sank. I gave her Richard's mobile phone number and said that we were on our way home. As I put the phone down, I asked no questions; I didn't want to waste a second. I was miles away, and I just needed to get home as quickly as possible to be with him.

Turning to Peter and Richard, I uttered, "Your Dad's poorly – please take me home."

My poor sons, who sensed that something awful may have happened, responded immediately, and without asking why. Richard picked up his keys, locked the house and we walked to the car and drove off in silence. We left the outskirts of Nottingham and I spared any criticism as we drove at a reckless speed on the motorway, although I knew Richard was a good driver, and I had great faith in his ability. My mind was in a turmoil, and I reached out behind me and held Peter's and Nathan's hands as they sat in the back seat. When the mobile phone rang in the car, Richard insisted on taking the call and I could feel myself going into shock. I heard him reply, "In about an hour," obviously referring to our time of arrival. He said nothing, concentrating on his driving. How stupid I was. All I kept thinking, was please, God, don't let it be a stroke – at the time it was the worst thing I could think of. My head was in a fog and I went numb. As we rounded the corner for home, Richard squeezed my hand and said, "Mum try to be brave." I knew then what Richard had known all along, that John had died. As I entered the house, I was greeted by two uniformed policemen and a policewoman. My sons immediately took charge of everything for me.

No one can ever prepare you for the loss of someone you love. Suddenly my happy ordered world was turned upside down. He was a kind, caring, generous and unpretentious man, who had shared with me the most intimate thoughts and feelings, my worries and my doubts, and who had given me the best and most memorable times of my life. Not only did I love him, I adored him.

For sometime, I just wanted to die – to not feel the hurt and despair anymore, but I had Nathan to think about. While we were at the house, I suddenly remembered that John Elliott didn't know. Richard rang him at home in Bishop Stortford. My family rallied, and friends phoned, sent cards and flowers. In my grief I forgot for a moment Nathan's feelings. While I sat crying in the bedroom one afternoon, a little voice said, "Please don't cry Grandma, remember I've lost Grandpa too!". In my grief, I had forgotten that, around me, I had three sons, and a young grandson, who were all a part of John, and who were hurting too.

I rang our friends, Bill and Betty Hiles, the following morning to tell them my awful news. Most of our friends had known over the months that John had had a heart problem, but even to them the news came as a shock because he looked so well. When I rang Sandra and Andy at home, poor Andy was flat on his back and on morphine injections from severe back pain. I tried to contact as many of our friends as possible to let them know but, of course, in times like these there are friends you forget to tell and I was sorry for that. My good friends Mickey and Mary Witherow contacted other friends for me. I had to get my act together and start planning and making arrangements for the funeral. In all this time, my sons were wonderful and took control of everything for me.

I faced the day of the funeral in a daze. I was overwhelmed and moved at the sight of so many of our friends in the church who had taken the time to travel up from the south of England, many dear friends from far and near who came to say their last farewell.

John had been retired from the RAF Regiment for about six years but everyone knew that he had the Regiment in his blood and I felt proud of once being a part of that life. The Senior Officers present, and David Bremner in his uniform, standing alongside Kingsley, gave the whole proceedings a military, united family feel, and Kingsley spoke a few kind words.

The day was sweltering and well into the high eighties before we reached the crematorium. The service was quick and I arrived back to the house with the family to be told that at the crematorium, Martin's car was broken into by some youths, unaware that they were being observed by Group Captain David Bremner's driver, sitting in the staff car nearby. What followed will be talked about and dined out on for years to come. My brothers, Peter and Robert, both policemen in the MET, and David Bremner, in his RAF uniform, plus driver, took off after the villains and apprehended them about half a mile away. Unbeknown to us at the time, although wondering where everyone had got to, they all found themselves at the local police station waiting to give statements. I think John would have been most amused at the proceedings.

I was amazed at such kindness, the wonderful fragrant flowers, the cards and the caring letters which I received, but one letter will stand out as very special to me. It was one written by a Senior NCO, Sergeant Jerry Gladwell (ex-Sgt – 63 Sqn), who I hope to one day to meet. It read:

> Flying Officer Thackeray, as he was then, was my Flight Commander on 'A' Flight of 63AA at Felixstowe in 1956. When the unit hastily converted to a Field Squadron and was sent to Malta in September of that year, I managed to stay on the strength. This involved a cross-posting to another flight, but a colleague of mine, Sgt. Tony Attwell stayed on 'A' Flight with your husband. Soon after arrival at Malta, 'A' (or as it became known No. 1 Flight) was detached to Idris, Libya. We lost touch for several months. Fond memories of Mr. Thackeray abound. He was a popular Officer and a fair and just Flight Commander. My only regret is not to have served for longer with him.

When I read the letter it brought tears to my eyes. To me he was a wonderful husband, a great communicator, a man with strong family values and my best friend whose pictures still warm my room.

Epilogue

Return to Africa

When my brother, Martin, first suggested a family reunion to Tanzania in East Africa in 2000, to visit the places that we had all known as children, I had my reservations.

I gave the idea quite a lot of thought; not least because my father had said to me, "Remember the good times, always look forward, never go back!". I felt some sadness and loneliness that John would not be with me to enjoy such a trip. Everyone else would be able to enjoy and share in the magical times with their partners. Furthermore, trying to get everyone together at the same time, could prove a logistical nightmare which I felt would all end in tears.

On the other hand, my curiosity, the sheer madness of such an undertaking, and the love and fun of my brothers and sisters, as well as the distant call of the wild, was too great an opportunity to miss; and I also thought that perhaps, it would give me the opportunity to set a few ghosts to rest, and draw to a close, the final part of MY story.

And so, forty years on, return we did – ten of us.

From making all the arrangements to finally seeing the family together at Schiphol airport safely to begin our holiday was no mean feat. Martin, according to Jackie, his wife, kept a file, sent e-mails and, like the methodical man he is, everything was planned like an army movement order! Four of us flew from Manchester, and six from Heathrow. Both KLM aircraft landed at Schiphol airport on time, to await the long flight on another KLM flight to Kilimanjaro Airport, on the 5th February – on what would have been my father's birthday. It was to be a holiday with no preconceived ideas, just our own trip down memory lane, forty years on.

The memory of the flight out to Africa will be of the amount of eating we all did. No sooner had we completed one meal, than another was being prepared. The flight was comfortable and we were looked after, fed and watered well, so that by the time we arrived at Kilimanjaro Airport, in the darkness and warmth, the last thing we wanted was food. As we disembarked to the familiar, mysterious sounds of the evening, the air was mildly cool but comfortable and the stars in the black sky were so clearly defined, that they appeared to welcome us back. Walking through the terminal building, we were greeted by red-waistcoated members of the hotel staff with armfuls of red and white roses for each of us, a welcome to Africa from the Dik Dik Hotel – a wonderful gesture I thought – but that was not all.

In the darkness almost in front of the airport entrance, discreetly hidden under the lights in a canopy of trees, was a small table covered with a white lace tablecloth and set out with a couple of opened bottles of champagne, a number of glasses and a tray of delicate canapés, prepared for us. We were all quite overcome by such a kind gesture and were able to savour the night air, oblivious of the mosquitoes which were perhaps enjoying their main meal of the day – on us! There was a lot of jollity and, afterwards, a number of young native hangers-on volunteered to load the bags on to the bus which was waiting to collect us. None of us had any local shillings with us for tips, so by the time we were ready to set off we were only carrying two holdalls apiece, plus a couple of boxes of goodies for the school; we were spreading so much largesse with five dollar bills, that we established that we had paid tips to every hanger-on and his friend, and his friend's friend, to the tune of at least sixty dollars – they must have thought Christmas had come.

We drove through the darkness, our faces pressed hard against the glass to try and catch glimpses of any animals, and at one stage we saw some small antelope grazing near the verge, highlighted by the oncoming headlights of other vehicles. The bus ride from the airport was slow, punctuated by road humps, and took about an hour. The bus was halted a couple of times along the route by stern-looking, white-uniformed traffic police, who walked around the bus checking: what, we didn't know.

At the hotel we were greeted by the Swiss owners, a pleasant bearded man, Erich Buckman, and his wife, Rose, and ushered into the dining room to a beautifully set dinner-table. How could we refuse? Although none of us felt like eating, we graciously sat down, our stomachs positively bulging, to a wonderful, five-course, international cuisine and even more wine, while a live band played some music for us.

The Buckmans had originally gone out to Africa for a three-month holiday and instantly fallen in love with the country. When they saw the somewhat run-down hotel, they bought it, spending much of their next few years transforming it from the state it was in to the welcoming place it is today, for friends, climbers and tourists alike. The hotel itself is situated about a mile along a turn-off from the main Moshi-Arusha road. Large, wide, wrought-iron gates, manned daily by a native warden, welcome the visitors, and the drive to the courtyard is swathed in a profusion of assorted-coloured Bougainvillaea.

The old colonial-style bungalow, with its red-tiled roof, nestles in the hills below Mount Meru. The natural springs from the mountain are harnessed at various points downstream. An excellently run family business, they improved and added more chalet accommodation and facilities such as a neatly-designed swimming pool. Their attractive daughter, Carmon, looks after the catering side while their son-in-law, Marcus, is the mechanical guru, responsible for the many vehicles that they run for their safari business.

The neat, chalet rooms were comfortable and offered every modern convenience with a shower that had ample hot water which was very invigorating after our long journey. The main electricity generator went off at midnight, but every room had a bedside light which worked on a smaller generator after hours.

Each evening the rooms were tidied and the beds turned down, and a complimentary biscuit and fruit was placed on the table. There were some wonderful touches and the whole place was a delight; the staff were always smartly turned out and were helpful and courteous –

nothing appeared to be any trouble.

Our itinerary was relaxed and laid-back, and on the days that we were not on safari, we went for walks, rested in our hammocks or simply relaxed by the pool, listening to the sounds of water rippling down through rock channels by the chalets, flowing in amongst the beautifully colourful flower gardens – of frangipani trees, banana trees and shrubs – to disappear into the river downstream in the valley, where the monkeys chased each other, cavorting and entertaining us with their acrobatic feats, and evoking memories of the past.

In their extensive garden, each plant, tree and shrub was labelled with its botanical name – which made me enquire as to whether Erich was a botanist – but it transpired that he had all the plants in his garden labelled because he got fed up with folk asking him their names! I wonder how many times he was asked if he was a botanist?

The following day, Sunday, four of us – Peter, Rowena, Mary and myself, took a taxi drive to Moshi. At eleven o'clock, the heat of the sun baked the earth, and the shimmering haze rose from the tarmac road. Our driver was quite pleasant and talkative and was keen to show us around. Along the main road, we were instantly made aware of the necessity for speed restrictions, as he swerved violently to avoid a donkey which strayed across our path. Along the whole route, there were small homesteads, habitations of wooden huts and half-built corrugated sheds dotted around with dukas (shops) selling local beers and soft drinks, and workshops and cafes. Some children played happily by a couple of rusting old car bodies; a reminder that accidents along the road are still commonplace.

The wild animals which had once abounded along the stretch of open grass plain, were long gone, as human habitation took hold and much of the virgin land had been tilled, from the road side to the hills, as far as the eye could see. We saw oxen working the land, as well as old Ford tractors – most of them rusting, with balding tyres – which appeared to outnumber the local cars. The dry, thirsting soil, which awaited the rains, appeared to sustain the few scattered banana trees and coffee acres here and there; while a number of roaming goats browsed and nibbled their way among the untrimmed, coarse grass by the roadside.

As we neared the town of Moshi, the sight of the snow-capped peak of Kilimanjaro brought a lump to my throat – perhaps there was not as much snow as I remember – but a magnificent and powerful sight, nevertheless. We passed the old colonial-style government buildings by the large roundabout and followed the road into town. The KNCU building, once the focal point for commerce and conferences, had fallen into slight disrepair, with the walled gardens gone, leaving bare, well-trodden earth. The steps to the arcade were crumbling. How well I remember those steps – old memories came flooding back – I had stood near them waiting for my lift home from work. My parents and friends, and Joan and myself had walked up and down them each day to work, and I remember John walking up them too. Oh, how at that very moment, I wished that I could have turned the clock back! The long, picture-glass, window-front of the old bookshop had not changed, but the Twiga is long gone – we peered in through the grille shutters (we didn't have shutters in my time) and into the darkness of the shop, but could only see a few curios, carvings and batiks displayed near the window. A group of young native children played along the corridor of the arcade, their wide-eyed, cheeky little faces staring with curiosity at us, appeared a familiar sight. The soul had not gone out of the town or its people, as every face we met seemed rather curious but friendly.

I understand that the local coffee growers still come to the town to get the best deal for their coffee crops, and with rail links to Dar-es-Salaam, Tanga and Arusha, they are assured of good prices; and around the world we can be assured of a good cup of coffee!

Although it was Sunday, we did find a local coffee house that was open to stop for a drink with our driver and, sitting down at our table, we were reminded that white faces were now in the minority. The centre of town had become an expanse of run-down, old-style, colonial-type, concrete buildings and sprawling, wooden outhouses with hundreds of people congregating and chattering in their doorways, or going about their daily chores. Along the many narrow, rough roads in the old areas, the four-wheel-drive vehicles, which were in abundance, churned up the fine dust, coating the outside of every white, chalk-painted building in a film of red ochre. We stopped along the road outside the church of St. Margaret's where Peter had been christened in the fifties; and while the inside of the church rang out to voices of the worshipping congregation, we discreetly took some photos of the outside. The pretty church, once surrounded by neatly-trimmed Bougainvillaea hedges and lovely lawns, was still a symbol of light, but the green lawns surrounding it were now bare, patchy, red earth and the once neat hedge was wild, sparse and wilted; but in the peace and quiet of that Sunday morning, we could hear the outside chirps of bird song and the humming of the bees.

Well before our departure from England, all the family had got together and purchased footballs and other sports and writing equipment for Arusha School, so we were all particularly pleased that we had the opportunity of offloading our cache with the Deputy Headmaster the following day at the school. Martin had pumped up all the footballs, and we bagged all the equipment and boarded our large, comfortable, airy thirty-seater bus and drove to Arusha School.

Although the town had grown dramatically since we were last there, with many of the old shops gone, as soon as we neared the clock tower I recognised exactly where we were. At the school, we were all greeted warmly and shown into the Deputy Headmaster's office, where Martin did the introductions. The visit of ten of us, all suitably attired and looking like a visiting delegation, caused some curiosity and interest among the children, especially as we seemed to have acquired the attention of most of their teachers for a good part of the morning. Everywhere we went, the youngsters, in their uniforms – unchanged since our days at the school – went about the place in their orderly and purposeful manner, and when we met them they greeted us with politeness and beaming smiles.

The school is highly regarded as being the best in the country and was well over-populated with fee paying pupils; there were over sixty youngsters to one teacher, we were told, and, on occasions, three children to a desk. We were shown around and were somewhat shocked at the general run-down state of the buildings. The trees around the school had grown to giant heights, and some lay felled and bleached beside the drive to the school, awaiting transport to be taken away to the saw mill, we were told. We were all in fits of laughter as Martin, Mary and Peter recalled their time as pupils at the school, relaying snippets of the pranks they used to get up to there, and the harsh discipline which was imposed at that time for being caught playing such pranks.

The most wonderful sight was the giant Galapagos tortoise, now a very old man with a thinning shell, showing signs of wear and tear from years of being sat on. A group of youngsters were asked to collect some lily leaves for his lunch, which they brought back by the handful. He is no longer as alert as he used to be, and doesn't move around much anymore, preferring to stay in his own well-worn bare patch of garden which he knows as home. He seemed as popular as ever and remains a great pleasure to everyone. It was incredible to think that this wonderful, gentle giant of a creature had seen generations of us come and go, and experienced the change of time in his own way, and was still loved by everyone!

We ended with a visit into Arusha town, now the

centre for commerce, trade and tourism, and growing fast, with its endless curio shops, tourist and safari companies and countless four-wheel-drive vehicles, which showed every disregard for the highway code. Erich had kindly loaned us the bus for the whole day, so we stopped outside the New Safari Hotel for coffee, where our presence quickly drew the attention of every hawker around. Showing the slightest signs of interest in any of the curios, brought a frenzy of outstretched arms, bearing every item you could think of. The biggest draw was my brother, John, who said he would pay five dollars to the first person who could tell him the football score. There was a sudden exodus, and to my delight, of course, the news came back that Newcastle United had beaten Manchester United. I knew that at home, my grandson, Nathan, would be happy, so I felt it was worth John's five dollars!

The following day, all of us piled into the back of three, four-wheeled-drive vehicles and headed for our first safari to Tarangire National Park, which Martin and Erich had organised for us.

On the long, wide, straight Arusha to Dodoma road – built and financed by the Italians, we were told – we stopped at the Cultural Heritage Centre, boasting a splendid array of carvings and handicrafts, and beautiful batiks. Across the road, we visited the Meserani Snake Park, not suitable for the squeamish though! The grounds were neatly laid out, with delicately flowering pepper trees to give gentle shading. A rather horrific picture poster met our eyes on entering, which served as a reminder that the snakes well deserve the respect they get! The young African guide who showed us around, really knew his craft and greatly impressed us with his knowledge, care and handling of the creatures in his charge; enough to persuade Martin and Joan to dangle a couple of the friendly reptiles around their necks, although some of us were not totally convinced! Further along the road, we stopped near a mature, forked tree which housed the largest bee nest. It must have been about four feet high and a couple of feet wide and was smothered with bees. I had never seen the like of this before, but I became somewhat nervous when the driver insisted on reversing nearer so that we could take some photos, as I was reminded that these were African bees and we were standing in an open vehicle.

A couple of young, elaborately dressed and painted Masai Moran in indigo togas and carrying spears, ran along the side of the road on their way to join some of their colleagues who had herded a large number of cattle into a boma on the open plain. Everywhere you looked, herdsmen were driving their animals to this one place, as others could be seen converging along the road. We were told that it was an outside open market, where the Masai bring their cattle to buy and sell.

We drove on to the Tarangire National Park, which lies south west of Arusha. The place offered so much, its main feature being the Tarangire River which flows from south to north and into Lake Barungi. It's a magnificent landscape: savannah over the Masai Steppe, grassland plain, and lush green vegetation, with hundreds of giant baobab trees, sausage trees and tall palms; owls, martial eagles and vultures flew above us or perched high up on the branches. Despite the heat of the day, the whole area teemed with wildlife: we saw lions, elephants, giraffes, impalas, zebras and buffaloes; a number of troops of baboons chased across our pathway, some groomed each other, and a tiny nursery group, clung on to one another's tails and ran up and down the trees, in the safety of the thick canopy.

We reached the tented lodge as the sun began to set, shining firelight rays across the plains and into the valley below, where herds of game made their way to the river to drink, and we watched two bull elephants with long tusks gently spar with each other. We sat for a while on the balcony with our evening 'sundowner', looking down at the shallow flowing Tarangire River – which must be an incredible sight during the rainy seasons! The high river banks on either side were home to rock hyrax and birds, which made their nests along the length of them. We breathed in the smell of the cooling air and listened to the sounds; later, lightning flashed around the sky and thunder roared in the distance, but it was all too far away to worry us.

Mary and I shared the very last of a whole row of tents, near a marginal clearing a few metres from the dense thicket, which meant a long walk to and from the dining area, which was incredibly scary in the dark. A few elephants had wandered through the area the evening before, we were told, and lions could occasionally be glimpsed nearby. The dim light outside the tent, attracted every flying night bug in the area to our tent's canvas walls, and by the time, we had negotiated the zip fasteners and entered into the darkness of our accommodation, half the pests had joined us. We heard the noise of a lion that evening and movement, but couldn't make out how near or far it was, neither of us caring to take a look: it was very unnerving.

Early the following morning before sunrise, a tiny dikdik delicately stepped out of the bush into the dim light in front of us and stood looking at us for quite a while, and as Mary left to go and get her camera, it nervously tiptoed its way along the hedge, and disappeared into the thicket. The abundance of colourful bird life around us was incredible. At breakfast, it was amusing to watch a couple of them sneak an opportunity to raid the sugar and cereal bowls and being shoo-ed away by frantic arm-and-napkin waving staff, only to return minutes later for another beak full of food. It was highly entertaining.

The early-morning, game-viewing run in the park brought even more spectacular sights. At first it hadn't occurred to us to look up above ground level. We were so focused at eye level looking for game that, when we spotted a Marshall eagle above us, we did look up, and were amazed at the numbers of baboons and monkeys that had taken shelter high in the palm trees and the variety of birds that frequent the area. The whole place was alive and unspoilt and abundant with wildlife. But we had to return to our tents to pack up and load our baggage once more and head for our next destination.

Lake Manyara, is one of Tanzania's smallest National Parks which covers only about one hundred and twenty square miles, of which the lake takes up about eighty-five. Manyara is a Masai word for a particular pencil plant which is used for making sturdy hedges and grows in abundance. The entrance to the park is heavily forested, and long strands of green moss hang limply from the trees nourished by the morning mists, while tall fig trees embrace and smother other more vulnerable trees beside them. We were told by our driver, Simba, that the Manyara area had been devastated two years earlier by flash floods, which came down from the hills, uprooting trees and killing many of the wildlife. The area was rife with tsetse fly, and none of us were to escape their vicious bites as they homed in on us after flying into the vehicles through the open windows; they were persistent critters. Luckily, we had the foresight to carry insect repellent, which we sprayed liberally around ourselves every few miles. We drove to the hot springs, a small, smelly, bubbling opening in the ground, where the hot water emerges from between the rocks and flows gently downhill into the lake, and I couldn't resist taking off my shoes and dabbling my feet in it just to feel its warmth. In the heat-haze of the midday sun, the area resounded to the whistling of the blackthorn acacia. The sun was blisteringly hot, and the area around the lake, appeared dry, arid and lifeless, save for one young flamingo sifting its way through the water, and a few ostriches. Most of the game appeared in singles or twos and threes, there certainly wasn't the vast herds of buffalo that I remembered. The wildebeest and odd buffalo, we observed only from a long distance. The large swathes of trampled ground vegetation were the only evidence that there were wild animals about. There were certainly well-worn tracks and pathways between the dry scrub and thorn bushes which were made by the elephants, but the great herds remained elusive – perhaps they had sensibly taken to the shade. The lush vegetation near to the park gate was a complete contrast to the barren-like lake floor on that day.

For lunch, we stopped at a small out-of-the-way spot, and soon became used to the hole-in-the-ground toilets. Water is very precious everywhere, and even more so in the dry season. However, when a small bowl of warm water was offered to us for washing our hands before lunch, I realised how much we all took for granted this precious natural resource which flows freely with just the turn of the tap.

All three drivers, Simba, Michael and Joseph, were not only excellent guides, but they pitched in to give Michael, the cook, a helping hand to prepare lunch, which was served on china plates on trestle tables, with napkins and utensils – a credit to Carmon and her planning.

We drove on to spend the evening at the beautiful, unobtrusive, tented lodges at Kirurumu. So luxurious were they inside, with every modern facility yet, under their thatched bandas, they gave you every feel of Africa, and I would have loved to have stayed there longer! We arrived just as a rain shower began, which was a welcome relief from the very hot afternoon, and we were met by a number of tall, elegant Masai, dressed in their traditional red and indigo robes, rubber tyre sandals and carrying spears – a great traditional welcome, I thought. We had entered true Masai country, high above sea level on the Gregorian Escarpment of the Great Rift Valley.

The balconies looked out over wild, seemingly untouched wilderness, and the chorus of cicadas and cheerful bird-song began and ended the day. A winding, rock-paved path led to each lodge, every one named after a member of the cat family; ours was called Genet after a small, shy member. At dusk, every pathway was lit by lamps, which led to the main dining and reception areas. We were all awake before our arranged 'wake up call' and sitting outside with binoculars or taking photos. A waiter brought teas and coffees to each chalet before breakfast. Sadly our stay was over too soon, and we had to pack and be on our way again to our next spot.

We drove off to the Ngorongoro Crater, along the smooth dirt road which is now wide enough for about three vehicles. We stopped for a while at a lookout near to a commemorative monument which recorded the names of those killed by poachers, or in accidents, in the name of conservation. Looking down into the great crater, with the sun shining on the lakes, brought back many memories of my last visit in 1959, only weeks after Michael Grzimek lost his life in his light aircraft. The stone slab bearing his name is further along the rim in its original spot, with another plaque below it, bearing the name of his father Bernhard, who chose the crater to be his last resting place.

The journey to the crater floor which took about forty-five minutes, was certainly much quicker and easier these days. The Masai still herd their cattle daily down into the area to drink, leaving great dust clouds in their wake. The place is still the game viewer's paradise, since the animals are more or less captive within the area. We disembarked from our vehicles, walked around taking in the essence of this magnificent place, and stood amongst zebra and wildebeest who strolled calmly among the tyre tracks and took little notice of our presence. The lake brimmed with flamingos, purple herons, pelicans, egrets, and sandpipers, while the hippos wallowed, half-submerged and looking like rocks. Nearby a couple of hyena dipped and sloshed about in the cool of the lake. We saw jackals lope by in the distance just showing above the tall grass. Scattered about were the odd, bleached bones of animals, and three vultures were happily feeding on the dead carcass of a flamingo nearby, until a Rupell's vulture flew down among them and they gave way to his larger size. As we drove around we scanned the area and every shape of fallen tree or grassy mound, is a potential lion or leopard. There were plenty of buffalo about, and three of the magnificent beasts stopped to stare, menacingly bucking their bossed horns at us, as we stared back. A rhino and calf happily grazed some distance away. We followed on to a spot where a number of vehicles had stopped to observe a lion, well camouflaged in some tall thicket, but when we got near to him, he looked rather old and mangy – and he certainly wasn't impressed by us either!

We drove along the road and down an incline in to the picnic area, and were amazed at the sight of the hundreds of four-wheel-drive vehicles which were parked there. You would imagine, that from all this tourism, the whole country would be brimming with wealth but, in fact, it is totally the opposite. Near the hippos' watering hole, we sat down to a wonderful picnic and cool beers, ever vigilant and wary of the hundreds of brown kites which flew menacingly above us, ready to swoop. We were told that a few people had actually been injured by these brazen birds, when they snatched food from picnickers' hands!

Jacqueline, my sister-in-law, who had been unwell before the start of the safari, suffered in silence, but the searing and rising heat of the area began to take its toll on her, so I decided to cut our trip short and the two of us headed out of the crater for the hotel, leaving the others to complete their trip, and join us about an hour later. The way out of the reserve, up a rough, steep road, was quite hazardous and dangerous, with deep ruts and rocks to negotiate. The bumping and buffeting only made matters worse for Jacqueline, who by now was looking deathly white. Our ascent took about forty minutes and, despite the roughness, was quicker and shorter than the way in, and we were both relieved to get to the top of the crater rim and head for our next night stop – the Serena Lodge.

The five-star lodge was comfortable and we were able to get to our rooms to shower and rest before the others returned. The place was hugely popular and full of people coming and going, but it wasn't my favourite place. There was little of the real atmosphere of Africa about it; in fact it could have been any other five star hotel in the tropics. However, the sight from the viewing telescope in the morning sunrise was magical, the crater-floor lakes, glowed like sheets of silver, until the sun rose higher, casting great shadows over the vast opening, revealing the slow movement of the animals across the plain.

Our last day on safari took us along the rim of the crater once more. My dearest wish was to see the Manyara Hotel which was not far away, and our driver kindly obliged. The last time I had seen the place was with my father, when the hotel was nearing completion and we sat and had tea with one of the District Commissioners. I was not disappointed; the place had changed little. The hotel had been added to, and the gardens were now mature and colourful, and had been lovingly tended. I stood once more at the edge of the escarpment overlooking the valley below, with a warm breeze in front of me. I took in every sight and sound, and looked at the surrounding areas below, almost bleached white, and where a few scattered trees lay half submerged in the lake. The smell and the sounds of the afternoon heat were just as I remembered. I left there, overwhelmed by the place and overdosed on nostalgia.

On the way home, we stopped to have lunch, pulling off the main road across rough ground and over part of the old Arusha road. In the distance, we could see children playing outside their school, during their lunch break. Our boxed lunches were filled to the brim with goodies, biscuits and apples, but none of us really felt like eating much, so Peter, decided to pack half a dozen of the boxes with the unopened fare and give it to the three Masai children who were sitting under the shade nearby, tending their goats. We were unaware, however, that we were being closely observed by the youngsters from the school, who came running across the main road towards Peter, who had his hands full, and he was unprepared for the frenzy that followed. Suddenly, small, flailing hands were grabbing at the boxes and there was food and boxes flying everywhere, as we were faced with an outbreak of open war between eight- and nine-year olds, almost coming to blows over them. The outburst startled everyone, and as the drivers tried to subdue them, ushering them back to their school, we were fearful that they would get run over. The incident was over in seconds, but it was a sad and horribly unnerving incident.

I was glad, after our great safari, to be back at the Dik Dik Hotel where we were able to relax, go for a swim or catch up on some sleep.

The next day we visited the Karanga Prison, where my father had worked and where we had spent most of our childhood growing up. I had also hoped to combine the day with a visit to Chief Tom Marealle's home to see him, but with so many of us together, it would have been a bit of an imposition, and so we called the visit off that day. Sadly, as it turned out, I couldn't make alternative arrangements as we were then rather pushed for time, and I couldn't get back to the area again to see him on my own.

Our visit to the prison was quite an event. We drove in through the old side entrance – now the main entrance to the prison – between the avenue of tall trees, which had now grown to about seventy feet. Their incredible height gently shaded neat flower and vegetable nursery beds on one side; and where tall, thick elephant grass once wafted in the wind, tiny pawpaw trees were growing side by side with banana and other fruit saplings. There were shambas everywhere you looked, making the prison quite self-sufficient.

We were greeted cordially by a number of dark-suited senior prison staff, introduced to each in turn and then briefly shown around the front area of the prison. The watch towers and the front facade had altered. The additional buildings which now exist, make up the women's prison. The outside wall verge was surrounded by mature tightly packed sisal plants, about four feet high with two-inch, black, needle-like thorns – surely a deterrent to any escapee.

It was lovely to see that not much had altered on the farm side. The cattle were out on their daily walk, but there were only five head. There were pigpens and rabbit runs, and even the old cattle-dip was the same. We were taken through the prison gates and shown my father's old office. Hanging on a wall, was a board, bearing the names of the people who had been in charge over the years, and the sight of my father's name at the top, brought a tear to our eyes. Mr. James Celestine, who is the current Regional Prison Officer, read a statement to us which had been sent to him from the Principal Commissioner in Dar-es-Salaam, outlining the current prison's organisational structure and reforms. We were invited to sign the visitors' book in his office, and then accompany the staff for a leisurely stroll around the grounds, taking in a visit to the Big House, where James, his wife and family of four now live. The last of the three tall trees lay felled across the old road to the fish ponds, waiting to be despatched. That road is no longer a road, having been gradually swallowed up by wild plants and grasses. The big house has a new corrugated roof, and neatly stacked by the side of the road were the old roof tiles which were the original roof cover for the house. Although the garden looked different, we all recognised places, with Peter, John and Martin reminiscing over the tree house outside the bedroom window, which stands many feet higher now, but still bears the scars! We walked on to the fish ponds, which somehow looked a lot smaller than I remembered. We were told that the largest pond again broke its banks in 1996, flooding the area. Talapia still thrive in the ponds, and a few were hauled out for us to see. The brown woodcocks and herons still stalk the banks – perhaps relatives of the ones we used to see. The fig trees had grown, fattened, and sprawled along the banks by the fresh stream, resembling strange animal-like shapes.

Our hosts and their children, happy and smiling, were interested to see the old photos which we had in our possession of various recognisable places around the area – most of them were not even born then, but they were enthusiastic and eager to hear about how everything used to be just the same. With the sun bearing down on us all, we broke for lunch and offered our transport to give them a lift into the hotel in town for lunch. Everyone was in a joyous mood and the company was good fun, with Joan putting her Swahili to good use. The plumbing at the hotel where we lunched lacked any running water and we resorted to cupped hands held out while a jug of water was provided.

After a couple of greetings speeches, and presentations, we sadly had to say our good-byes to our kind and generous hosts, but we took with us wonderful memories of a very happy day.

We concluded the afternoon in Moshi, with a trip to the old, iron bridge across the Karanga river, which used to be the way to the main entrance of the prison. The last time I saw films of it (old cine film), the iron struts, were painted white to receive VIPs crossing it after the opening of the Kilimanjaro Airport in 1971. Now, unpainted and left to fall into disrepair, it stands a shadow of its former self, with rotted planks and wide, gaping holes ready to snare and trip the unwary. The hills around the thickly-forested gorge have opened up to rough, bare earth and pathways made by grazing cattle and goats, and the troops of baboons and monkeys have gone, and, no doubt, the leopard! The wild, forested gorge had finally given up its secrets, and the Karanga River can be seen gently rolling over the large granite boulders, where mothers do their washing and young children happily play. We left Moshi just as the clouds were thickening to cover Kilimanjaro, and the afternoon sunlight was shining on the peak of the ice cap. The day had been satisfyingly nostalgic.

On our last trip to Arusha, to do our final souvenir shopping, the local 'hawkers' were overjoyed to see us back again, and were even happier when we bought some of their goods. Even as we returned to the bus, the young men were still prepared to barter, shoving and waving their wares through the window to us, until it was getting out of hand, and we had to ask our driver, Simon, to drive on. We returned to our hotel to pack and settle our bills, ready for our journey home. On our last look around, five of us went for a long walk into the hills with our guide, a member of the hotel staff, while others went off to climb the hotel's high 'look-out' tower and take last-minute photographs of the area. Later, we met Erich and his family for a farewell drink. Poor Rowena, the 'poorly bug' finally caught up with her just hours before our departure, and she was unable to enjoy the final, early-evening meal which was wonderful. We sat down to a beautifully decorated table and a meal fit for kings. A choice of meats had been barbecued and delicately carved from a long skewer on to our individual plates – wildebeest being one of the choice of meats – and it tasted delicious; in the background, music played to see us on our way. We said our farewells to Erich and his family, said good-bye to the staff who loaded our baggage, and departed just before complete darkness was once again upon us, heading for the airport. It had been a memorable occasion and I was happy that we had all returned to Africa together, with husbands and wives and, collectively, we would take home enough lovely moments to remember, and talk of, for years to come.